'Economics, as the science that should aim to tell us how to provide people with what they need and want, is of obvious and fundamental importance to human well-being. Yet the dominant tendency in contemporary economics has been widely perceived as largely irrelevant. This philosophical examination and critique of contemporary economics aims to address this situation from two directions. First, Reiss insists, against the tendency of economics to drift into self-contained mathematical formalism, that economics must be an empirically grounded science. And second, he insists that the content of economics cannot be divorced from the fundamental values the science aims to serve. These two themes together provide a sophisticated and important philosophical argument that economics can be both credible and useful. At the same time he provides a compelling illustration that the philosophy of science, also prone at times to self-absorbed navel-gazing, can be vital and useful'.

John Dupré, *Director of Egenis and Professor of Philosophy of Science, Department of Sociology and Philosophy, University of Exeter, UK*

'Julian Reiss' exciting new book, *Error in Economics: Towards a more evidence-based methodology*, challenges economists to live up to their self-conception as tough-minded respecters of facts. Its bold and ambitious case for relying more heavily on subtle inductive methods and less heavily on abstract theory is detailed and well-informed, and it should be taken seriously'.

Daniel M. Hausman, *Herbert A. Simon Professor, Department of Philosophy, University of Wisconsin-Madison, USA*

'This is a terrific book and a paradigm of good work in philosophy of economics in my view. It uses numerous, carefully discussed pieces of real economic research and applies philosophy of science tools in a concrete way to analyze the successes and failures of the research discussed. It makes general philosophy of science points but does so in a way that is directly relevant to and supported by the specific economic research presented. Reiss also argues, successfully I think, that policy and value issues are never far from the surface in economic research and need to be confronted head on. The end product is something economists and philosophers of science should both find very helpful'.

Harold Kincaid, *Director of the Center for Ethics and Values in the Sciences and Professor of Philosophy, Department of Philosophy, The University of Alabama at Birmingham, USA*

Error in Economics

What is the correct concept behind measures of inflation? Does money cause business activity or is it the other way around? Shall we stimulate growth by raising aggregate demand or rather by lowering taxes and thereby providing incentives to produce? Policy-relevant questions such as these are of immediate and obvious importance to the welfare of societies. The standard approach in dealing with them is to build a model, based on economic theory, answer the question for the model world and then apply the results to economic phenomena outside. Data come in, if at all, only in testing a limited number of the model's consequences. Despite some critical voices, economic methodology too has, by and large, subscribed to a 'theory first' approach to applied economics.

Error in Economics systematically develops an alternative to the theory-based orthodoxy. It places the methodical study of evidence at the centre of the scientific enterprise and thus provides a foundation for a methodology of evidence-based economics. But the book does not stop at the truism that claims should be based on the best available evidence. Rather, detailed studies in the areas of measurement, causal inference and policy analysis show what it means for a claim to be evidence-based in the context of a concrete case. The examples discussed concern topics as diverse as consumer price indices, radio spectrum auctions, the transmission mechanism, natural experiments on minimum wages and the evaluation of counterfactuals for policy.

Error in Economics will be essential reading for economic methodologists, philosophers of science and anyone interested in how claims about socio-economic matters are validated.

Julian Reiss is Assistant Professor in the Department of Philosophy at Erasmus University, Rotterdam, and a Research Associate of the Centre for Philosophy of Natural and Social Science, London School of Economics.

Routledge INEM Advances in Economic Methodology

Series edited by Esther-Mirjam Sent

University of Nijmegen, the Netherlands

The field of economic methodology has expanded rapidly during the last few decades. This expansion has occurred in part because of changes within the discipline of economics, in part because of changes in the prevailing philosophical conception of scientific knowledge, and also because of various transformations within the wider society. Research in economic methodology now reflects not only developments in contemporary economic theory, the history of economic thought, and the philosophy of science, but it also reflects developments in science studies, historical epistemology, and social theorizing more generally. The field of economic methodology still includes the search for rules for the proper conduct of economic science, but it also covers a vast array of other subjects and accommodates a variety of different approaches to those subjects.

The objective of this series is to provide a forum for the publication of significant works in the growing field of economic methodology. Since the series defines methodology quite broadly, it will publish books on a wide range of different methodological subjects. The series is also open to a variety of different types of works: original research monographs, edited collections, as well as republication of significant earlier contributions to the methodological literature. The International Network for Economic Methodology (INEM) is proud to sponsor this important series of contributions to the methodological literature.

1. Foundations of Economic Method, Second Edition
A Popperian perspective
Lawrence A. Boland

2. Applied Economics and the Critical Realist Critique
Edited by Paul Downward

3. Dewey, Pragmatism and Economic Methodology
Edited by Elias L. Khalil

4. How Economists Model the World into Numbers
Marcel Boumans

5. McCloskey's Rhetoric
Discourse ethics in economics
Benjamin Balak

6. The Foundations of Paul Samuelson's Revealed Preference Theory
A study by the method of rational reconstruction, Revised edition
Stanley Wong

7. Economics and the Mind
Edited by Barbara Montero and Mark D. White

8. Error in Economics
Towards a more evidence-based methodology
Julian Reiss

Error in Economics

Towards a more evidence-based methodology

Julian Reiss

Routledge
Taylor & Francis Group
LONDON AND NEW YORK

First published 2008
by Routledge
2 Park Square, Milton Park, Abingdon, Oxon OX14 4RN

Simultaneously published in the USA and Canada
by Routledge
270 Madison Ave, New York, NY 10016

Routledge is an imprint of the Taylor & Francis Group, an informa business

Typeset in Times New Roman by
Book Now Ltd, London
Printed and bound in Great Britain by
Biddles Ltd, King's Lynn

British Library Cataloguing in Publication Data
A catalogue record for this book is available from the British Library

Library of Congress Cataloging in Publication Data
A catalog record for this book has been requested

ISBN10: 0–415–39141–5 (hbk)
ISBN10: 0–203–08679–1 (ebk)

ISBN13: 978–0–415–39141–2 (hbk)
ISBN13: 978–0–203–08679–7 (ebk)

To my mum, Peter and my father in memoriam

Contents

Analytical table of contents

Figures and tables

Figures

Tables

Preface and acknowledgements

According to a widely shared perception among economic methodologists, philosophers and other commentators on the discipline, economics is in a serious muddle. Indeed, the evidence for the prophet of doom is sweeping: economics has a grizzly success record at standard measures of scientificness such as predictive success or success at implementing policies; few if any matters have reached consensus – in particular, no *theory* is accepted by a majority worth mentioning; in economics, knowledge seems not to accumulate: even claims once accepted as facts are often challenged subsequently.

Though perhaps on the extreme side, the following opinions give an impression of the sentiment felt by many of those who are unhappy with the condition of the dismal science:

> If economics were a boat, it would be a leaky tub. The pumps would be straining and the captain would be trying to prevent it from capsizing. Which is to say: Our ideas for explaining trends in output, employment and living standards – what we call 'macroeconomics' – are in a state of disarray.
>
> (Samuelson 2005)

> Economists don't believe one another. [. . .] I think it's worse in economics than in what we English speakers call 'science.' And I know it's worse than in historical science. Historians don't believe everything they read in the library. But they expect, rightly, to be able to rely on sheer factual assertions by their colleagues and to have some confidence in their interpretations, if signs of haste or of party passion are absent. [. . .] I could claim that in economics we have nothing like this degree of scientific agreement.
>
> (McCloskey 2003: 230)

> I start from a recognition that, as an intellectual pursuit, much of modern economics is not in a healthy condition at all. This much is

> frequently affirmed even by many of the discipline's mainstream spokespersons . . .
>
> (Lawson 2003: xv)

Explanations for this predicament are ready to hand: unrealistic assumptions; excessive degree of abstraction; a rapidly changing subject matter; mistaken metaphysical presuppositions; bad as well as exaggerated use of mathematical formalism; bad as well as exaggerated use of statistical significance testing. Frequently, they boil down to a complaint that economists are more concerned about developing highly abstract mathematical theories rather than the analysis of real economic phenomena.

While the belief that there is something wrong with economics is widespread and while there is even some agreement what that is, opinions differ widely about what can be done about it. On one side of the spectrum are radical pessimists such as Alex Rosenberg who don't believe that economics could ever be a full-fledged empirical science (see Rosenberg 1992). On the other are optimists such as Deirdre McCloskey who think that economics could be much more like other sciences if only economists started attending to the economy rather than theories about it (see for instance McCloskey 1994). One can regard positions such as Tony Lawson's as middle of the road because he appears to believe that economics, if done properly, can be successful with respect to some of its aims (say, explanation) but not with respect to others (say, prediction) (see Lawson 1997, 2003). Similarly, a position such as Milton Friedman's instrumentalism (Friedman 1953) can be regarded as middle of the road because he too forfeits some aims (say, explanation) in favour of others (say, prediction).

The perspective conveyed in this book is completely (and, perhaps, naïvely) optimistic. Unlike Rosenberg I am utterly unimpressed by the fact that intentionality may play a role in economics (see also Kincaid 1996, Ch. 6, who shares this lack of enthusiasm for the problem of dealing with intentions). Unlike Lawson and Friedman I don't think economics has to give up any of its aims – if the latter are properly understood (though I do indicate in a number of places that there are contexts in which some aims can be more important than others).

The optimism is fuelled by a belief that the empirical resources of economics have not been exhausted yet; in fact, in some areas they still have to be discovered. Economics, as practised by the majority of players in the field, is driven by theoretical, not empirical, concerns. This is true of many areas of economics – most importantly, of many areas of *applied* economics (that pure economics is driven by theoretical concerns should be no surprise). When a key economic variable such as consumer-price inflation is measured, the index number used to aggregate individual price and quantity data is frequently chosen on the basis of a theory such as consumer theory; when an economic experiment is conducted, it is often conducted to test a theory such as game theory; sometimes, inferences about causal relations are drawn exclusively on the basis of a mathematical model, which was constructed on the basis of a theory such as partial equilibrium theory; theory, say Keynesian macro-economic theory, helps to identify an instrument in an econometric investigation; and theory, say monetarism, plays an important role in policy advice.

The analysis of the various case studies contained in this book provides a thorough inspection and criticism of the use of theory in a number of areas of applied economics. But it is important to point out that the aim of this book is not merely, or even dominantly, negative. Rather its objective is to supplement the theory-based orthodoxy with an evidence-based alternative.

Putting it this way may raise the worry that the contrast I draw – theory-based versus evidence-based methodology – is misleading. Doesn't all scientific progress depend on a fruitful collaboration between theory and evidence, between speculating and observing? Hasn't the view that science in general, and economics in particular, can proceed on the basis of evidence alone been refuted a long time ago?

Empiricists have regularly subscribed to the thesis that 'evidence is prior to theory' (the 'priority thesis') but it has been hard to flesh out exactly what the thesis is saying. For it is neither clear what precisely is meant by 'evidence' (sense data? observations? statements whose non-logical terms refer to observables alone? verified statements?) nor by 'theory' (a set of sentences and their deductive closure? do these sentences have to be individually verifiable or falsifiable or verifiable or falsifiable as a whole? a collection of models?) nor in which way one is prior to the other (temporally? semantically? epistemically?; for these three versions of the priority thesis, see Kelly 2006). In order to avoid getting into this philosophical minefield and, perhaps, attempting to give a general answer where there is none, I have chosen a case-based approach for this book. I believe, and to my mind the cases discussed in the remainder of this book make evident, that in the context of a specific inquiry it is not only possible to distinguish neatly between 'theory' and 'evidence' but also that the priority thesis is very plausible.

The case studies are organised into three parts. Part I discusses issues of measurement. Measurement is a hugely important topic but sadly neglected, both in the general philosophy of science and more particularly in economic methodology. That measurement is important is already clear from the fact that accurately measured variables are a presupposition for the success of those activities that are usually regarded more highly such as causal inference or prediction. But, as we will see, measuring variables accurately can be an important aim in itself. Now, the road from individual data on, say, the prices and traded quantities of goods, household unemployment or income to the corresponding aggregate variable – inflation, unemployment, aggregate income – is long and windy. Along the way, numerous assumptions must be made; for example, about the distribution of goods, about the value of some novelty, about the accuracy of survey results, about the treatment of outliers. One way to justify the use of this or that assumption in a measurement procedure is to refer to a prediction made by some economic theory regardless of whether this theory has been confirmed in the relevant population. For example, an assumption frequently made in the measurement of consumer-price inflation is that all consumers choose such that the resulting bundle maximises their utility subject to a budget constraint. An alternative is to demand that such assumptions be made on the best available evidence. This alternative would pay attention to the evidence to the effect that, say, people don't always make the choices that are in their best own interest or that some markets are rationed – if there is any such evidence. The cost of ignoring this evidence is to get the measurement right only with serendipity.

Part II is concerned with causal inference from experiments of a variety of kinds. In order to identify an experiment too numerous assumptions must be made. If for example we would like to analyse a natural experiment with the econometrician's instrumental-variables technique, we should make sure that the instrument is correlated with the putative cause variable but uncorrelated with the error term of the putative effect variable (in fact, we need a somewhat different set of assumptions, as I am going to show in Chapter 7; I use this example for illustration only). Whether or not a variable is correlated with another again can be decided on the basis of theory. For instance, we might argue that rational employers will observe the Vietnam-draft random sequence number of their employees and decide upon the investment in training according to the probability of an employee's being drafted (see Chapter 7 for a discussion of this case). The alternative is to decide about the presence or absence on the basis of evidence.

Part III is concerned with policy matters. It asks how to translate the knowledge gained for instance by the experimental means of Part II into effective policy strategies. This translation is in no way straightforward. From knowing that, say, a causal relation is present in some experimental population (the population on which the experiment was conducted) it is a long way to knowing that the same causal relation is present in the target population (the population that is targeted by the policy). For example, it is widely accepted today that not every policy that has proved to be effective in developed countries will continue to be effective when implemented in a developing country. Causal relations can also change within a single country. If, for instance, a new institutional setup is created by a law, new causal relations may be created along with it and old relations may discontinue. Once more, we can make judgements as to whether knowledge is exportable in this sense on the basis of theory. We can, quite naïvely, suppose that evidence for a causal relation is in fact evidence for some general theory. But since that theory is general, it has to apply in the target population as well. The alternative is again to regard the question about exporting knowledge from experimental to target populations as an empirical question, to be settled on the grounds of evidence.

To prepare the reader for what follows I want to make a couple of announcements. First, this book is not a textbook. It is a research monograph and, as such, it presupposes many matters instead of providing introductory discussions of them. If the reader expects neat accounts of Popperian falsificationism or scientific realism or Bayesian updating (on the philosophical side) or general equilibrium theory and its discontents or permanent income theory or the quantity theory (on the economic side), he or she won't find any. My focus in this book is on a topic or, perhaps more broadly, on a theme: How do we conduct economics such that it resembles our best sciences? How do we base economic claims on evidence and what types of evidence do we need? In my attempt to respond to this theme, I make free use of any philosophical tool that appeared useful and case studies from any area of economics I have some (even if limited) expertise in, and which proved interesting. My hope is that the advantage of this methodology is to have produced an attractive perspective on an interesting and, or so I think, important topic. But the drawbacks are obvious: it presupposes a fair amount of both philosophy and economics or some preparatory study. For economists unacquainted with the contemporary philosophy of science, I'd suggest they read at least one textbook on economic methodology that on the one hand does not presuppose much philosophy and, on the other, does discuss important philosophical themes. Francesco Guala's book on experimental economics (Guala 2005) is excellent in this respect (also good as a complement to this book as I have only one chapter on experimental economics) and so are Dan Hausman's *The Inexact and Separate Science of Economics* (Hausman 1992; check out its appendix), Wade Hands' *Reflection Without Rules* (Hands 2001) and Uskali Mäki's edited collection *Fact and Fiction in Economics* (Mäki 2002). (Guala's book is to my knowledge the only other monograph concerned mostly with applied economics.) One or more of these, read in conjunction with a good textbook on the analytic philosophy of science (e,g, Ian Hacking's *Representing and Intervening* [Hacking 1983], Peter Godfrey-Smith's *Theory and Reality* [Godfrey-Smith 2003], Peter Kosso's *Reading the Book of Nature* [Kosso 1993], *Introduction to the Philosophy of Science* by the Pittsburgh Department of the History and Philosophy of Science [Salmon *et al.* 1992] or the classic with the same title by Lambert and Brittan 1987), should provide some of the background required.

What I would suggest for the philosopher of science unacquainted with economics is to 'backtrack' from the case studies in as much as it seems requisite. If, for example, a more detailed understanding of the quantity theory is required, I'd read the pertinent chapter in a textbook such as Blanchard 2005, Mankiw 2002, Samuelson and Nordhaus 2001 or Stiglitz and Walsh 2006, then some historical account (such as David Laidler's *The*

Golden Age of the Quantity Theory [Laidler 1991]) and some of the original texts (Irving Fisher's *The Purchasing Power of Money* [Fisher 1911], Milton Friedman's *Studies in the Quantity Theory of Money* [Friedman 1956] and Friedman and Schwartz 1963 are indispensable). But how much background is needed depends on the case study and on how much the reader is interested in following up the issues raised here. For the aid of both philosophers and economists I have provided a Glossary of technical terms I use but do not discuss in detail at the end of the book for quick reference.

Despite its non-introductory level, I do think this book can be used as a backbone for a course in the philosophy of economics for advanced undergraduate or graduate students. For what it is – a monograph on methodological problems in applied economics – it is quite comprehensive and it raises many issues young philosophers and methodologists should think about. At any rate, parts of the book have been used for teaching, and without disastrous consequences.

If regarded as a philosophical treatise, this book takes a somewhat unconventional approach. The standard philosophical approach to a subject is to begin with a philosophical question, which is usually either conceptual (and of the form 'What is *X*?', where *X* might be evidence or causality or scientific representation or knowledge) or interpretive (and of the form 'What stance shall we take towards *X*?', where *X* might be a scientific theory or an unobservable or a result derived by a thought experiment), then to discuss the inadequacies of the standard philosophical theories on the subject and finally to come up with a more satisfactory answer. The frolicking becomes really intense when answers in the form of necessary and sufficient conditions are provided for the first type of question (such as 'A causes B if and only if $P(B \mid A) > P(B)$' or 'An agent knows if and only if she has justified true belief'), or with some -ism (such as realism and antirealism, constructive empiricism or rationalism) for the second type. The main difference of the approach taken here is that I start with a methodological problem that arises in the context of a concrete case taken from the practice of applied economics. Philosophical theories in the sense of necessary and sufficient conditions for some concept of interest are virtually absent because I think that the search for necessary and sufficient conditions isn't particularly fruitful in the present context; -isms are invoked only in so far as they prove useful in illuminating aspects of the methodological project.

Another particularity might be that every chapter has been written independently as a stand-alone paper. Again, there are obvious virtues and drawbacks of this technique. A virtue is that each chapter is readable in its own right. In fact, the chapters can be read in any order (although there are some advantages in looking over the first chapter prior to studying the remainder of the book). One does not have to go through five introductory chapters before reaching the meat. On the other hand, there may be some lack of continuity between the chapters. Overlap I have tried to reduce to a minimum.

I first got interested in methodological questions in economics when reading for a Masters in Economics (*lic. oec.*) at the University of St Gallen. In my final year I worked as a research assistant to Jörg Baumberger with whom I had many memorable discussions about economics, its history and methodology, which greatly helped in setting me off on this project. I then transferred to the London School of Economics to study for a PhD in Philosophy. My supervisors were Nancy Cartwright (for the whole period), Dan Hausman (for the first two years) and Mary Morgan (for the next three). My intellectual debts to all three are enormous.

Some of the ideas presented here (especially those of the first part) were developed while I was working with the LSE–Amsterdam Measurement in Economics and Physics Group. Apart from Nancy and Mary, Jordi Cat, Hasok Chang, Marco Del Seta, Peter Dietsch, Roman Frigg, Till Grüne-Yanoff, Francesco Guala, Carl Hoefer, Makiko Ito (now Harrison), Cynthia Ma, Antigoni Nounou, Christoph Schmidt-Petri and George Zouros were members of the London arm and Marcel Boumans, Hsiang-Ke Chao, Harro Maas and Peter Rodenburg were members in Amsterdam. Thanks to all of them for all discussions we had together, and in particular for comments on papers I gave to the group.

Some of the ideas of Parts II and III first saw light when I managed the *Causality: Metaphysics and Methods* research project at the Centre for Philosophy of Natural and Social Science. Apart from Nancy, I wish to thank Damien Fennell, Elliott Sober, Michael Stentenbach, Jon Williamson and John Worrall for valuable discussions and comments on papers I gave.

The manuscript has been read in part or total by Rachel Ankeny, Luc Bovens, Nancy Cartwright, Roman Frigg, Francesco Guala, Kwela Hermanns, Kevin Hoover, Anton Hufnagl, Harold Kincaid, Ted Porter, Marina Roehrs, Dan Steel, David Teira and Jesús Zamora, all of whom I owe my most sincere thanks.

Papers that would later become chapters of this book were read at conferences in Amsterdam, Austin, Barcelona, Grinnell, Konstanz, Leeds, London, Madrid, New York, Rome, San Diego, San Sebastian, Tacoma, Vancouver and Witten-Herdecke. Thanks to the audiences at these occasions for valuable discussions.

Financial support I received from the Friedrich-Naumann-Stiftung (for a PhD scholarship, 1997–2000), the Arts and Humanities Research Council (for the project *Causality: Metaphysics and Methods*, 2001–4), the Spanish Ministry of Education and Science (for my Ramón y Cajal research project *Models of Probabilistic Causality in the Special Sciences*, since 2005) as well as the Urrutia Elejalde Foundation (for support of several seminars and conferences at which some of the ideas contained in this book were presented).

- Chapter 7 was published as 'Practice Ahead of Theory: Instrumental Variables, Natural Experiments and Inductivism in Economics',

Causality Technical Report 12/03, London: CPNSS, 2003 and, in an abridged version, as 'Causal Instrumental Variables and Interventions', *Philosophy of Science* 72:5 (PSA2004), 964–76, 2005.

- Chapter 8 was published as 'Do We Need Mechanisms in the Social Sciences?', *Philosophy of the Social Sciences* 37:2, 163–84, 2007.
- Chapter 9 was published in *Nancy Cartwright's Philosophy of Science* (Luc Bovens and Stephan Hartmann, eds), London: Routledge, forthcoming.
- Chapter 10 was published in *Economic Policy Making Under Uncertainty: The Role of Truth and Accountability in Policy Advice* (Peter Mooslechner, Helene Schubert and Martin Schütz, eds), Cheltenham: Edward Elgar, 204–32, 2004.

1 Evidence-based economics

What it is and what it isn't

I

The various perspectives we find in the philosophy of science in general, and in economic methodology in particular, tend to come with a more or less illuminating label each of its own: constructive empiricism; critical rationalism; realism; constructivism; rhetoric; historicism; falsificationism; positivism; critical realism. As if this wasn't confusion enough, one aim of this book is to propose and advance yet another perspective with yet another label attached: evidence-based economics.

Choosing this as the label brings some rhetorical advantages with it: it will be hard for critics to argue that evidence-based economics is what we do *not* want, that we need less rather than more evidence. For what else should economics, or any other empirical science for that matter, be based on but evidence? But while it is clear (or should be clear) that economics should be based on evidence, a plethora of questions, worries and open issues lurks behind this platitude. What besides evidence has economics been based on till now (after all, the subtitle of this book is 'Towards a *more* evidence-based methodology')? What is this evidence economics is supposed to be based on and what does it mean to 'base' a science on evidence? Is economics supposed to be based on evidence *alone* or is there a role for theory? If so, what is this role? In particular, is 'evidence-based economics' a more deductive enterprise à la Popper's or Lakatos's falsificationism that has been so influential in economics and economic methodology or is it a more inductive enterprise à la Schmoller's German historicism and parts of American institutionalism? If the former, how does it address the scathing criticisms that have been levelled against falsificationism? If the latter, how does it address the even more scathing criticisms levelled against inductivism in economics?

The aim of this introductory chapter is to take up some of these issues and worries. But, to start with a caveat, the position advanced in this book is thoroughly contextualist (as is, for instance, Harold Kincaid's; see Kincaid 2004). That is, I believe that most important issues in the epistemology and methodology of science have to be addressed in the context of concrete cases. Perhaps, after studying a range of specific cases, it is possible to draw some more general lessons. But the reader who expects to find claims in this book that are supposed to be true of all science or even of all economics will find little material of this kind. The methodological stance taken here is plainly small-m rather than big-M, to say it in Deirdre McCloskey's apt words. Hence the discussion in the remainder of this chapter will be necessarily vague and in need of filling-in with detail; it will put forward a framework for thinking about the issues of interest rather than a full-fledged theory. Nevertheless, I do want to provide such a framework in order for the reader to see that there is some degree of systematicity in the bewildering details of the case studies that follow.

II

To begin with the most important but also most difficult issue, what is the view on evidence taken in this book? What's that thing economics is supposed to be based on? Traditionally, empiricists have demanded that all (meaningful or acceptable) claims be based on the perceptual aspects of the contents of our minds, such as observations or sense data. To base a claim on evidence thus means that it is supported by some perceptual state, as in 'Steve can tell a Chevrolet when he sees one'. But with the advance of technology in our everyday lives and science, such a radical empiricist stance has become more and more implausible. We don't only see with our eyes but also with contact lenses, spectacles, binoculars, as well as microscopes and telescopes of scores of types, technologies and resolutions. No advanced science, including economics, today 'observes' without the use of more or less technologically involved instruments. Furthermore, even when aspects of a scientific procedure are observable in a more literal sense, they are often meaningless unless analysed with the help of statistical techniques and interpreted (see for instance Bogen and Woodward 1988; Woodward 1989).

And even if we do not want to get into a general discussion about the virtues of an epistemology that places great weight on 'detection with the unaided senses', in economics such a position would be absurd. No aspect of economic life worth mentioning is observable in this sense, and this is true of micro- as well as macro-economics. Perhaps we can see a company's buildings, plants, machinery, management and employees but a 'firm' is a theoretical entity that is distinct from any and all of these observable aspects. We can see the house a household lives in and some of its members, but the 'household' of economic theory isn't exhausted by either. I can't observe my own preferences, let alone those of others. Of course, choices are sometimes observable. But most pundits today agree that preferences aren't reducible to choices (at any rate, surely not all relevant choices are observable). It is worse in macro-economics. An individual price label is observable but not the price change between now and the last period (which matters for inflation measurement), and inflation is measured by a hugely complicated procedure, only a few aspects of which could count as observable. Succinctly, the price label but not the price level is observable. At best I can observe a person, but usually not whether or not he or she is unemployed in a sense relevant for measuring the unemployment rate. Household income, too, is not observable and has to be inferred from reports given by a household member. And so on.

Although empiricist in nature, the position defended here therefore does not give great importance to observable aspects of our world. Rather, it accepts that there is a plurality of methods for gathering evidence: indeed observation with the naked senses; instrument-enhanced scientific observation; statistical methods (such as data-reduction and analysis techniques, index numbers, regression, ANOVA etc.); mathematical modelling; computer-based methods such as simulations; laboratory experiments, thought experiments and the analysis of natural experiments; testimony and expert judgement.

Nevertheless it is not surprising that observation (say, with the naked eye) has played such a prominent role in the history of epistemology: it is a remarkably reliable method for a wide range of purposes and in a wide range of contexts. 'Reliable' in the sense employed here means 'conducive to a given purpose'. The best test for whether I should take an umbrella on my seven minute walk to my favourite café is to stick my neck out of the window. Our senses allow us to orient ourselves geographically, they allow us to at least roughly classify the food before us (and are usually quite fit at distinguishing edible from non-edible food), and help us with a myriad of other everyday tasks. But for some, even everyday, tasks, evidence from the senses will be highly unreliable. If my plan concerns not a stroll to the café within the next few moments but rather a weekend break in a few days, looking at the sky will not normally help. We'd rather consider a weather forecast, which is brought to our attention through a complex network of instrumentally enhanced observation, measurement, statistical analysis, mathematical modelling and simulation, expert judgement and testimony. Nevertheless, even here we can tell, roughly, how reliable the method is. We know, for instance, that weather forecasts are accurate for horizons of a few days up to about 12 days but not beyond. We also know that the weather in some parts of the world is essentially unpredictable while in others forecasts are more reliable – and that even in such areas predictability can vary from day to day.

For yet other purposes, the range of methods we can use can be highly limited. We cannot run experiments on climate change for technological reasons and because the likely consequences of failure are too high. Thus computer simulations play a significant role in climate research. There are no reliable mechanical tests for distinguishing a real painting by a famous master from a fake. Expert judgement is all there is. Similarly, we rely on testimony in many legal trials. In these areas too, judgements about the reliability can be made. We know, for instance, that a trained expert is a very reliable predictor of the sex of young chicks. But we also know that there are many situations in which political experts fail to predict future political events reliably.

The upshot of this discussion is that it is experience itself that gives us ideas as to what evidence-producing method we can use to provide evidence in the context of a given purpose. I take this stance to be essentially Baconian in nature. Though Bacon is frequently regarded as one of the empiricists, he did not place a great weight on *observable* evidence. He did not worry about Hume's fork or Locke's innate ideas. What he did worry about was the reliability of our evidence-providing methods. He looked at the history of science for clues and found that grand-scale speculation and unsystematic experiment do not lead to results that further the purposes of science, the most important of which for him was finding ways to control the course of nature in order to improve human welfare. In Bacon's work there are no *a priori* criteria for the admissibility of concepts, beliefs or statements. But there are extended discussions of types of methods that have been successful at a given purpose in the past. And there is a further analogy in Bacon's work that is relevant for this book. At least according to some commentators, Bacon's approach to scientific methodology can be regarded as an 'error-correction approach' (see for instance Hon 2003). This, too, is the framework I have chosen to discuss some of the ideas that will come up in the remainder of this book.

III

Above I mentioned an array of methods capable of producing evidence in this or that context, for this or that purpose. It seems to me a matter of prudence to be pluralist in this sense: not to exclude any type of evidence *a priori*. For all methods come with their own advantages and drawbacks, and with their own limitations in their range of applicability. To *a priori* exclude types of evidence would thus amount to restricting the kinds of questions that can be asked and the kinds of ways with which they are addressed. And since we don't know the kinds of purposes tomorrow's scientists pursue with tomorrow's science, it seems a bad idea to ban such purposes even if some methods are indisputably better in the light of the salient purposes of today.

From now on, following standard usage, I will say that evidence is always evidence for a hypothesis. But under what conditions is an observation, a report, a measurement result or some physical exhibit evidence for a hypothesis? In other words, what ought the relationship between evidence and hypothesis be?

A number of suggestions have been made in the philosophical literature. An early idea, discussed among logical positivists and their heirs, was that there is a deductive relationship between *h* and *e*. But this idea has many flaws. One, perhaps not damaging, flaw is that deductive relationships hold between *statements* but evidence can often be a different kind of thing. Sometimes, 'evidence' can mean some aspect of the contents of our minds (the visual image of a black raven, say); at other times, it can be a physical exhibit such as a blood-stained glove, a photograph or a model. But even if we can translate all types of evidence into evidential statements, scientific hypotheses will not usually entail evidential statements directly or indirectly. First, one usually requires a host of auxiliary assumptions in order to derive anything of interest from a scientific hypothesis at all; second, usually the statements one can thus derive from scientific hypotheses are about phenomena, not data (for this distinction, see Bogen and Woodward 1988; Woodward 1989). To give an economic example, macro-economic theories at best predict facts about inflation but never about the individual data points that provide the evidence that the inflation rate is such and such.

Another relevance relationship that has been discussed is probabilistic: *e* is evidence for *h* only if $P(h \mid e) > P(h)$, that is, only if the posterior probability of *h* given the evidence *e* is higher than *h*'s prior probability. This theory has been discussed extensively in numerous variants, and it would go far beyond the scope of this chapter to discuss even some of this literature (but see for instance Achinstein 2001, Chs 3–6). Suffice it to say that the theory has quite serious problems, whether we regard the probabilities as objective or as subjective. If the probabilities are regarded as objective, it is not clear that the hypotheses have a probability in any meaningful sense of the word. The probability that 'all ravens are black' could for example measure the frequency of worlds in which all ravens are indeed black among all worlds. But, at least for all we know, there is only one world (ours). Other objective interpretations of probability have similar problems. The subjective interpretation, according to which a probability measures degrees of belief, is initially more plausible. Saying that P('all ravens are black') = 80 per cent could, for instance, express the confidence I place in that belief. But as an account of *evidence*, this theory puts the cart before the horse. If I want to know whether some perceptual state of affairs or statement or physical exhibit is relevant for a hypothesis, I must be able to learn so on the basis of a feature that the thing itself has (perhaps in conjunction with other pieces of knowledge I have), not essentially by observing myself. Thus, even if it were always true that knowing that something is evidence raises the degree of belief in a hypothesis, this is only a symptom of that thing being evidence and not that which makes it evidence.

The third relevance relationship discussed in the literature is explanatory connection (Achinstein 2001). This is the most promising theory so far. It says that if *e* is evidence for *h*, then either *h* (if true) helps to explain *e*, *e* helps to explain *h* (if true) or some other statement helps to explain both *e* and *h* (if true). Indeed such a connection seems to hold in many instances of evidential relevance. The most frequent case is probably the first: a hypothesis, if true, helps to explain its evidence. A racoon having been in my front yard helps to explain its sorry state; the knife being the murder weapon helps to explain that it is blood-stained; the presence of a disease helps to explain the symptoms. But as effects can be evidence for (hypotheses about) causes, causes can be evidence for (hypotheses about) effects: John taking an overdose of arsenic is evidence for a prediction that he dies in a few moments; a political expert in the early 1980s may have taken Ronald Reagan's Strategic Defence Initiative (SDI) as evidence for his prediction that the Soviet Union will have collapsed by the end of the decade – and with hindsight we may even find out whether he was right in believing that the SDI played a causal role in that story. Lastly, a common cause can help to explain both evidence and hypothesis. If my evidence is 'the coin has come up tails 1,000 times in 1,000 consecutive flips' and the hypothesis 'the coin will come up tails on the next flip', a third statement, 'the coin is biased', helps to explain both (this is Achinstein's example; see ibid.: 150).

The problem with Achinstein's suggestion is that the relevant kind of explanation isn't always a causal explanation, and that the relationship isn't always explanatory. Correlations are sometimes (rightly) taken as evidence for a causal relationship. But even though a causal relationship does in some sense help explain the correlation, the mode of explanation is not causal in this case: correlations are mathematical relationships between numbers, not empirical relationships between causes. When the evidence explains the hypothesis, the mode of explanation can be non-causal too. Chapter 6 will investigate in detail the question whether knowledge about a mechanism that connects two aggregate variables can serve as evidence for a hypothesis about a causal relationship between these variables. Let us suppose it can. But the mechanism can hardly be said to *cause* the aggregate causal relationship. Rather the causal relationship operates through the mechanism or, perhaps, is constituted by it.

And the explanatory model cannot cover all cases of evidence, not even all cases described in this book. As I will describe in more detail in Chapter 8, forecasting models can outperform causal models in terms of predictive accuracy. A result produced by a forecasting model may be taken as evidence for a hypothesis concerning the future but there is no clear explanatory story to be told. Or consider expert judgement. Expert judgement is clearly a potential source of evidence (see Chapter 2). But it is hard to construct a plausible account of an explanatory connection between a judgement on the one hand and a hypothesis on the other. This is perhaps possible when the 'experts' are witnesses in a murder trial. The killing happened – and played a causal role in the witness's observation, and memory of it may play a causal role in the utterance of the testimony. But consider using expert advice in determining whether a painting is genuine or fake. The expert's opinion will count as evidence – but there's no explanatory story connecting his or her judgement and the genuineness of the picture.

Luckily, all these problems for a *theory* of evidence, for an account that provides necessary and sufficient conditions, are not necessarily problems for the contextualist. In a given context, background knowledge will make plain which kinds of clues can be evidence for a hypothesis and which cannot. The raven paradox (the paradox that a red shoe comes out as evidence for the hypothesis that all ravens are black under Hempel's theory while it does not seem to be evidence) and related problems for *theories* of evidence are thus mainly of philosophical or theoretical interest. We can thus define:

Prima facie evidence. An observational or experimental outcome *e* is prima facie evidence for *h* if and only if knowing *e* is relevant (in a sense to be determined in a concrete context on the basis of background knowledge) for believing or acting on *h*.

Not every piece of information that is relevant for a hypothesis at stake will, however, always turn out to be good or what I would like to call *valid* evidence. How do we turn prima facie evidence into valid evidence? Consider, by way of analogy, Patrick Suppes's two stages of causal inference (Suppes 1970). First, he identifies as prima facie cause an event that precedes another event and that raises the probability of the second event (p. 12). But a prima facie cause can be spurious or genuine. If there is a partition such that, given any event in that partition, the prima facie cause does not raise the probability of the later event, then the prima facie cause is spurious. If there is no such partition, then the prima facie cause is genuine (p. 28).

In Suppes's account of causal inference, the move from prima facie causes to genuine causes is simple. Generalising slightly, Suppes turns a prima facie cause into a genuine cause by ruling out alternative causal explanations for the observed statistical relationships. Effectively, this is what happens in many evidential inquiries too. A cough is prima facie evidence for bronchitis. But it won't be valid evidence unless alternative causal hypotheses have been ruled out. For a cough is also a symptom for the following conditions:

- tonsillitis
- sinusitis
- gastrooesophageal reflux
- laryngitis
- pharyngitis
- diphtheria
- oesophageal cancer
- achalasia
- lung cancer
- lung abscess
- bronchiectasis
- throat cancer
- asthma
- pneumonia

and tens of other conditions. Most of the other conditions come with very clear additional symptoms, so they are easily ruled out. Nonetheless a cough isn't evidence for anything unless these alternative explanations can be ruled out. Very frequently, the move from prima facie evidence to valid evidence thus involves the elimination of alternative explanations. Some common examples are:

- ruling out alternative causal accounts;
- demonstrating that an expert is 'biased':
  - there is a conflict of interests
  - he or she has been bribed
  - he or she is not the expert in the right field
  - etc.
- a measured correlation is an artefact of certain properties of the time series studied and has no causal account;
- etc.

Since the evidential relationship isn't always an explanatory relationship, moving from prima facie to valid evidence is not always a procedure of ruling out alternative explanatory hypotheses. It is more generally a procedure of 'eliminating error'. It is only one relevant type of error that a cause different from the one mentioned in the hypothesis is responsible for the generation of the evidence. Consider the following. In Chapter 6 I will argue that having a model for a causal mechanism (for a causal relationship) can be prima facie evidence for some causal hypothesis. Accepting or rejecting the model will usually not consist in the ruling out (or not) of alternative hypotheses. One source of error might be in the derivation of the result – there may be a simple mathematical mistake. Another will be evidence to the effect that some causal link described in the model is not operative outside the model. Yet another might show that there is another mechanism that would destroy the first mechanism's effectiveness – were it in operation. Similarly, demonstrating that a forecasting model is or is not an effective tool for generating predictions will not usually imply the ruling out of alternative *explanatory* hypotheses. What needs to be ruled out is making errors in the inference from the evidence to the hypothesis. But the kinds of sources of such inferential error may be numerous – and open ended.

This is, then, where this book gets its title from. An inference is a good one if all possible sources of error have been controlled for. But only history can show us what kinds of sources there are. It is a truism that no test will yield certain knowledge about a hypothesis. So the best way to go is to try to make sure that at least known sources of error in the inference from evidence to hypothesis have been controlled for. Let us therefore define:

Valid evidence. e is valid evidence for *h* if and only if *e* is prima facie evidence for *h* and all known sources of error in inferring from *e* to *h* have been controlled for.

In order to illustrate this, consider randomised clinical trials (RCTs). An RCT is an experimental setup such that patients who suffer from a given condition are allocated to two experimental arms, the treatment group and the control group, by means of some random mechanism such as flipping a coin or a table of random numbers. The treatment group receives the treatment whose efficacy is under test while the control group receives an alternative treatment or a placebo. A causal hypothesis such as 'drug *d* is effective in reducing symptoms *x*, *y* and *z*' is then evaluated by measuring some aspects of the symptoms, averaging over patients in both groups and testing whether the difference is statistically significant.

RCTs play a prominent role in the now popular evidence-based medicine movement. The preceding discussion makes plain why: the design of an RCT aims at controlling a large number of sources of experimental error all at once. The major problem in causal inquiries is to distinguish between the operation of the causal factor under investigation – in this case, a new treatment – and confounders, that is, factors other than the factor studied that can be responsible for the same kinds of effects. A difference in outcomes between the treatment group and the control group can thus be due to the new treatment or one of various confounders. Randomisation is thought to take care of this problem because it is thought to produce groups that are homogenous with respect to confounders. If, say, age, gender and general health are causal factors other than the new treatment that can influence recovery, randomisation is thought to ensure that the treatment and control groups are identical with respect to the distribution of these factors. If there remains a difference in outcomes between the two groups, it must be due to the new treatment. Hence the method takes two steps at once: if successful, RCTs immediately generate valid evidence without the detour via prima facie evidence and subsequent copious attempts to rule out error.

Despite these supposed virtues, RCTs are neither necessary nor sufficient to generate valid evidence. On the one hand, we can rule out known sources of error one by one rather than in one go. There is no compelling reason, for example, to physically construct a situation in which only the causal factor of interest can produce a difference in the outcome. Another way would be to take an observed difference as a starting point and rule out alternative explanations for this difference severally. Even if certain confounders cannot be ruled out, we may be able to calculate their contribution and see whether there remains a difference after adjustment.

On the other hand, randomisation may contribute to but does not guarantee control of confounding factors. If by 'randomisation' all we mean is 'allocation using a random mechanism', then even perfectly randomised groups can still be severely biased because such devices guarantee genuine randomness only for infinite series of trials – but empirical trials are of course always finite (there is always a chance that the ratio of heads to tails differs from unity in a series of *n* tosses of a fair coin no matter how large *n* is, provided it is finite).

There is another problem with RCTs, which to my mind is more severe. RCTs may be good at establishing the average causal effect of a treatment in a test population (subject to the just mentioned caveats). Suppose the result is positive, that is, there is evidence for the hypothesis h = 'treatment t is effective in population S (the test population)'. Hypotheses like h are, however, almost never what one would like to know. If you are a doctor, say, what you'd often like to know is whether t is effective for an individual patient, not for a test population or even the population at large. If you happen to be a policy maker, what you would like to know is whether t is effective in the population of your constituency, not a test population. And so forth.

That is to say, there is a difference between having evidence for some hypothesis and having evidence for the hypothesis relevant for a given purpose. The difference is important because scientific methods tend to be good at addressing hypotheses of a certain kind and not others: scientific methods come with particular applications built into them. Consider a number of examples. Price indices calculate precisely the amount that must be expended in order to purchase a given basket of goods; however, this quantity may be of little relevance when addressing problems regarding the development of the cost of living for a certain population. Similarly, the advantage of mathematical modelling is that its method of deriving a result is that of mathematical proof: the conclusion is guaranteed to hold given the assumptions. However, the evidence generated in this way is valid only in abstract model worlds while we would like to evaluate hypotheses about what happens in economies in the real world. To give a third example, natural experiments can, if we are lucky, generate valid evidence for past experimental populations but we would like to know what will happen in future target populations.

The upshot is that valid evidence does not seem to be enough. What we also need is to evaluate the relevance of the evidence in the context of a given purpose. Let us thus define 'sound evidence':

Sound evidence. An experimental or observational outcome e is *sound* evidence for an h if it is valid evidence for h and h is the relevant hypothesis for attaining purpose p.

As in the previous step, a variety of errors can occur here. One may take the result of a causal model as evidence for predicting the future value of some variable but experience has told us that, under certain conditions, causal models are inferior forecasting devices. Vice versa, one can base a policy on a forecasting model and ignore the fact that the policy may change the basis for the model's past success by changing the relevant causal structure. One may simply ignore the fact that experiments are run under artificial conditions and not worry about extrapolation to the field. Or one carries out the experiment in the field and neglects to take into account that the target population may differ in important respects from the test population. And so on. The case studies in Part III concern mainly these types of errors.

In summary, we can say that:

- prima facie evidence gives a licence to *investigate*;
- valid evidence gives a licence to *believe*; and
- sound evidence gives a licence to *act*.

In the framework of this book, the three types of evidence can be evidence for three types of hypotheses (cf. Reiss 2004). First, there are hypotheses about the values of variables measured in a particular region and period. Let us call them 'measurement hypotheses'. Examples are 'consumer-price inflation in US urban areas was 4.1 per cent in the 12 months to July 2006', 'the unemployment rate in the UK was 5.5 per cent in the period April–June 2006' or 'the average contribution in a public goods experiment conducted at the University of Turin decreased from 14 in round 1 to 8 in round 20'. Second, there are 'causal hypotheses', hypotheses about causal relationships, which can be singular or generic. Examples for the former are 'a decision by the Federal Reserve Board caused the economic crisis in the Asian tiger states', 'the hyperinflation in Bolivia in the early 1980s was defeated by a sharp increase of the oil prices by the Bolivian state petroleum company' and 'the increase in the minimum wage rate in New Jersey on April 1, 1992, raised employment in the fast food industry'; examples of the latter, 'changes in the money stock cause nominal income', 'social norms influence behaviour' and 'asymmetric information lowers market volumes'. Third, there are hypotheses for policy advice, usually future-regarding. These are called 'policy hypotheses'. Examples are 'the German economy will grow by 2.1 per cent in 2007', 'raising public spending is an effective strategy for reducing UK unemployment' and 'bombing is an effective strategy against global terrorism'.

The three parts of this book mirror the three kinds of hypotheses. The first two parts are mostly concerned with generating evidence for measurement and causal hypotheses. The first part is about measurement. Chapters 2–4 develop an account of measurement, which is purpose- rather than theory-based. Chapter 2 recounts the story of the controversy about the ability of the US consumer price index (CPI) to correctly measure consumer inflation. The dispute was sparked by the publication of a report written by an expert panel to study the accuracy of the CPI, led by Stanford economist Michael Boskin. This report stated that the CPI overstates 'true' consumer price inflation by about 1.1 percentage points annually. A correction of this 'measurement error' along the lines Boskin and his colleagues suggested would have had enormous ramifications for the federal budget and income distribution in the United States. The chapter examines and criticises the arguments made by the Boskin Commission – because they are based at best on prima facie evidence – and considers ways to improve the role of expert judgement in measurement problems (and elsewhere). Chapter 3 focuses on one aspect of the controversy in more detail: the quality-change issue. Taking the idea that an adequate measurement procedure is one that is effective at serving a given purpose seriously, I examine a core recommendation made by the Boskin Commission and show that the recommendation is very likely to be flawed if the escalation of social security payments is the purpose considered. Chapter 4 ponders the question of the design of measurement procedures at a more theoretical level and sketches a pragmatist and coherentist account, following some ideas found in Hasok Chang's excellent study of the history of thermometry (Chang 2004).

Part II concerns causal hypotheses. Chapter 5 studies economic experiments in the laboratory and argues that orthodox experimentalist methodology is unlikely to yield fruitful results if the ultimate aim is to provide policy advice. That is, the results of economic experiments may or may not be valid evidence for certain hypotheses but by and large they will not constitute sound evidence for policy hypotheses. The results, in so far as they can be achieved, are often achieved by changing the question and experimentally testing the new question. It is quite clear, however, that scientists, when asked to give policy advice, should work on the given question and not on a question they think can be answered – they should provide sound and not merely valid evidence. This suggests that we need a new form of experimentalist methodology in experimental economics. Chapter 6 studies thought experiments. Thought experiments and results derived from mathematical models are often used as evidence for causal claims. I argue that they do play an evidential role but a fairly limited one: they provide prima facie evidence or hypotheses that call for further empirical testing. Chapter 7 studies the analysis of natural experiments. I examine in detail the instrumental-variables technique, which is often used for the analysis of natural experiments, and argue that the technique needs to be supplemented with strong causal background assumptions to yield valid evidence. But I also show that such causal assumptions are often made in applications of the method, and that these assumptions can be substantiated on the basis of causal rather than theoretical background knowledge.

Part III turns more explicitly to policy hypotheses. Chapter 8 examines a relatively recent movement in the philosophy of the social sciences that focuses on the study of explanatory mechanisms. I argue that the investigation of mechanisms is often ineffective and inefficient for evaluating policy hypotheses that concern accurate description, prediction and control. Chapter 9 examines the question whether there are social capacities – that is, social factors with relatively stable 'characteristic effects' that one can carry from situation to situation and therefore exploit for policy. I argue that the fact that few such factors have been found gives little reason to believe that future success is impossible. The reason for heedful optimism in the question is methodological: in my view, few serious – and methodologically sound – attempts to find social capacities have been made. Chapter 10, jointly written with Nancy Cartwright, examines the evaluation of 'What if' questions for policy. We investigate orthodox accounts of evaluating counterfactuals and sketch an alternative based on capacities systematised in causal models.

The title of this chapter alludes to the article 'Evidence-Based Medicine: What It Is and What It Isn't' (Sackett *et al.* 1996). Sackett *et al.* define evidence-based medicine thus (p. 71):

> Evidence based medicine is the conscientious, explicit, and judicious use of current best evidence in making decisions about the care of individual patients. The practice of evidence based medicine means integrating individual clinical expertise with the best available external clinical evidence from systematic research.

For a reader who likes concise statements, we can, in summary, define evidence-based economics or EBE by paraphrasing – and qualifying – Sackett *et al.*: 'Evidence-based economics is the conscientious, explicit, and judicious use of sound evidence in making decisions about the welfare of societies. The practice of evidence-based economics means integrating individual socio-economic expertise with valid external evidence from systematic research relevant for the purpose at stake.' This definition shall, however, be the only loan I take from evidence-based medicine.

IV

Above, I have likened the methodological perspective advanced in this book to some aspects of Francis Bacon's philosophy of science. Another aspect of Bacon's philosophy resounding in evidence-based economics is its policy orientation. Perhaps some sciences are practised for theoretical purposes only. That is, they focus mainly on advancing the theoretical understanding of nature, and applications are, if they exist at all, by-products. Economics, according to the stance taken here, is different. It is more akin to medicine, epidemiology, technology or other practice- and policy-oriented sciences. The adequacy of an economic claim stands and falls with its ability to contribute to the welfare of societies.

While this book focuses on methodological aspects of economics, and in particular on how to ground economic claims more firmly in evidence, in 'the facts' if you will, normative matters regarding the welfare of societies will show up time and again. And this should not be surprising. Economics, even in areas that would traditionally be counted as 'positive' rather than 'normative' economics, is an enormously value-laden endeavour. This is hardly surprising if one looks at some recent work on the fact–value dichotomy.

Philosophers such as Amartya Sen, Vivian Walsh and Hilary Putnam have argued that the thesis that there is a dichotomy between facts and values – in the sense of there being one natural kind of things, 'facts', that stands apart from a quite different natural kind of things, 'values' – cannot be upheld (see for example Putnam 2002; Sen 1999; Walsh 1987). One philosophical reason for denying the dichotomy is that it has turned out to be impossible to find an adequate definition of 'fact'. For Hume, factuality pertained to an individual *concept*. A matter of fact was an idea that copied a corresponding sense impression. But this criterion turned out to be too narrow as many interesting scientific properties do not directly affect the senses. The logical positivists later replaced Hume's theory with that of verifiability – which pertained to *statements*, not individual concepts. But soon it turned out that few individual statements could be verified by themselves. At best, whole scientific *theoretical systems* could. Willard van Orman Quine (Quine 1953) drew a conclusion for another empiricist dichotomy – that between the *analytic* (or statements that are true by virtue of logic, that is, convention, alone) and the *synthetic* (or statements that transcend pure logic and have to be confirmed by facts). Quine thought that the idea that within such a theoretical system individual statements could be classified as either purely analytic or purely synthetic was mistaken. But if there is no analytic–synthetic dichotomy (because there is no unequivocal criterion of factuality), it is only a short step to see that there is no fact–value dichotomy either. Vivian Walsh thus writes (op. cit.):

> To borrow and adapt Quine's vivid image, if a theory may be black with fact and white with convention, it might well (as far as logical empiricism could tell) be red with values. Since for them confirmation or falsification had to be a property of a theory as a whole, they had no way of unravelling this whole cloth.

Many of the case studies in this book document such an entanglement of facts and values. Values pervade seemingly factual enquiries at a number of levels. One level is concept formation. Moral philosophers now standardly distinguish between 'thin' and 'thick' ethical concepts. A thin ethical concept refers to some morally evaluative property without descriptive content such as 'good', 'right', 'just', 'virtue', 'duty' and so on. A thick ethical concept, by contrast, always conveys some additional descriptive content and can – for certain purposes – be used dominantly descriptively: 'cruel', 'crime', 'slap', 'courageous', 'generous' (for a discussion, see Putnam 2002, Ch. 2). Social science is full of such thick concepts, and it is very hard to get rid of their normative content.

The CPI case study of Chapters 2 and 3 demonstrates that 'consumer-price inflation' is such a thick – political – concept. What is fascinating about the CPI case is that at first glance inflation looks as objective as concepts get in economics. Surely most economists would say that inflation measurement is a part of positive and not normative economics. And yet, the measurement procedure associated with the CPI is replete with value judgements. To begin with, we have to decide what to keep fixed through time: a basket of goods? utilities? standard of living? And what concept of the latter? perhaps functionings? or relative positions in society? Second, we need to decide whose baskets or standards of living to fix: the whole society's? social security recipients'? tax payers'? How many indices do we need? Third, we have to decide how to weigh individual households: by their expenditures? household by household? by the number of people living in a household? If the latter, how do we weigh children? Further, how do we deal with change when it happens? At what point shall we, for instance, include DVD players, mobile phones and LCD screen television sets in the basket? And so forth. Thus, a seemingly innocuous factual question – What's the rate of inflation this month? – turns out to be enormously value-laden.

Another point at which values enter concerns methodology. No methodology – the methodology of conducting RCTs, say, or that of mathematical model building or that of investigating causal mechanisms – is an all-purpose methodology. Rather, different methodologies fare well at different purposes. An RCT is good for establishing average causal effects for experimental populations; a mathematical model is good for establishing claims about laws, causes and policies for abstract model worlds. Knowledge about a causal mechanism for a causal relationship increases our understanding of why the higher-level relationship holds. Many methodologies, thus, wear their purpose on their sleeve. But therefore promoting a given methodology will in turn encourage the pursuit of one purpose at the expense of others. This can have adverse effects if we think that science should respond to the needs of society, and not just of scientists.

Chapter 8 examines a movement in the philosophy of social science that emphasises the importance of investigating causal mechanisms at the expense of virtually everything else. But since models that represent mechanisms have mostly explanatory virtues, a large number of other virtues get neglected. In particular I discuss descriptive accuracy, predictive accuracy and control, and show how mechanistic models are systematically bad for realising these values. Again, it is a seemingly innocuous practice, investigating mechanisms, that carries enormous normative import.

The third context in which values matter has directly to do with the collection of evidence. Above I pretended that evidence is gathered in a disinterested arena where timing and other practical constraints do not play a role. Basically the stance was: in order to decide a matter in an evidence-based fashion, we need enough evidence of a well-defined kind. This is, in fact, a huge idealisation. In many real-life decision problems we won't have enough time or money to collect all the evidence we need in order to come to a fully fledged evidence-based decision. At some point, the cost of not making any decision will outweigh the cost of making a somewhat inaccurate decision. But how do we trade off the opposing desiderata of accuracy and expeditiousness? This, once more, is a value decision. Values will also determine the standards with which the quality of the evidence is assessed. What we know about anthropogenic climate change is often regarded as being based on relatively low-quality evidence. However, given that dramatic consequences are to be expected if our models are right, according to some people's evaluations there is enough evidence for action. Other people maintain their usual high standards of evidence and thus feel they have grounds for inaction. Such disagreements may be pure disagreements about value judgements – although evidence is directly involved.

This third area is touched upon also in the context of the CPI controversy. The CPI is a social aggregate. As such, it idealises away from the many details of individual households' choices. A maximally accurate index would probably be an index for a single household. Obviously, it would be impractical to design a household-specific policy. But on occasion analogous questions come up in actual debates. The CPI, for instance, is used for a variety of indexation purposes such as the escalation of federal spending programmes and tax brackets as well as the indexation of private contracts. Different subgroups of the population may face radically different price vectors. While many waged employees may make use of special price deals offered by new distribution channels such as online shops and discounters, many pensioners may not be able to buy at discount prices because they depend on traditional retailers in their neighbourhoods. Perhaps, therefore, different indices should be calculated for the different groups of, say, waged employees (for tax bracket indexation), benefit recipients and pensioners. But perhaps the additional accuracy is not worth the investment. Only a value judgement will tell.

In order not to dash the reader's hopes, let me make clear that this is a book on methodology and not political philosophy. But unlike many other methodological treatises in this area, it acknowledges that decisions about evaluations are part and parcel of the scientific enterprise. The position I take here is democratic: if value judgements are at stake, what should matter are the values of the people concerned. But I admit that a thorough normative discussion about the question 'Whose values?' is missing here, and thus at least some of the conclusions I draw are pretty tentative. In this respect I would like 'evidence-based economics' to be understood as a research project under construction rather than a finished methodological edifice. Parts of it surely raise more issues than are answered here. But I take this as a virtue because I think that many of these issues are important and often neglected.

V

Finally in this introductory note I would like to discuss one of the predecessors of evidence-based economics very briefly. At the beginning of this chapter I introduced a number of questions and worries that a methodological stance with the label 'evidence-based economics' could raise. I hope to have addressed some of these questions already. One that still remains is this: 'Evidence-based economics surely subscribes to a "evidence is prior to theory" thesis. But haven't there been devastating arguments against economic inductivism? And haven't earlier inductivist research programmes failed miserably?'

Among economic historians the most widely discussed attempt to do evidence-based economics was by the German historical school. This nineteenth-century movement in German economics was directly opposed to Ricardian classical economics, which in the view of German historical economists was abstract, deductive and ahistorical/acultural. In its stead they proposed a methodology that started from cautious observations of concrete facts, then subtly generalised inductively but kept in mind that even the generalisations arrived at by this procedure might have limited temporal and geographical validity.

The most explicit clash between proponents of these two methodological paradigms occurred in the *Methodenstreit* in the late 1880s and 1890s between the leader of the so-called 'younger German historical school', Gustav Schmoller, and the leader of the emerging Austrian school of economics, Carl Menger. Schmoller's methodology is Baconian in nature: economic phenomena are observed, recorded and classified and then generalisations are established on the basis of the observed phenomena. Menger countered that such an inductive procedure would not yield fruitful results because real economic phenomena are too complex for generalisations ever to be 'strict', that is, universal. Instead phenomena had to be broken down into their 'simplest elements' by a process of mental abstraction. Because each token element of any given type would be exactly identical (the mental process would assure this), generalisations about the exact types would also be universal. Such generalisations are of course abstract, plainly unreal. But information about more concrete phenomena could be gained by deduction from more abstract generalisations. This last part in particular was contested by the historicist opposition. Schmoller and his followers denied that any statements derived from abstract principles, which themselves are not established inductively from observations, could ever be informative about genuine, concrete economic phenomena.

As it happened, the deductivist approach emerged victorious in this dispute. Does this mean that inductivism has been disproved as a candidate for a sound economic methodology? Some appear to think so. For example, Bruce Caldwell notes in an article that comments on a proposal to merge all historically and institutionally sensitive approaches in economics to a common 'school' (Caldwell 2001: 651):

> The early Schmoller . . . defended a 'programmatically antitheoretical inductivism' . . . that directly contradicted Menger's approach. New institutionalists need to be aware of these differences, particularly given that one of those approaches, Schmoller's program, appears to have failed so miserably. It is bad enough to reinvent the wheel; ten times worse to reinvent phlogiston.

In my view, concluding that inductivism cannot work in economics from the lack of success of the German historical school would be a *non-sequitur*. For example, one common criticism against the historical school is that its proponents never proceeded beyond mere fact gathering, and if policy recommendations were made they were not based on a systematic analysis of these facts but rather derived directly from the facts in one great leap (e.g. Schumpeter 1954). Perhaps, then, proponents of the historical school did not follow their own methodological precepts. For nothing could be further from Schmoller's own methodological ideas than unsystematic fact-gathering. Quite clearly, at least in his later writings, Schmoller regarded a schema of causal concepts and hypotheses as a precondition for observation to be meaningful. He explicitly rejected the mere fact-gathering approach sometimes ascribed to his school (Schmoller 1911: 282f., my translation):

> Since the maturation of political science and particularly political economy we notice two beginnings of developments of this kind. First cameralism and mercantilism engaged in primary, indeed often quite superficial, gathering of facts, in descriptions of Holland, England and other states; endless encyclopaedias and compilations were written; this older orientation couldn't stop delighting in the material and ended up in thoughtless polyhistory. [. . .]
>
> The difference between the descriptive orientation of economics today and that of the previous century is that the economists of today stopped gathering notes haphazardly but rather demand scientifically perfected observations and descriptions to be made in accordance with a strict method.
>
> When especially German social science followed this orientation it never imagined that observation and description is by itself of scientific interest, that this was more than preparation for establishing general truths.

Moreover it is clear that a number of institutional and historical reasons were responsible for the demise of the German historical school (which at the time of the *Methodenstreit* was dominant in German academia). One reason for its demise as a 'school' was certainly the so-called 'Althoff system'. Friedrich Althoff was one of Schmoller's colleagues at the University of Strasbourg (where Schmoller taught between 1872 and 1882) who later became ministerial director in the Prussian Ministry of Education. Already in Strasbourg he had begun to build up a vast network of confidants, to whom he now referred when making decisions about the appointments for which he was now responsible. He often followed his friend Schmoller's recommendations, if only because he had little academic judgement of his own (he had received a full professorship without either a doctoral dissertation or the necessary qualifications, even then a rarity). Now, Schmoller seems to have exploited this friendship in order to place candidates that were not only sympathetic to the historical approach of his school but also to his more particular political views. One of the consequences of this system was of course a deep resentment among younger scholars, but also a rejection of some of the core ideas of the Historical School (for example, that economics is at least in part a value-driven business). Clearly, the two World Wars further contributed to the demise of the Historical School (see for instance Häuser 1989).

At any rate, the main pillars of Schmoller's methodological system are nowadays much easier to swallow than they were in his own time. As exemplars consider the following three disputes in the *Methodenstreit.*

Inductivism versus deductivism Pure deductivism (say, à la Popper), that is, the epistemological view that we learn about the world exclusively by conjecturing hypotheses (where it does not matter where these hypotheses come from) and testing them against observable data – in case the hypothesis conflicts with the data, it is given up, otherwise temporarily retained – is as dead as a position in philosophy can be. So is, of course, pure inductivism – the position that has sometimes been ascribed to Bacon, according to which we learn about the world exclusively by observing particulars and using a 'more of the same' rule to generalise. Every scientific epistemology worth considering constitutes a mix of inductive and deductive elements. So too does Schmoller's. He never denied that deduction from hypotheses is a part of the scientific enterprise. At times he added that the deductive step has to be preceded by an inductive step, at others that induction and deduction are complementary – as we need both the left and the right foot for walking (Schmoller's metaphor; on Schmoller's views on induction, see Homann 1989).

What the debate is really about is, perhaps, not whether one of the two inference methods should be used exclusively but rather whether the context of discovery (of scientific hypotheses) and the context of justification can be neatly separated, and whether one can say something philosophically interesting about the context of discovery. On this question, the philosophical consensus today sides firmly with Schmoller (who held that the context of discovery is indeed worthy of our philosophical attention).

Laws as universal generalisations versus laws as culturally and historically specific Perhaps not universally (no pun intended) but still widely accepted is the concept of a scientific law as qualified by an implicit or explicit *ceteris paribus* clause. That is, a majority view today holds that law-like generalisations are true only when certain conditions are met. Thus, when conditions change, the laws can change. Of course this does not mean that when investigating human behaviour we can never generalise beyond a single local context. It does however mean that whether or not we can infer the truth of a generalisation in one context from its truth in another depends on the factors that operate in the two contexts and thus has to be investigated empirically (on this problem specifically in economics, see Hodgson 2001).

Value-free versus confidently politically oriented science No one denies that values matter in the application of scientific results as, for example, in policy. But Menger thought that economic policy was one thing – an art best left to the policy maker – and economic science another. I have argued above that the image of a value-free, 'positive' economics is a myth. Values are all over the place, even in areas that, at first glance, look decidedly 'positive'. But, as I will argue below, the attempt to separate economic 'science' from economic 'policy' (in the way Menger suggested) has detrimental consequences for attaining the goals of our science. The major problem is that, since values are intimately linked to at least some of the concepts, claims and methods that economists employ, pretending that economics can be conducted in a value-free way often leads to sweeping contentious issues under the carpet and assuming some set of values that is not necessarily the set that ought to be adopted. The view that values have an important role to play in science, though perhaps not accepted by a majority, is gaining more and more ground in philosophy today (see for example Kincaid *et al.* 2007).

Of course, none of this implies that there are no factual claims in economics or that economics has to be partisan. But in his acknowledgement that evaluations are an important part of economic science, Schmoller in this respect too appears as the more modern methodologist.

Much of Schmoller's programme is therefore quite defensible in the light of contemporary perspectives on science. Let us now see in detail what a modern counterpart could look like.

Part I

Error in measurement

2 Methodology and expert judgement in evidence-based economics

Lessons from the CPI controversy

'How can that happen? Aren't paintings examined by experts?'

'Of course they are. But famous paintings come with a pedigree, a history, a string of learned opinions and endorsements, rather like precedent in law. When a painting has been accepted as genuine for a number of years, that's a very powerful recommendation. Experts are only human; they believe experts. If they're not expecting to see a fake – and if the fake's good enough – there is a better than even chance they won't spot it. Under normal circumstances, I'd have said Denoyer's Cézanne was genuine, because it's so beautifully done. But thanks to you, dear boy, I had my eye skinned for a fake.' Cyrus paused.

'And a fake is what I saw.'

(From Peter Mayle's *Chasing Cézanne*)

I

It is rare that a specialist controversy in economics carries over to the broader public. Measuring prices seems to be an exception to this general rule. Time and again, when details of the measurement procedure associated with the US Consumer Price Index (CPI) have been debated among government statisticians and academic economists, the public has showed a great interest. The most recent controversy was fuelled by the Final Report to the Senate Finance Committee, prepared by the Advisory Commission to Study the Consumer Price Index or Boskin Commission (after their chair, Stanford economist Michael Boskin), which announced that the CPI was overstating consumer-price inflation by 0.8–1.6 percentage points annually. Following the publication of the report at the end of 1996, newspaper and television reports were filled with late-breaking stories on the CPI.

The outburst of public interest in academic economics was understandable and well warranted: measuring inflation is of immense significance for the wider public, both present and future generations. Since tax brackets and public spending programmes as well as many private contracts are inflation-indexed, the measured inflation rate affects disposable incomes for most employees and recipients of government benefits and pensions, government receipts, expenditures and national debt. To cite just one figure, the Congressional Budget Office estimated at the time of the report's publication that if the CPI were reduced by 1.1 percentage points per year (the Boskin Commission's best point estimate of the bias) the federal debt would be reduced by $691 billion in a decade.

Measuring prices is also of unrivalled importance for economic *analysis*. Many, if not most, empirical analyses of economic phenomena concern what economists call *real* variables, that is, variables deflated by an inflation index. Finding that our index seriously misrepresents the aspect of the phenomenon we are interested in potentially invalidates much of what we know about the economy, not only in terms of describing different economies and comparing them but also in terms of understanding the causal relationships responsible for the phenomena of interest. If we find a significant bias in the measured inflation rate many of our ideas and results regarding economic quantities, such as income, growth, productivity, money and their interrelationships, may have to be reconsidered (for instance, for the effect of a CPI-adjustment on what we know about consumption, see Triplett 1997). A transformation of that empirical knowledge, in turn, may have further policy consequences.

It is therefore indispensable that a hypothesis such as 'consumer-price inflation in the urban areas of the United States 12 months to July 2006 was 4.1 per cent' or 'the US CPI overstates consumer price inflation by 1.1 per cent annually' be based on good evidence. The aim of this chapter is to provide a discussion of what it means when a hypothesis regarding the measurement of an aggregate economic variable is evidence-based in the context of this case. After a brief introduction to CPI measurement in Section II and a summary and explanation of the Boskin recommendations in Section III, I will criticise many of the recommendations made as being based on less than valid evidence in the sense of Chapter 1. As we will see in Section III, expert judgement played an influential role in establishing the claim about the CPI's bias. This naturally raises the question as to whether and to what extent expert judgement can and should play a role in evidence-based economics. I will try to answer that question in Section V. Section VI concludes.

II

Prior to some recent changes introduced in response to the Boskin Commission report, the CPI used to be a *price index*. A price index tracks the cost of purchasing a fixed basket of goods through time. If q_{i0} denotes the quantity of good i in the base-period basket at time 0 and p_{i0}, p_{i1} denote its base and current-period price at times 0 and 1, respectively, then $L_{01} = \Sigma q_{i0}p_{i1}/\Sigma q_{i0}p_{i0}$ is the price index for the current period relative to the base period or *Laspeyres price index*.

In the United States, the CPI is measured by the Bureau of Labor Statistics (BLS), which collects monthly price quotations on 71,000 individual goods and services at about 22,000 retail units in 88 regions throughout the country, known as primary sampling units. In addition to that, the BLS collects information from about 40,000 tenants or landlords and 20,000 homeowners for the housing components of the CPI. These individual goods and services are aggregated in two steps. In the first step, the individual prices are aggregated into 9,108 *strata*, one for each of 207 *items* in 44 *areas*. An item stratum is a low-level index for groups and services such as 'Men's suits, sports coats and outerwear' and 'Gardening and lawncare services'. Within each item stratum entry level items (ELIs) are defined. Some strata may have only one ELI (e.g. 'Apples') while others can have a number of more or less heterogeneous ELIs (e.g. 'Physicians' services'). An area is either an actual geographical region (32 areas correspond to locations in 29 cities) or a construct that represents smaller and mid-sized cities in several regions in the United States (that is, the remaining 12 areas are constructed from 56 primary sampling units).

Since a price index measures the cost of purchasing a *fixed basket of goods*, decisions have to be made on how to treat cases where the characteristics of goods change in one way or another. Here are some examples of relevant changes: some goods grow in their relative importance for consumers whereas others decline; the production of some goods discontinues while new goods are launched; the quality of goods improves or deteriorates; distribution channels change and new channels emerge; environmental factors of relevance for the consumer change. Already before the Boskin-induced alterations in the CPI-measurement procedure, the BLS employed an array of methods to deal with a changing world. Although the CPI was nominally a fixed-basket index, it was BLS practice to update its weights every decade or so. The weights themselves are obtained from the so-called Consumer Expenditure Survey (CES), which collects detailed information on all out-of-pocket expenditures from a national sample of households. Thus one could simultaneously tackle the substitution as well as the new goods problem, though admittedly crudely.

The weights obtained from the CES are used to aggregate higher-level price indices from indices for item strata. Below the level of the stratum, the weights used in the aggregation of individual prices stem from two sources. First, the Census Bureau conducts a so-called Point-of-Purchase Survey (POPS) which attempts to measure the distribution of expenditures across different retail outlets. Based on the results of the POPS the BLS selects a sample of outlets in a given area. The probability of being sampled is proportional to the share of that outlet in total expenditures in the area for the item selected. Second, BLS economists visit these stores and choose one or more specific items from which the broader category of items is to be priced. The probability of being selected for any given item is proportional to its estimated share in the outlet's revenue.

In this process, about 20 per cent of all items undergo sample rotation every year, that is, they are replaced by other, not directly comparable items. This means that full rotation takes place about every five years. For those items rotated into the sample, the BLS performs various quality-adjustment procedures.

Sample rotation is not the only source of item substitution. The BLS tries to make sure that each month exactly the same kind of item is repriced. This is, however, not always possible because an item may be temporarily or permanently unavailable. In this case the BLS representative can judge the new item to be comparable to the old one, following certain standardised guidelines. If the item is judged to be non-comparable, one of a number of adjustment procedures will be applied. Quality changes are the subject of the following chapter; for a more detailed discussion of these procedures, skip forward to Section II of that chapter.

III

The Boskin Commission was an expert committee formed by the economists Michael Boskin of Stanford University, Ellen Dulberger of IBM, Robert Gordon of Northwestern University, and Dale Jorgensen and the late Zvi Griliches, both of Harvard University. The experts made over a dozen specific recommendations regarding the measurement of the CPI, including the following (Boskin *et al.* 1996, Section VIII):

- (Boskin Recommendation No. 1) The BLS should establish a cost of living index as its objective in measuring consumer prices.
- (from No. 3) A 'superlative' index formula should be adopted to account for changing market baskets, abandoning the pretence of sustaining the Laspeyres formula (specifically, the recommendation is to move to a 'trailing Tornqvist' index, i.e. a regularly updated, weighted geometric mean of price relatives, at the stratum and ELI level, and to geometric means of price relatives at the elementary aggregation level).
- (No. 9) The BLS needs a more permanent mechanism for bringing outside information, expertise, and research results to it.
- (from No. 12) The BLS should develop a number of new data collection initiatives to make progress regarding the impact of new commodities and services and the changing economic, social, and environmental climate within which the consumer is operating.
- (No. 15) Congress should establish a permanent (rotating) independent committee or commission of experts to review progress in this area every three years or so and advise it on the appropriate interpretation of the then current statistics.
- (No. 16) Congress and the President must decide whether they wish to continue the widespread overindexing of various federal spending

programs and features of the tax code. If the purpose of indexing is fully and accurately to insulate the groups receiving transfer payments and paying taxes, no more and no less, they should pass legislation adjusting indexing provisions accordingly.

Not all of these recommendations are easily understandable to outsiders. In this section, I explain each recommendation in slightly more detail; the next section provides an analysis and criticism.

The most salient and important recommendation is that the BLS should establish a cost-of-living index (COLI) framework for the CPI. That the CPI should be a COLI is widely accepted among (US) economists (though there are dissenters; see for example Deaton 1998), and indeed it was already recommended by the Stigler Committee when it studied the accuracy of the CPI in the late 1950s. In contrast to a price index, which measures the change in the cost of purchasing a fixed basket of goods, a COLI measures the cost of purchasing a given amount of 'utility' or 'welfare' or 'standard of living' (in discussions about the CPI, these terms are used interchangeably). Introducing this abstract quantity solves a number of conceptual problems simultaneously because it makes all goods commensurable, at least in principle. Simply put, according to this framework, purchasing a good means to purchase a quantity of utility, and consumers know how different goods compare in terms of the amount of utility they are worth. Hence, there is a principle solution to all problems caused by the fact that the universe of goods traded in the market continually changes.

If prices change, consumers will react to that by shifting their purchases from now relatively more expensive to relatively cheaper goods – thereby trying to maintain their standard of living. Moreover, when aspects of the goods themselves change, old good and new good are now commensurable. If, say, an old fashioned TV set used to provide 1,000 units of utility on average and cost $500, and a new flat LCD screen now provides 1,500 units of utility but cost $1,500, the net price change is not 200 per cent but only 100 per cent – the price change discounted by the additional utility provided.

In this framework, a Laspeyres index is inadequate. When relative prices change, consumers can optimise by switching from relatively more expensive to relatively cheaper goods at the same level of utility. Since in a Laspeyres formula the weights are fixed, the effect of this substitution behaviour is excluded. In other words, a Laspeyres price index *overstates* a (base-period utility) COLI.

An obvious problem is that statistical agencies do not know the level of utility attached to each of the goods in the basket. Hence, a 'true' COLI must be approximated on the basis of assumptions about the underlying utility functions of the consumers. A *superlative* index formula is one which approximates a true COLI using only price and quantity data (though only under a suitable set of assumptions about consumers' preferences).

For instance, under such assumptions, a Paasche index, that is, a current-period weighted price index $P_{01} = \Sigma q_{i1}p_{i1}/\Sigma q_{i1}p_{i0}$, with q_{i1} = current-period weights, can be shown to understate a true (current-period utility) COLI (see for instance Diewert 2001: 172–73). This together with the earlier result that a Laspeyres index provides an upper limit for a true base-period utility COLI implies that there is a utility level in between the base- and current-period levels such that the COLI at that level of utility lies in between the observable Laspeyres and Paasche indices (ibid.). A Fisher index, that is, the geometric mean between a Laspeyres and Paasche index, is thus a superlative index. The Tornqvist index, similarly, is such a superlative index.

Many factors apart from narrowly defined economic goods and services may have an impact on consumers' utility levels. Just think of factors such as pollution, crime, longevity, health and many other general socio-economic aspects that do not neatly fall into product categories for which there are markets. One might also mention increasing or decreasing product variety in this context, which may influence utility over and above the impact of the goods themselves. The Boskin Commission thus recommended using funds to study the effect of those factors.

Finally, the Commission recommended closer collaboration of the BLS with academic economists and a hearing of those economists when indexation decisions are made. The presupposition seems to have been either that the recommendations made by the Commission would not be fully implemented or that an upward bias, the extent of which academic economists are in a better position to estimate, would remain even after full implementation.

The Boskin Commission estimated that the CPI overstates a COLI by 0.8–1.6 percentage points annually, their best point estimate being 1.1 per cent. Table 2.1 specifies the Boskin estimates for each individual category.

Upper-level substitution refers to substitution *between* item strata, for example between 'Apples' and 'Pears'. Lower-level substitution is substitution *within* strata, for example between Royal Gala and Golden Delicious. The biases due to new goods and quality changes are jointly estimated, which makes sense since the distinction is quite arbitrary. Finally, the new outlets bias is due to the appearance of novel kinds of retailing channels such as discounters and the fact that consumers gradually shift from traditional to these new retailers.

Table 2.1 The Boskin estimate of the CPI bias

Sources of bias	*Estimate*
Upper-level substitution	0.15
Lower-level substitution	0.25
New products/quality change	0.60
New outlets	0.10
Plausible range	0.8–1.6

In the period following the publication of the report, its findings were hotly debated inside and outside academic economics. Some critical voices regarding the Commission's results and methods (see Abraham 1997; Baker 1997) notwithstanding, many of the recommendations have been implemented subsequently (the remainder of this section largely follows Gordon 2000).

First, and foremost, the BLS agreed that the objective of the CPI is to measure a COLI (Bureau of Labor Statistics 1997). It is only consequent, then, to employ geometric weighting at the lower level because geometric weighting reduces the substitution bias. The BLS introduced geometric weighting for almost two-thirds of product categories, effective with data from January 1999. At the upper level, the BLS switched from a period of about ten years to a two-year period in updating budget weights. This shift is thought to eliminate or at least reduce upper-level substitution bias.

A change that had been planned before the publication of the Boskin report was to increase the speed of sampling rotation. Now telephone surveys are used more extensively, allowing an increase in the sample size and a more rapid focus on categories where products turn over and new goods are introduced.

A number of adjustments concern quality changes. The pricing of hospital services is treated differently as of January 1997. In the old methodology, hospital visits used to be priced on a 'dollar per day' basis. By contrast, the new methodology obtains prices for a sample of specified treatments for particular diseases. Further, the use of hedonic methods was extended (for a discussion of these methods, see p. 50). In particular, television sets and personal computers are now priced using hedonic regression methods. Finally, pollution control measures receive a different treatment. Prior to the report, changes in automobile or petrol characteristics due to air pollution mandates used to be treated as quality changes. As of January 1999, the BLS regards such changes as changes in price rather than quality. That is, pollution mandates are treated as implicit taxes.

IV

In this section, I assess whether and to what extent the Boskin estimates and recommendations were evidence-based, where by 'evidence-based' I mean 'grounded in a systematic empirical investigation of the phenomenon of interest'. The most salient and significant recommendation is that the objective in measuring consumer prices should be a COLI. The belief that the CPI should be a COLI is widely accepted among economists, in the United States and elsewhere. But economists provide little if any justification for this choice of measurement objective.

There is no such thing as 'the' consumer-price level. This is clear from the fact that different indices address different questions. A Laspeyres price index, for instance, answers 'How much does a consumer's income have to change between a base and a current period for the consumer to be able to purchase the same selection of goods?', while a COLI answers 'How much does a consumer's income have to change between a base and a current period for the consumer to be able to achieve the same level of utility?' Every index carries its application with it in this way. Hence, given a certain purpose, the right or correct index number is the one that is most effective at serving the purpose (Diewert 2001; Fisher 1921; Mitchell 1915; Reinsdorf and Triplett 2004). Now, prominent uses for the CPI are the following (Schultze and Mackie 2002: 192):

- as a compensation measure to calculate how much is needed to reimburse recipients of social security and other public transfer payments against changes in the cost of living and for formal or informal use in wage setting;
- for inflation indexation in private contracts;
- as a measure of inflation for inflation-indexed Treasury bonds;
- as a measure with which to index the income tax system to keep it inflation neutral;
- as an output deflator for separating changes in gross domestic product (GDP) and its components into changes in prices and changes in real output; and
- as an inflation yardstick for the Federal Reserve and other macroeconomic policy makers.

Because the indexation of federal programmes has received the greatest attention in the public and academia, let me focus on this purpose. The idea behind indexation is to insulate benefit recipients from rising price levels, which would reduce the value of the transfers if these stayed nominally the same. In the United States, benefit indexation was introduced in 1969 by the Nixon administration. In his Special Message to the Congress on Social Security, the president said the following (emphasis added):

> The impact of an inflation now in its fourth year has undermined the value of every Social Security check and requires that we once again increase the benefits to help those among the most severely victimized *by the rising cost of living.*
>
> I request that the Congress remedy the *real losses* to those who now receive Social Security benefits by increasing payments by 10 per cent.
>
> Beyond that step to set right today's inequity, I propose that the Congress *make certain once and for all* that the retired, the disabled and the dependent never again bear the brunt of inflation. *The way to prevent future unfairness is to attach the benefit schedule to the cost of living.*
>
> This will instill new security in Social Security. This will provide peace of mind to those concerned with their retirement years, and to their dependents.

> By acting to raise benefits now to meet the rise in the cost of living, we keep faith with today's recipients. By acting to make future benefit raises automatic with rises in the cost of living, we remove questions about future years; *we do much to remove this system from biennial politics*; and *we make fair treatment of beneficiaries a matter of certainty rather than a matter of hope.*

Let us first focus on the idea that indexing social security payments to the CPI insulates recipients from 'rises in the cost of living'. If this is the ultimate aim behind the CPI, then the Boskin recommendation that the CPI be a 'cost-of-living index' seems to be validated (but cf. Diewert 2001 who regards the measurement of a cost-of-living index as an important purpose in itself and distinguishes this purpose from that of payment escalation).

But this conclusion is a bit too quick. The economists' technical notion of 'cost of living' as 'cost of achieving a given level of utility' is only one among many connotations the term has. The reader is invited to verify this by consulting a number of English dictionaries. Here are some salient meanings (cf. Banzhaf 2001):

- 'the cost of meeting certain basic requirements';
- 'the cost of purchasing goods which are included in an accepted standard level of consumption'; and
- 'the cost of maintaining one's usual standard'.

Each of these has different implications for the associated measurement procedures, mainly, of course, as regards the choice of the basket of goods. The first and second definitions contrast with the subjective nature of the economists' conception and call for intersubjectively accepted conceptions of 'basic requirements' and 'standard of consumption', respectively. While the first includes only essential goods such as food, clothing and shelter the second covers any definition as long as it is somehow socially legitimised. The third may include a household's standing *relative to others*, and thus comes closer to an income rather than a price index.

Different definitions have different consequences for the wellbeing of benefit recipients. This shifts the discussion from 'What is the right index number?' to 'What is the right concept of "cost of living"?'. At this point we leave the territory of solid empirical facts and enter the realm of evaluations. For no matter how much we investigate prices and goods, their traded quantities, their qualities and how they change over time, such analysis will not give us any clues as to the correctness of our concept of the cost of living. What kind of investigation should we seek instead?

The answer is, in my view, that this question should be settled in the exact same way as other questions regarding the aims of a society are settled. Societies must make up their minds about such decisions all the time: What's the age of consent? Should there be capital punishment? Should we allow smoking in bars? How do we treat users and dealers of recreational drugs? Should there be a national speed limit? Ought we to allow stem-cell research? And so on and so forth. Since this is not a treatise in applied political philosophy, I hesitate committing to a definite answer to our specific question (or any of the above, for that matter). But from the point of view of the methodology of economics it is important to see that such a question cannot be addressed by scientific means alone. There simply is no naked fact there, waiting to be picked up by a scientist. Rather, just as society decides whether to support certain groups in the first place, it should decide in the same way about the concept of cost of living because that concept determines the cash value of the support.

Without a decision being made by society about the correctness of the concept of cost of living (be it by explicit vote, some representational mechanism, a benevolent dictator, a philosopher king or what have you), it is hard to argue that the COLI is necessarily the wrong choice (but consider the discussion in the next chapter). In what follows I will, for the time being and the sake of the argument, take the COLI concept as given.

If the CPI ought to be a COLI, it is correct to try to estimate the substitution bias, which arises from the fact that there is no substitution whatsoever in a fixed-basket price index. We need to be alert though. A superlative index approximates a true COLI only when certain assumptions can be made. The approximation result presupposes the truth of general equilibrium theory, that consumers' preferences are stable over time and have a certain form, and their distribution is relatively homogenous in the group considered. None of these assumptions are necessarily or universally true or even true for the most part. The COLI approach implies that item substitution is caused by no other factor than price changes. In fact, item substitution may also be due to many other factors such as changes in tastes, limited availability, chance and error (see for instance the discussion about the difference between forced and voluntary substitution in Reinsdorf and Triplett 2004: 11, as well as the discussion below). Assuming general equilibrium theory tacitly supposes that these other factors are not at work but whether they are or not can and should be determined empirically.

The most controversial issue is, however, the treatment of quality changes. Including the bias due to new outlets the error in this area estimated by the Commission amounts to 0.7 per cent of the 1.1 per cent total. As mentioned above, the BLS employs an array of tools to deal with quality changes. Given these tools are already in place, the Boskin Commission is effectively saying that the BLS methods are insufficient to determine the exact effect of 'true' quality changes on utility. But how would the Commission know? The answer must be that they (think that they) employ superior methods to determine the impact of quality changes. This is surprising because they did not have any special research funds at their disposal to empirically investigate the issue. Hence, the Commission based their results on extrapolations from previous research and guesswork.

In the Final Report, the estimates of the bias are organised by product categories following the seven main categories of the CPI. Let us take a brief look at the arguments given (all quotes are from the relevant sections in Boskin *et al.* 1996).

1 *Food and beverage* The Boskin Commission notes that there is little if any published evidence on the impact of quality changes in this category. They argue, however, that this category has experienced great improvements over the past 30 or so years due to increased product variety, increased freshness of the produce and a greater selection available at supermarkets, eliminating the need to do time-consuming trips to specialised shops. They reckon: 'A conservative estimate of the value of extra variety and convenience might be 10 percent for food consumed at home other than produce, 20 percent for produce where the increased variety in winter (as well as summer farmers' markets) has been so notable, and 5 percent for alcoholic beverages where imported beer, microbreweries, and a greatly improved distribution of imported wines from all over the world have improved the standard of living. Increased variety and convenience in food away from home, in every price category from McDonalds to luxury restaurants..., can also be credited with a 10 percent premium', which amounts to a total bias in this category of 0.4 per cent per annum (weighted by CPI shares and converted into annual geometric growth rates).

2 *Housing* The most important component within housing is shelter, and the Boskin Commission thinks that the BLS underestimates the value of appliances such as modern refrigerators, stoves/ovens as well as air conditioning and improved plumbing. Their 'conservative' estimate of this bias is 10 per cent over 40 years or 0.25 per cent annually. The Commission further argues that the BLS misses important quality improvements in the non-shelter components of housing such as telephone and cable TV services. New communication technologies have improved clarity and reliability of phone calls, and 60 per cent of households now have cable TV along with its improved picture quality and variety of channels. The 'conservative' estimate in this category is 10 per cent per decade or 1 per cent annually. Unlike most other product categories, that of appliances and consumer electronics has been systematically researched – incidentally by one of the Commission members, namely Robert Gordon (Gordon 1990). On the basis of this research the Commission estimates the bias to be 3 per cent for appliances, 4 per cent for radio–TV, including VCRs and camcorders, and 15 per cent for personal computers, which amounts to 0.1 percentage point annually after weighting.

3 *Apparel* In this category too Robert Gordon has conducted a systematic study (Gordon 1996). On the basis of year-by-year comparisons of identical items from the Sears catalogue, Gordon estimates that the CPI overstates

true apparel inflation by 1.92 per cent annually. Yet, the Commission 'conservatively' concludes that the bias is 1 per cent per year for apparel.

4 *Transportation* Within the transportation component of the CPI new and used cars occupy a central place. In their calculation of the bias, the Commission treats mandatory anti-pollution devices as price rather than quality increases. Curiously, mandatory safety equipment such as seatbelts and crash-resistant bumpers continue to be treated as quality improvements 'since our feeling is that consumers see the connection between their own safety and the devices more directly than they do between anti-pollution devices and air quality'. This is irrelevant, however, for the determination of the current bias of the CPI since most of these new regulations were introduced in the period before 1983. But since 1983 the longevity of cars has improved markedly, another fact overlooked by the BLS. The Commission argues that cars should be treated on a rental-equivalent basis similar to owner-occupied housing. If the lifespan of a car increases, the annual cost goes down as the same purchasing price can be distributed among more years. The bias due to this factor is estimated to amount to 0.59 per cent annually for the post-1987 period. Similar considerations apply to transportation-related products such as petrol. The Commission thinks there is a bias in this category of 0.25 per cent due to increased convenience from automatic credit-card readers built into pumps. Finally, Baily and Gordon (Baily and Gordon 1988: 416) estimated a substantial bias due to the failure of the BLS to take discount air fares into account.

5 *Medical care* There are three primary categories in this area: prescription drugs, professional medical services and hospitals. The CPI for drugs is upwardly biased because of the treatment of generic drugs (prior to 1995) and the introduction of new drugs, according to the Commission. This conclusion is based on research by Commission member Zvi Griliches and his collaborators (Bernt *et al.* 1996; Griliches and Cockburn 1994). The bias is estimated to be 2 per cent annually. In the physicians/hospital services category there is a bias due to the treatment of services based on input rather than outcome (cf. above discussion). According to a number of studies of particular treatments, which assess the bias due to the BLS practice to measure 'days in hospital' rather than 'services pertaining to a specific condition', the CPI overstates true inflation by roughly 4.5 per cent. The Commission regards 3 per cent as a conservative estimate.

6 *Entertainment* The Commission finds no bias in newspapers and magazines but assumes that sporting equipment and toys are subject to a slightly smaller bias than Gordon found for appliances (2 per cent per year as compared to 3 per cent for appliances).

7 *Other goods and services* This category includes small personal care appliances such as hair dryers, which are subject to the same bias as other appli-

ances according to the Commission. Further, personal financial services are 'conservatively' estimated to suffer from an annual bias of 2 per cent, due to improved technology such as cash machines.

The results found in each category can and have been questioned on the basis of considerations very similar to the ones given by the Commission. For instance, the Commission members argue that the quality of the available food has constantly improved over the past 30 years due to better variety, refrigeration technology and so forth. With the same degree of justification we can argue that the quality of our food has deteriorated in this period. The flip side of the greater convenience that accompanies the larger market share of big supermarkets is a greater concentration of business, which means greater market power of retailing companies, who often use this power to put pressure on food producers. This, in turn, forces food producers to cut costs and thus to use cheaper ingredients, more intensive farming methods and so on. Food scandals like BSE are only one effect of this process. Another is the use of cheaper inputs like hydrogenated vegetable fats instead of good oils, butter or lard and the use of animal waste products instead of muscle meat. The health effects of these and similar factors are well known, and looking at US obesity figures lets one wonder whether the quality of nutrition really improved by as much as the Boskin Commission reckons.

Certainly, I do not want to argue that the Commission's *results* in the food and beverage category are necessarily mistaken. Maybe the factors cited by the Commission outweigh the just mentioned opposing factors by exactly the amount estimated. The problem is that we cannot tell – on the basis of the evidence given.

The exact same reflections apply to all categories. Maybe the average quality of housing improved over the past decades. At the same time the United States experienced the phenomenon of the 'urban sprawl' – suburbanisation – with all its potentially negative effects on wellbeing. Maybe cars have much better durability than they used to. But maybe we only use them for more years because we're forced to by income constraints or because we simply like to. Maybe the prescription drugs available today are much better than those 20 years ago. But maybe the pharmaceutical industry convinces us to suffer from diseases we would not have were it not for the drugs that treat them. We need to recall that the relevant quantity is not an objective fact about quality changes of various products. It is rather the effect of perceived quality changes on subjective wellbeing of consumers, on consumers' 'utility'. Guesswork in this area cannot substitute for systematic research into consumers' opinions.

In summary, there is little systematic evidence for the correctness of the Boskin estimate of a 1.1 percentage point upward bias of the CPI. Accepting that the CPI should be a COLI, a judgement for which there is itself little supportive evidence, it is correct to calculate the bias that is due to consumers' substitution behaviour. The technique employed by Boskin *et al.* presupposes that all substitution is due to relative price changes, an assumption that lacks plausibility and should be substantiated empirically. Moreover, bias due to substitution makes up only 0.4 per cent out of the 1.1 per cent total. The remainder is due to changes in the quality of goods and retailing channels, and the impact of such changes on consumers' utilities should be estimated empirically and not guessed at.

It looks therefore as if the Boskin estimates and recommendations were based on dogma rather than the appropriate political process; and on guesswork rather than systematic empirical investigation. But perhaps this conclusion is too hasty. Don't many socio-political decisions require expertise rather than explicit vote, say, and judgement rather than standardised empirical test? The following section takes this suggestion seriously and examines the prospects for basing such decisions on expert judgement.

V

Let us now return to the Nixon quote and focus on a different aspect. Here is the last sentence again: 'By acting to make future benefit raises automatic with rises in the cost of living, we remove questions about future years; *we do much to remove this system from biennial politics*; and *we make fair treatment of beneficiaries a matter of certainty rather than a matter of hope*.' In other words, the underlying aim of benefit indexation is to substitute *political judgement* with an automated or *mechanical procedure*.

In his *Trust in Numbers* (Porter 1995), Ted Porter argues that one driving factor behind the increasing mechanical quantification of political matters is the attempt to overcome mistrust in expert judgement. Much of the history of CPI measurement is an almost paradigmatic case study for this process. The CPI was first introduced in 1919 (though under a different name), following the Shipbuilding Labor Adjustment Board's decision to escalate wages by a price index. Federal programmes were first CPI-indexed in 1969 (see Nixon's Special Message above), and the number of indexed programmes has since risen greatly.

Recall the Boskin Commission's recommendation number 15: 'Congress should establish a permanent (rotating) independent committee or commission of experts to review progress in this area every three years or so and advise it on the appropriate interpretation of the then current statistics.' One way to interpret this recommendation is to say that the Boskin Commission wants to resist this process of mechanisation or objectification of socio-political decisions. Porter points out in his book that such counteracting tendencies have been common in the past. Importantly, he shows that there is often a struggle between two conflicting aspirations: our desire to make *transparent* decisions on the one hand (by applying mechanical decision rules, which, in principle, can be checked by the public) and our desire to make *accurate* decisions on the other (by invoking experts).

We mistrust experts because they are humans and as such sometimes err. They will always act on some interests, and these interests may conflict with the purpose of the investigation. Moreover, expert judgement has an irreducible subjective element. This creates a problem for the public accountability of the decision making. An explicit procedure is transparent and can, in principle, be checked. Human judgement, by contrast, cannot be rationalised in the same way. Using it may create the impression that scientific decisions are up to a committee of elitist insiders whose exact working is foreclosed to ordinary people.

There are thus methodological reasons, as well as reasons having to do with the public interest, in deriving scientific decisions to limit the role of expert judgement. And yet, there are few areas in science (and many other areas of inquiry) that are characterised by problems simple enough to be addressed adequately by purely mechanical procedures. Porter describes one case where the experts were able to sustain the pressure to generate mechanical, quantitative evidence from the government bureaucracy for a comparatively long time: the Victorian 'gentleman actuaries'. An argument frequently used by the actuaries was that company principles, investments made and lives insured differ too much from case to case such that a set of standardised rules would necessarily lead to bias (in fact, this claim by the Victorian actuaries seems to be supported by evidence; see Ericsson and Lehmann 1996). What was called for was thus 'judgement and discretion'. But the necessary expertise was not based on a particular elite from which the actuaries were recruited or even their academic training. Rather, it was the acquaintance with the local particularities of the business concerned that mattered. Porter summarises a lecture by actuary Henry Porter thus (op. cit.: 106):

> Men of experience recognize the crucial importance of 'judgment' in actuarial practice. Porter's lecture was a paean to 'judgment and experience,' which 'cannot be taught' but only acquired through an apprenticeship, as in all professions.

Stories about the expert wine taster, chicken sexer, chess or bridge player or art dealer are legend. The chicken sexer merely looks at the back of the day-old chick and knows its sex on the basis of very subtle cues without really being able to explain how he came to the decision (Horsey 2002); the chess player 'sees' the next move without going through a complicated algorithm that could be instantiated on a machine; countless tests have been developed to tell a fake from a genuine piece of art – but they can all be tricked more easily than the trained expert.

The same is true of many areas in science. Experts reliably outperform novices in cases of difficult medical diagnoses, especially when diagnoses are visual; for example diagnoses from X-rays or diagnoses of skin disorders. Experienced physicists exceed younger colleagues in problem solving because they have developed superior mental representations of paradigmatic situations and so on.

The trade-off pointed out by Porter then seems to be real. Many domains of science and everyday inquiry involve a tacit element that often resists formalisation into a standardised rule. Experts can fill in the gap but at the cost of bringing in methodological and normative problems.

In order to trade off the conflicting desiderata adequately, a reasonable strategy may be to require that experts meet certain tests if their judgement is to be accepted as evidence. We calibrate a measurement instrument against a standard or investigate its proper functioning empirically in other ways. Analogously, we want to ascertain that experts 'work well' when their judgements are called for. In terms of the concepts introduced in Chapter 1, we can say that any expert judgement is prima facie evidence for a claim; the judgement is valid or sound evidence only if the experts are free of bias – if they pass the tests. The following set of principles is intuitively appealing (indeed, see the six conditions in Walton 1989: 60, which overlap with the following to some extent):

- *Subsidiarity principle. Experts should be invoked only when there is reason to believe that they perform better than mechanical rules or that mechanical rules cannot be applied in the context of a given task.*
  If it is true that there is a trade-off between accuracy and transparency, we should seek to get at least one pole of the trade-off. It hardly makes sense to seek evidence from a procedure that is both inaccurate and intransparent.
- *Supporting evidence principle. In so far as possible, experts should underpin their judgement with supporting evidence.*
  Experts should judge *with* numbers rather than *instead of* numbers (Levy 2001; see also Ted Porter's response in Porter 2001). A prudent physician will, when making a complex medical diagnosis, support his or her judgement with external evidence in as much as this is possible and reasonable. Similarly, experts in any area should not ignore any piece of information that can improve the accuracy of a judgement.
- *Relevant expertise principle. We should seek advice only from an expert who is a specialist in the relevant area.*
  Why do experts sometimes outperform laypeople and standardised procedures? This is often because of an intimate acquaintance with the relevant subject area, that is, because of superior experience with the matter at hand. There is no reason to suppose that experts in *some* area produce accurate judgements in *any* area. We should not trust authorities per se but rather the years of training and practice in a given subject.
- *Democratic principle. Expert advice should be made on the basis of the goals and values of the advice seeker, not the advisor.*

Suppose you have a certain condition and there are two medical treatments to choose between. One promises a longer life on average but more pain; the other is risky but if it works there are good chances that you'll be pain free. Consulting your doctor, he can tell you his best guess what the figures are in your case, about the effects and side effects of each treatment and so forth. But he cannot take for you the decision whether you prefer a higher risk of dying or a longer but more painful life. This is a value-decision that should be up to you, the patient. The same holds for all instances of client–expert relationships. Experts are experts about the likely consequences of alternative courses of action; but the aims the decision about the course of action is going to pursue should be chosen by the client.

- *Impartiality principle. As a rule, the expert should not have a stake in the matter considered.*
  This can be used as a catch-all principle seeking to avoid obvious instances of bribery, partisanship, sectarianism and so on. Of course, there is no guarantee that the medical expert who is paid by the pharmaceutical industry will misjudge the efficacy of a new drug; nor is there any guarantee that the superannuated catholic priest will ill advise a teenager about the risks and virtues of birth control. But judgements by partial experts should be taken with special care and, if possible, avoided.

These seem intuitive enough. And yet all five principles appear to have been violated in the CPI controversy. Let us go through them one by one and, for the sake of variety, back to front.

Impartial experts Far be it from me to insinuate that the Commission members were partial in the sense of having pursued a definite political or economic agenda with their work on the price index. However, it has been claimed that only those economists who had testified to the effect that the CPI *over*stated consumer-price inflation were invited to join the Commission (Baker 1997). This, together with the fact that there were (and continue to be) dissenting views, indicates that the Commission as a whole wasn't neutral on the topic. Perhaps each member gave his or her best judgement about the accuracy of the CPI, independently of any own or third-party interests. On the whole, however, the verdict the Commission reached – that the CPI significantly overstated consumer-price inflation – had been predictable before the Commission started their work.

Democratic experts As discussed above, making alleged scientific judgements on the basis of utility theory smuggles in specific values that may or may not be the values a society would endorse by an explicit political procedure. Without evidence that such a procedure would have resulted in a different set of values, I of course cannot claim that the goals and values implicit in the Commission's reasoning were necessarily mistaken (though I will give some arguments to that effect in the following chapter). The point here is methodological: the mistake was to leave implicit the fact that many measurement decisions behind the CPI are normative, not to put the goals and values behind the CPI on the table and discuss the matter. Perhaps, for practical purposes, we can't do better than the Boskin Commission. But we shouldn't ignore the fact that the CPI is a value-laden concept.

Relevant authorities All Commission members were economists. That raises the question whether economists, and only economists, are experts in the right field. I do not want to deny that economic expertise can contribute to making the CPI a more accurate measure of consumer-price inflation. After all, consumers, prices and goods are involved here, and what is economics but the systematic study of the relationships among these? Nevertheless, there are at least two problems with appealing *exclusively* to economic expertise. First, one of the purposes of measuring consumer-price inflation is, as we have seen, to keep social security benefit recipients' standards of living constant. If that is so, one type of relevant expertise concerns the lives of benefit recipients. Thus, expertise from social workers, sociologists or perhaps political scientists, that is, specialists who study these lives, should have been included.

Second, economists tend to look at the world through economics looking glasses (no more and no less than any specialist looks at the world from the perspective of his or her speciality). They tend to regard economic phenomena as being produced by a giant machine that satisfies the assumptions of general equilibrium theory (GET). And thus they tend to make inferences on the basis of what would be the case were GET true. But we need to know what is the case in this world, not what would be the case had GET been true. This matters in particular in the area of assessing the impact of quality changes on consumers' wellbeing. Quite clearly, these should be studied empirically, and not on the basis of casual observation and GET.

And yet, one of the Commission members, Robert Gordon, suggests that such detailed research is not needed (Gordon 2000: 27, original emphasis): 'For instance, even though we will never precisely measure the value of the invention of the jet airplane, as economists we *know* that consumer surplus triangles have an area that is positive rather than zero.' This is an intriguing statement. Of course, it is *plausible* to assume that substituting jet airplanes for propeller-driven ones bumps up consumer welfare. One may even agree that it would be *objectively rational* for consumers to prefer jet to propeller planes. But neither claim is a substitute for evidence to the effect that consumers value jet planes more highly than propeller planes. The first claim is a piece of guesswork. The second, an instance of what one may call the 'reverse naturalistic fallacy' – an argument from an 'ought' to an 'is': since people ought to prefer jet airplanes, they in fact do so.

An inference the Boskin Commission used time and again is that from 'the market share of some good x_i in a market X increases' to 'consumers prefer x_i to its alternatives x_j ($i \neq j$)'. But this inference rule is fallacious in the same way that 'post hoc ergo propter hoc' is fallacious. This is because many other factors apart from consumers' preferences may be responsible for the shift in market share. To name but a few, the relevant outlets (or producers, as in the case of airplanes) may just stop selling the older good; consumers' preferences are induced to change (by, say, aggressive advertising or peer pressure); a third or environmental variable changes so that the preference between i and j is reversed; consumers are forced or tricked into buying i without having a genuine preference for it. Unless we control for these other factors, the inference may always be misleading.

The advisors in the Boskin Commission are experts in economic theory. But advice based on economic theory, that is, economic theory *alone*, can lead to damaging consequences. I could not state it better than Paul Klemperer (an auction theorist!) who traces this point back to Alfred Marshall (Klemperer 2004: 124):

> Some academics also need to widen the scope of their analyses beyond the confines of their models which, while elegant, are often short on real-world detail. Marshall always emphasized the importance of a deep 'historical knowledge of any area being investigated and referred again and again to the complexity of economic problems and the naivety of simple hypotheses' (Sills 1968). Employing 'know it all' consultants with narrowly focused theories instead of experienced people with a good knowledge of the wider context can sometimes lead to disaster.

Therefore, there is one reason to believe that economic expertise is not sufficient; and another reason that it might positively impair good judgement.

External evidence As we have seen above, in most categories the Boskin Commission provided *some* numbers to support their estimates of the bias. But the external evidence the Commission cites often appears to be of little relevance for the problem at hand. In terms of the distinctions made in Chapter 1, we can say that the Commission provided at best *valid* but not *sound* evidence. That is, what they cited may or may not have been good evidence for hypotheses regarding certain categories – but not for the hypotheses at stake.

To mention a few examples: It may be the case that what is true of breakfast cereals is true of food and beverage in general (Hausman 1996, cited in the section on Food and Beverage). Maybe results for anti-depressants are true of drugs in general (Bernt *et al.* 1996, cited in the section on Medical Services), and maybe what is true of heart attack and cataract surgery is true of all physicians' and hospital services (Cutler *et al.* 1996 and Shapiro and

Wilcox 1996, respectively, also cited in the section on Medical Services). But without further argument, there is no reason to believe that this should be so.

A curious piece of reasoning also appears in the section on Medical Services. Boskin *et al.* point out that the biases estimated in two studies on heart attack and cataract surgery, respectively, almost agree: 'The closeness in the Cutler et. al. [sic] and Shapiro–Wilcox studies of quite different medical procedures is striking', and conclude that this must mean something about the bias in the whole category (Boskin *et al.* 1996).

The argument indeed resembles an argument to the effect that if the results of two different procedures purporting to detect the same phenomenon coincide, the phenomenon is real rather than an artefact of the procedure. However, we cannot ignore the 'purporting to detect the same phenomenon' here. The two procedures considered by the Boskin Commission measure the quality-adjusted price change of heart attack surgery and cataract surgery, respectively – and the two are clearly two different things. A coincidence of the two numbers is not indicative of anything.

Are experts better than mechanical rules? Do we need expert judgement to determine the effect of quality changes on consumers' wellbeing? On the basis of the known evidence, this is hard to decide conclusively but it is important to note that this area surely is not inaccessible to alternative evidence-generating methods (cf. the Stigler Committee's recommendation that psychologists and other specialists could use surveys to appraise consumers' perceptions of the relative qualities of varieties; Stigler *et al.* 1961: 37). Evidence about the impact of new goods on consumers' wellbeing can be investigated by means of surveys, experiments, field studies and econometrically. Therefore, unless it can be demonstrated that experts systematically beat these methods in terms of either accuracy or efficiency, there is no reason to believe that experts should have been called for this task.

In case of a conflict between a normative theory (in this case given by the five principles) and practice (in this case given by the work of the Boskin Commission), in order to restore consistency, we should either revise the theory or we have to maintain that practice is deficient. How shall we proceed in this case? I think we need a bit of both. The rules clearly need revision; but it is just as clear that something went wrong in the CPI controversy. To reach some conclusions let us, once more, look at each principle in turn.

Subsidiarity The problem with subsidiarity is that knowledge of which of a set of alternative measurement procedures is more accurate is often hard to come by. There exists an extensive literature about expert judgement in many areas (for a recent discussion in the context of economic methodology, see Angner 2006; for a recent book on expert political judgement,

Tetlock 2006). Most of this literature, however, presupposes that experts' performance can be assessed relative to some objective standard. For example, some studies measure the 'overconfidence' of an expert as the difference between the stated subjective degree of belief in the correctness of an answer in a questionnaire and the true frequency of correct answers of a given kind in the same questionnaire. Another method is to make experts predict a future event of a certain kind for a definite date and simply to wait till that date and see whether or not the event has occurred (which is assumed to be straightforwardly observable). Thus we know that corn judges systematically misforecast crop yield and misgrade corn because we can wait and observe yield and have accurate methods to grade the product (see Shanteau and Stewart 1992). In the same way we know that expert chicken sexers beat mechanical procedures. Chicken sexing is an art only with a very young chick – its sex is obvious even to the layman when it is five to six weeks old. We therefore only have to wait and see.

The problem we are facing here, and no doubt the methodologically more involved and interesting problem, obtains when there is no such objective standard. There is no alternative method to determine whether an arts dealer has correctly judged a painting to be genuine or fake, even with hindsight. Perhaps sometimes new evidence comes in, for example, that a given painter has used a certain technique or material (which was also used for the disputed piece) for works whose origin is uncontested. Often, however, the expert's judgement will be all there is. In these cases we simply don't know how accurate expert judgement as a whole is at a given task.

In such cases, does it seem reasonable to require to have a good reason to believe that an expert is better than a mechanical procedure at a given task? I think that the core of truth in this principle is that it should never be presupposed that only experts can be reliable generators of evidence in a given area. Like all evidential methods, expert judgement comes with its own set of virtues and vices attached. Its biggest virtue is also its biggest vice, namely that experts are humans. As such they are more adaptable to particular circumstances and they can 'judge' as opposed to merely follow an algorithm. And as such they also take bribes, act on interests other than the client's, display overconfidence and get tired. In any domain that has even a mild degree of complexity, we will never get rid of expertise altogether. It is important thus to keep in mind the disadvantages it is necessarily associated with, decide accordingly and try to supplement expert judgement with alternative methods wherever possible and reasonable.

Supporting evidence It is a minimum requirement of rationality to take any relevant evidence into account and thus I don't think that there is anything wrong with this principle, even as formulated above. It should be qualified that the evidence be sound in the sense introduced in Chapter 1. This is precisely the qualification needed in the CPI controversy. It is not that the Boskin Commission ignored external evidence; but the evidence they took into account was of a notoriously bad quality. Prima facie evidence is, prima facie, not evidence for anything. And evidence, even if it is good (i.e. valid) evidence for some hypothesis, might be entirely irrelevant to the hypothesis under investigation. Only sound evidence should therefore play a role.

Relevant expertise The discussion of this and the preceding principle has shown that experts should not be assessed one by one but rather as a group or committee. In many cases it will not be possible to find one person who knows enough to count as an expert in the relevant domain. This is especially so when problems call for interdisciplinary approaches. But this does not mean that the relevant expertise cannot be found in a committee of experts. The more complex the problem, the larger the committee will have to be. To repeat, in this area too the Senate could have done better, namely by appointing a more heterogeneous Commission.

Democracy I think, as a rule, it is correct to say that, if goals and values are at stake, it should be the goals and values of the client, not the expert. Consider the following case by Gerd Gigerenzer (Gigerenzer 2002). According to the psychologist, many women 'ascribe almost magical powers to mammography' in reducing the risk of breast cancer, due to the information they receive from the media, physicians and health organisations (p. 74). They thereby ignore the fact that mammography also incurs costs in the form of adverse psychological and physical effects of false positives, similar adverse psychological and physical effects of detected non- or slow-progressive cancers, radiation-induced cancers, and, in addition, the financial costs for the health system for carrying out unnecessary tests and treatments, etc. Gigerenzer argues that women should be informed about these likely costs as well as the benefits of mammography prior to the physician's recommendation so that they can make an informed decision. He concludes (p. 71):

> Before age 50, mammography does not seem to have benefits, only costs. Women at age 50, however, face the question of whether the potential benefits outweigh the costs. Each woman must decide for herself what the answer is. Her physician can help her understand what the benefits and costs are, but not how to weigh them. Her decision depends crucially on her goals, such as peace of mind, keeping her body unscarred, or a willingness to take (or not to take) the chance that she is one of the few who benefit from screening.

The same should, in principle, be true of the socio-economic decision-making process. But we have to qualify this in a number of ways. First, not everybody has the mental capacity to know what is best for him or herself. This is quite obviously true for young children and the mentally impaired but there can be situations in which an otherwise completely rational person should leave decisions about his or her aims to a benevolent outsider. Second, goals and values, even to the most rational among us, are not always there to be observed straightforwardly and clearly. Rather, they form slowly and gradually in a process of deliberation – in which experts can and should take a part. I still think it is dumb to ask an old catholic priest for advice about family planning – mostly because we know his answer. But what the priest might help the client do is formulate her aims more clearly, see what the moral choices are and simply assist her in finding out what she wants (in the best of all possible worlds, that is). In this area too, it is a great lacuna in the Boskin report not to have made clear that moral choices are involved. Third, when political decisions are concerned it might not always be clear who exactly is the client. The Boskin Commission reported to the Senate Finance Committee (SFC). Ideally, the SFC should act as a mere representative – but for whom? The relevant group in this case is the (US) consumers. But the consumers are in fact a quite heterogeneous group. In particular we have to expect conflicts of interest between benefit recipients and tax payers. Such conflicts of interest arise whenever there are important choices, and they should be arbitrated (in principle) in the same way as conflicts in other cases. Of course, there cannot be an explicit vote on minute details of the measurement procedure associated with the CPI. But there is no reason to suppose that such details cannot be determined in a way that is as satisfactory as the bringing about of decisions about other moral choices.

Impartiality The problem about the requirement that experts be impartial is that there won't always be impartial experts. Who outside the Catholic Church will be an expert on matters catholic? If that's not enough, think of Opus Dei or of the Free Masons. More seriously, the nature of the problem at hand will often make it likely that all available experts are partial in one way or another. Issues with global consequences are a case in point. No matter whether the expert is an environmentalist, a rural farmer in the Amazon, a representative of the car industry or the head of the George W. Bush administration, he will always have *some* stake in the issue of global warming. Even the most selfless and well-meaning physician will be subject to some external forces, be they constituted by national health care systems, patients' direct payments, superiors and administration (say, when employed by a hospital) and so on and so forth. If sacrificing the goals and values of one patient will result in helping many other patients to pursue their goals and values, this physician might, and quite reasonably, not make the recommendation that is in that patient's best interest.

These difficulties notwithstanding there are a number of clear cases of partiality that should be ruled out, such as bribery and obvious sectarianism. In more subtle cases, it will help to publicise affiliations. It is one thing to hear an expert reporting on the efficacy of a new drug; it is quite another hearing that expert when it is known that he works for the pharmaceutical industry that will profit if the drug is licensed. Other cases will be far less obvious. The UK public policy regarding sunlight exposure was formulated by dermatologists – which, prima facie, does not seem to be a bad thing as sunlight most directly affects the skin. One consequence of this is that the policy focuses too much on the potential risks of sunlight exposure (because sunlight is implicated in melanoma and other forms of skin cancer) and not enough on the potential benefits (because the most substantial benefits are not directly related with the skin). The dermatologists are partial because they see only part of the problem, and not necessarily even the most important part (or so argues Oliver Gillie; see Gillie 2004). Here too it could help to make clear that this policy was formulated having in mind the consequences for the skin alone (or better still, to try to formulate a more balanced policy that weighs up risks and benefits for overall health).

VI

What, thus far, are the lessons from the CPI controversy for methodology and expert judgement? When does a report by the Bureau of Labor Statistics that 'The Consumer Price Index for All Urban Consumers (CPI-U) decreased 0.5 percent in October [2006], before seasonal adjustment' provide evidence for the hypothesis that (US urban) consumer prices have decreased by half a percentage point in that period? And what kind of evidence?

To satisfy readers who enjoy labels, let me point out that the lessons have a pragmatist, an empiricist and a political aspect. The major methodological problems in CPI measurement are:

- How do we aggregate prices (that is, what's the right index formula)?
- How do we deal with changes in the market place?

There is no one correct answer to the first question. Whether or not an index-number formula is 'correct' depends on the purpose pursued. The point I am making here is thus roughly pragmatist in character: there is no 'true' inflation rate; but there are numerous inflation indices that are more or less useful relative to the given purpose. Once the purpose is given, the numerical determination of the index should be based on empirical evidence. This is the empiricist aspect of the lessons. If, as I have taken for granted in this chapter, the CPI purpose is to measure a constant-utility index, then the effects of various changes in the market place on consumers' utility should be estimated empirically. This is the second major methodological issue as measuring utility is hard. Perhaps estimating the effect of changes in the market place on utility is practically speaking impossible; perhaps utility can only be measured (by standard empirical methods) under restrictive conditions regarding consumer behaviour, and these conditions are not met, by and large, for typical consumers. But then the

Boskin Commission had an answer to this problem: expert judgement. Expert judgement is often called for when standardised or mechanical procedures do not yield satisfactory results. When regarded as a measurement instrument, an expert should be tested for reliability just like any other instrument. To this effect I have described five principles or tests that seemed intuitively appealing. We saw, however, that none of them was met in the CPI controversy. This led us to both revise and qualify the principles as well as to deduce that the Boskin Commission had a number of shortcomings in this respect.

The American pragmatists saw that values pervade science through and through. The CPI is no exception. Values come in immediately when the index-number purpose is determined. The Nixon administration chained social security payments to the CPI in order to keep benefit recipients' cost of living constant. But what is the 'cost of living'? We have seen that the economists' answer, namely the 'cost of achieving a given level of utility', is only one among many, and that different answers have different implications for the measurement of the CPI. Which answer is right? My view is, again, that there is no one correct solution. Rather, answers to questions of this kind have to be legitimised in the same way as other normative decisions in a society are legitimised. The following chapter investigates whether we cannot go beyond this platitude with the information at hand.

3 Readdressing the quality-change issue

I

The recent history of the US Consumer Price Index or CPI is an ideal case study for the project of evidence-based economics because it highlights very nicely its two salient aspects: the methodological and the normative, and the ways in which the two are intertwined. This chapter continues the discussion of the previous chapter but focuses on one facet of the debate in particular: quality changes.

The quality-change issue has been called the 'house-to-house combat of price measurement' (Shapiro and Wilcox 1996). First, the phenomenon of quality changes is pervasive. On the basis of 1995 data it has been estimated that about 4 per cent of all price quotations involve a replacement article in the CPI each month. Every year, a quality adjustment is necessary for about 10 per cent of the items in the CPI (Moulton and Moses 1997). Second, dealing with quality changes is fiendish. As we have seen previously, it is now standard to assume that the measurement objective of, or concept behind, the CPI is a cost-of-living index or COLI. Consequently, when goods change in one respect or another, the effect of any modification in the basket of available goods on consumers' utility has to be calculated. The prices that enter the CPI are then discounted by their estimated quality change. But utility is, as is well known, unobservable. Hence, the effect must be inferred on the basis of more or less doubtful assumptions about the relationship between consumer behaviour and their wellbeing or between objective features of the quality change and consumers' subjective experience of these features. But any such assumption can and has been contested. The quality-change issue thus remains vexed (apparently, already Adam Smith was troubled by the problem; see Hulten 1997: 87).

In this chapter, I want to approach the issue from a new perspective. In order to avoid the usual impasse, I modify the standard approach in addressing the issue. It is now standard to decide about the *concept* behind an index on the basis of its *purpose* and then about details of the *measurement procedure* on the basis of the concept. For instance, we decide that for indexation purposes the COLI concept is adequate, and if the CPI is a COLI we design the measurement procedure accordingly.

The alternative I suggest is to assess details about the measurement procedure directly in the light of the index-number purpose. This, in turn, will provide some information about the adequacy of the concept behind the index. Therefore, whereas most of the previous chapter took the COLI concept for granted, this chapter scrutinises this framework. Given what I said in the previous chapter about values – that decisions about value-laden aspects of a measurement procedure should be politically legitimised in just the same way as other normative decisions in society – it is clear that my results are tentative. However, I will indicate that the treatment of quality changes presented here has some plausibility and that it is more consistent with the US political practice than the treatment under a COLI regime.

In what follows, I will first briefly introduce the quality-change issue and argue that aspects of the measurement procedure have to be determined by the index-number purpose. Section III contains the main argument regarding the treatment of quality changes. Section IV uses the results of Section III to argue that the COLI framework is inadequate for the CPI if indexation is the purpose. It also contains some thoughts about what could be a more adequate concept.

II

As indicated above, the root of the difficulty in dealing with the quality changes within the COLI framework is that the concept refers to an unobservable quantity, namely consumers' standard of living or utility. To give a simple textbook example, suppose the relevant basket of goods consists of 1 unit of housing ($q_{h,1} = 1$) and 10 units of food ($q_{f,1} = 10$) in the base year or year 1. The prices are $p_{h,1} = 100$ and $p_{f,1} = 10$, respectively. Quality can be represented by an additional parameter ζ, which is normalised to unity in the base year: $\zeta_{h,1} = \zeta_{f,1} = 1$. The cost for purchasing the base-year basket of goods is thus $q_{h,1}\, p_{h,1} + q_{f,1}\, p_{f,1} = 200$. Let the utility function of the representative consumer in our toy economy be $U_t(q_{h,t}, q_{f,t}, \zeta_{h,t}, \zeta_{f,t}) = \min(10q_{h,t}\zeta_{h,t}, q_{f,t}\zeta_{f,t})$, which yields 10 units of utility in the base year. (This choice of utility function treats housing and food as perfect complements, like left shoes and right shoes. While perhaps on the extreme side, this assumption is not implausible altogether as both housing and food are indispensable and few people, especially when they are poor, will be able or willing to trade off food for housing or vice versa.)

Suppose now that in the second year all prices go up by 10 per cent, that is, $p_{h,2} = 110$ and $p_{f,2} = 11$. Further, the quality of housing changes due to, say, improved amenities such as air conditioning and increased number of square feet per housing unit, etc. Let us say that the quality improved by 5 per cent, that is, $\zeta_{h,2} = 1.05$. Because of that quality improvement, in order to receive the same amount of utility as in the base year, consumers will have to purchase 0.95 units of housing, and the same 10 units of food, so that their expenses are now 0.95*110 + 10*11 = 214.5. Hence, while all prices increased by 10 per cent, the quality-adjusted price change is a mere 7.25 per cent (= 214.5/200 – 1). In other words, in the second period consumers need an additional 7.25 per cent of income in order to achieve the same level of utility as in the base period.

In practice neither utility function nor its subjective quality change parameter ζ is observable. Hence, the impact of quality changes on utility has to be *imputed* rather than directly measured (some even speak about a 'large subjective component' in the estimation of the CPI; see Lebow and Rudd 2003: 163). The usual method is to assume certain law-like connections between observable characteristics and the utility function. At some point it was standard BLS practice (for BLS practice prior to the Boskin review, see Moulton and Moses 1997) to attribute the price change between the old item and that which replaced it fully to their difference in quality when an old item became unavailable. This assumes that producers accurately estimate the impact of the quality change on consumers' utilities and change prices accordingly. In our example, the price for housing would have remained at 100, so that the index would have risen by a mere 5 per cent. This practice is obviously unsatisfactory when price adjustments concur with quality changes, as in our example. In the years prior to the changes partly initiated by the Boskin report, the following methods were in place:

1 *Overlap method.* If in the given period (say, t) both the new and the old item are available, the change in the index is calculated by using the change in the price of the old item between t–1 and t, and that of the price of the new item between t and t+1. This implicitly treats the price differential between the old and the new item as reflecting their quality difference and nothing else. Because old and new items are hardly ever available in the same period, this method is seldom used except in sample rotation.
2 *Mark-up method.* In some categories, producers are asked to estimate the cost of a given quality improvement. This cost (marked up to an estimated retail value) is then deducted from the price change to reflect the quality improvement. The widest application of this method is in the area of motor vehicles.
3 *Hedonic method.* The BLS makes limited use of hedonic estimation techniques, mainly in the area of housing and apparel. In hedonic estimations, the value of a good is broken down to various characteristics such as square feet, number of bathrooms and age of an apartment. Given estimates of the individual characteristics and observations of these characteristics in a good or service, a price change can be analysed into change due to quality change and that due to other factors (for an early treatment of hedonic methods, see Griliches 1971).
4 *Link method.* The link method exploits information on closely related items. If the old item is last observed in t–1, and the new one is first

> observed in t, then the price change between t–1 and t is calculated using the price change of the closely related item between t–1 and t and, thereafter, the change in the price of the new item. This is the most commonly used method outside sample rotation. It also implies a quality adjustment: in this case the price difference between the closely related good and the new good is treated as reflecting nothing but quality change.

After the Boskin report, the BLS extended the use of its quality-adjustment tools to a wider range of product categories. In particular, hedonic methods, which prior to 1998 were used only in the apparel category, have been introduced for personal computers, washers and dryers, microwave ovens, refrigerators, televisions, VCRs, DVD players, camcorders, consumer audio product components and college textbooks (Abraham 2003).

Because unverifiable assumptions about the relationships between an unobservable quantity and various observable quantities have to be made, the quality-change issue is extremely controversial. As is well known, a full 0.7 per cent of the 1.1 per cent total bias estimated by the Boskin Commission was due to neglected quality changes (and new products, which were treated jointly). But the Boskin findings were criticised by other economists. Some have pointed out that the estimates are likely too high and criticised the lack of evidence Boskin *et al.* provide (see Abraham 1997, Baker 1997, Triplett 1997; to some extent also Hulten 1997), while others regard the estimates as probably conservative (see Diewert 1997). Given that no more direct evidence is available because any estimate is based on unverifiable auxiliary assumptions, is there any way to adjudicate between the differing opinions? I think there is, but one has to put the concept behind the CPI itself at stake. One way to argue that the COLI framework is not quite as useful as most economists working in the field would have us believe is to point out the difficulties it generates with respect to its measurement. This has been argued before (see Deaton 1998), and the argument is quite convincing from a practical point of view. Measurability is clearly a condition of usefulness for an index number.

But while I am sympathetic to this standpoint, in my view it is overly positivistic. It is too reminiscent of the logical empiricists' attempt to police our language by banning talk about unverifiable states of affairs. It seems rather that a concept can be adequate even though no measurement procedure is associated with it. Certainly, measurability is a plus, but a plus that, perhaps, cannot always be had.

The next section will address the quality-change issue from the point of view of the index-number purpose. That is, it will ask whether the treatment of quality changes in the CPI is adequate given the epistemic or practical purpose that is pursued with the CPI.

III

The idea that the ultimate criterion for assessing whether measurement procedure associated with an index number is adequate in whether it serves the index-number purpose has a long history in economic measurement. But it is not always clear what it amounts to: '[Wesley Clair] Mitchell made the connection between the design of an index number and its purpose so much a part of his approach to price indexes that it was repeated as a mantra by others years after, sometimes apparently without a clear sense of what was meant' (Reinsdorf and Triplett 2004). In my terminology, the expression 'an index number serves its purpose' signifies that the index number helps in realising an accepted epistemic or practical end (for this terminology, see Kitcher 2001). Epistemic ends are those aims of science that relate to its cognitive dimension, such as scientific explanation or other theoretical analysis of phenomena. Irving Fisher, for example, constructed index numbers in the context of his work on the quantity theory of money. Being able to test the quantity theory helps us in explaining the business cycle, which is of great epistemic significance. Practical ends are those that relate to action. The escalation of wages, income tax brackets and social security programmes as well as devising a target for monetary policy are prominent practical index-number purposes.

Of course, what is an end from one point of view is a mere means from another. Diewert (2001) cites 'measuring a cost-of-living-index' as an index-number purpose. Surely, this will double up as a means to a different end such as 'insulating benefits recipients from changes in the cost of living'. The latter, in turn, may be a means towards reducing inequality in society, which in turn may be a means towards achieving greater social justice (and so on).

We therefore have to stop somewhere and as in the last chapter I want to focus on the escalation of federal social security programmes. The reason to focus on this index-number purpose is that it has great practical significance, both for benefit recipients as well as the federal budget, and consequently it's the one that has received the greatest media and academic coverage.

The core instrument in my argument is a taxonomy of quality changes. One can distinguish three types of quality change: *quantitative* changes or 'mere repackaging'; *spurious* quality changes (that is, changes that do *not* improve consumer wellbeing); and *genuine* quality changes (that is, changes that improve consumer wellbeing). In practice, many product modifications will be a mix of the three but for the purposes of the argument to be made in this chapter it is valuable to distinguish them.

Quantitative changes or 'mere repackaging' occurs when the standard unit of trade for an otherwise qualitatively identical good changes; for example, the size of soda bottles, the number of square feet of an apartment or the package size of a dry good. The good is the same, but one buys more or less of it. Sometimes we can think of a modification in terms of repackaging even though the good has changed qualitatively, by an appropriate redefinition. If the quality of petrol has improved such that it yields an increase in the number of miles per litre for all types of vehicles, then we can think of the traded good as 'miles from fuel' rather than 'petrol' and conceptualise the quality change as a mere repackaging (for this example, see Schultze and Mackie 2002: 108).

Some economists seem to think that *all* quality changes can be treated as instances of repackaging (see Fisher and Shell 1968, 1972). Indeed hedonic methods to estimate the value of quality changes presuppose this. But many changes are more than a mere repackaging. Increasing the CPU speed in a computer may, within a certain range, be treated as 'more of the same'. However, at some point a faster computer becomes a qualitatively different kind of thing than its slower predecessor because it allows new kinds of applications to be run and supports new kinds of peripherals. Among such genuine quality changes there may be some from which the consumer benefits, others from which he or she suffers a loss, and still others that are neutral. Often, it is much easier to tell *that* the quality has genuinely changed than to tell *in which direction* it has changed. Imagine the good we are interested in is music records, and we try to compare vinyl and CDs with respect to consumer benefit. Everybody will probably agree that CDs are genuinely *different* from vinyl. But are they better or worse? One aspect from which consumers are likely to benefit is the smaller size and lighter weight. But at least some consumers prefer the warmer analogous sound of vinyl to the colder digital sound of CDs. (In fact, today it is debated whether we should move from a 16-bit standard to a 24-bit standard, one reason for which is surely that a trained ear can tell that a song recorded with a 16-bit depth sounds 'digital'.) And it is completely unclear whether CDs are really more durable than vinyl records – despite what was advertised when they were introduced back in 1982. Another example is word processors. New generations of word processors certainly introduce new functions and thus may be regarded as quality improvements. With an increased number of functions, however, also comes increased complexity and often decreased user-friendliness and, at least in the case of *some* word processors, decreased reliability. I know more than a few users who prefer working on LaTex not only because of its handling of mathematical typesetting but also because of the reliability with which one can produce results. The trade-off is, of course, that a typical LaTex editor has about as few fancy features as word processors used to have before Windows was introduced over 20 years ago. But it simply isn't clear *a priori* whether 'fancy feature' or 'reliable output' is a more important characteristic.

A third example is provided by increased product variety. It is undeniable that to some extent consumers benefit from an increased variety. The usual economic rationale is that consumers' preferences can be more effectively satisfied when product variety is greater (see Feenstra 1992; Hausman 1996; Trajtenberg 1990; and for a brief discussion, Griliches 1997). With the same degree of justification one can say that increased product variety reduces welfare because of increased search costs in the form of time, stress, deliberation and so on. Furthermore it is clear that more is not always better. While it is nice to now have cereals available in supermarkets, there is probably little additional value in having yet another variety of Cheerios (Triplett 1997).

To give meat to the idea of distinguishing between spurious and genuine quality changes, some standard of 'consumer benefit' that is different from consumer preference is required. Developing a precise account of this distinction is beyond the scope of this chapter. Nevertheless, I do want to indicate the kind of idea I have in mind. Roughly, the distinction is that between 'actual' or 'brute' and 'reflective' or 'considered' preferences. Actual or brute preferences are those people display spontaneously when facing a choice situation, while reflective or considered preferences are those they would have *all things considered* (such a distinction is now standard in the literature on deliberative democracy; see, for example, Elster 1998; Pettit 2001; Sunstein 1993). 'All things considered' encompasses a variety of sources of information. I have a strong actual preference for going out and getting a drink tonight rather than sitting at the desk and finishing this chapter. But a little contemplation tells me that it will not only cost me the rest of the evening but also a considerable part of tomorrow. Some research reveals the health effects. A call to my girlfriend reveals she won't be amused. An email from my editor reveals a new deadline for submitting the manuscript. And so on. It is important to note that part of the sought information is factual in nature while another part concerns the points of view or tastes of others. After the process of deliberation my actual preferences will be in line with my reflective preferences. But we can distinguish between the two because we will not always go through the process of deliberation even though we could and sometimes should.

Clearly much shopping behaviour is based on actual rather than reflective preferences. And the deviations are not random but systematic. It would be hard to explain many stylised facts about advertising, supermarket layout etc. otherwise. Interestingly, although the distinction between actual and reflective preferences seems like a far cry from standard welfare economics, it is in fact part and parcel of price measurement practice. Indeed, both the BLS as well as the Boskin Commission implicitly draw a distinction along similar lines. If they did not, neither BLS practice nor the arguments given by the Commission would make sense. Each of the BLS methods to deal with quality changes tries to extract some objective information about the product and estimates the value for the consumer on this basis. Just take the so-called direct methods. Here an attempt is made to estimate the effect of product modifications on welfare on the basis of information about the investment made to introduce the change or a vector of product characteristics. But unless reflective preferences matter, either information is irrelevant – consumers would prefer the way they prefer, independently of such 'objective features'.

Similarly, the Boskin Commission sometimes tries to argue that there is a lot of reason to believe that the quality of the products in various categories has genuinely changed for the better – safer cars, fresher fruit and vegetables, greater variety, faster and more reliable surgeries, etc. None of these considerations would be relevant if the focus was on *actual* preferences. If that was the case, the only relevant source of information would be the consumers themselves. Indicating that information about objective properties is relevant shows that reflective, not actual, preferences are to be measured here.

Now let us turn to the purpose of escalating federal programmes. The idea behind escalation is to insulate benefit recipients from changes in the general level of consumer prices. Usually, the question of how to calculate the correct escalation formula is addressed by deciding about a precise concept of 'cost of living' first, and then to adjust details about the measurement procedure on its basis. As I have argued in the previous chapter, the decision about the 'cost of living' concept is ultimately a political (rather than scientific) one because it concerns a societal *aim*, and decisions about societal aims have to be politically legitimised.

Therefore, here I want to bypass the conceptual issue and ask whether we could not say something substantial about the treatment of quality changes, given what we know about the index-number purpose, but without invoking a precise concept of 'cost of living'. I do think that this is possible: in a large number of cases, quality-induced price increases are real increases in the level of consumer prices quite independently of whether consumers benefit from them.

To see this, consider the three above-mentioned kinds of changes. The first concerns quantitative changes. Imagine, as in the example, the budget in the first year is 10 units of food and 1 unit of housing in our toy economy. There are 50,000 calories in each unit of food. In the second year, food is repackaged so that each unit now contains 52,500 calories, an additional 5 per cent. The price goes up by 10 per cent, say. In general, when products are repackaged there are two possibilities: either the old packs continue to be sold or they are withdrawn. If they are still available, nothing changes because we can still use the old version in the calculation of the price index. But if they cannot be bought any more, as in the example, consumers may face real constraints. For example, in order to satisfy their year-one diet of 500,000 calories, in year two consumers have to continue buying 10 units. Even though the price *per calorie* has risen by only 4.75 per cent, in order to be as well off as in the first year consumers have to spend the whole additional 10 per cent. Of course, if they do so, they receive an extra 5 per cent of food. But they receive the extra amount whether they want it or not. The price *level* has thus increased for them (for a similar reasoning, see Gross 2004). Now suppose we address this type of quality change in the way Boskin *et al.* suggest (Boskin *et al.* 1996). That is, we allow the price index for food to increase by only 4.75 per cent. Because of the indivisibility of traded units, consumers would now be able to purchase only 9 units of food with 27,500 calories less than in the previous year. Federal payments are indexed exactly in order to prevent such losses.

The next type concerns spurious quality changes – changes with no genuine value for the consumer. In the terminology introduced above, consumers do not reflectively prefer the new over the old good, although they might actually prefer the new good. It should not be controversial to say that, from the point of view of insulating benefit recipients from increases in the price level, a price change that is induced by a change in a characteristic of a good that does not constitute a genuine benefit for the consumer has to be considered a pure price change. I don't see any way to argue that a benefit recipient should bear the cost of a product modification if he does not genuinely gain from the modification.

Third are quality changes that have genuine benefits for the consumer. Here as in the first case it depends on whether the old product is still available. If it is, nothing changes because the old product can (at least temporarily) remain in the basket. If the product is discontinued, consumers have to purchase the new version, whether they want it or not. Suppose a third good is added to our toy basket, a hip operation. From year one to year two the quality of hip operations changes for the genuine benefit of the patient: shorter required hospital stay; less pain; higher chance of success, etc. The price changes from 10,000 to 15,000. How is this price change to be treated? From the point of view of the consumer, the price level has increased by a full 50 per cent. If a hip operation is required, and there is no choice between the two treatments, then, in order to protect the consumer from the losses due to price increases, he has to be compensated for the higher price – even if the utility increases by the same amount as the price (parameter ζ in our example changes from, say, 1 to 1.5).

The hip operation was, of course, a *forced* substitution and as such already a departure from the assumptions of general equilibrium theory. *Forced substitutions are to be treated as mere price changes.* While it is probably the case that forced substitutions are more common than general equilibrium theory suggests, it is certainly true that some substitutions are deliberate. How ought one to treat deliberate substitutions?

Suppose now that there are two strata in our society, waged workers and benefit recipients. There is considerable heterogeneity among consumers, especially within the waged workers group. Suppose further that plasma TVs are a new variety of television sets, and that all consumers actually and reflectively prefer plasma to conventional TVs at *some* price $p_{\text{plasma}} > p_{\text{conventional}}$, but that the price difference varies among consumers. The new TV sets are sold at very high prices first, either because of vertical discrimination behaviour of monopolistic producers or because of high production costs, but over time their prices gradually decrease. Thus more and more consumers are able to buy plasma TVs. I think there are two reasons to believe that plasma TVs should, at some point (albeit much after their initial appearance on the market), be introduced into the index without adjusting for their quality difference.

It is of course a political decision whether a society wants to support certain groups, a decision that needs political sanction. However, it seems inconsistent on the one hand to support a group for whatever reason but then on the other hand to exclude them from the progress the society makes (or, to say it in a more value-neutral way, from the change the society undergoes). If, at some point, it becomes standard to consume one kind of product in the rest of society, it would seem unfair not to let benefit recipients change with the rest of society.

Keeping utility constant means freezing recipients' lifestyles in the base year. Basing social security payments on a COLI thus means (to say it with a vivid image) that benefit recipients write their letters on mechanical typewriters, drive in huge, heavy and noisy cars, watch films on black-and-white screen TV sets and live in houses without central heating (if these products happen to be available still and cheaper than the more recent replacement). This is absurd. Given that we want to support the disadvantaged groups in the first place, it would be antithetical to ask them to live the lifestyles of an age gone by (or else, if they buy the goods that are contemporary standard, to buy less and less of them).

The preceding discussion also reveals a second reason for including new goods at some point without adjusting for the quality change. Frequently, at some point new product varieties tend to become cheaper than their predecessors as their relative market shares change. When it was introduced, colour photography was more expensive than black and white but now it's the other way around. Vinyl records today are only available from specialised stores at relatively high prices. The same is in the process of happening with DVDs versus videos, digital versus analogue photography and so on. Thus, it might not only be fair to substitute older with newer product varieties, at some point it might be the cheaper thing to do.

IV

Surprisingly, an earlier review of the CPI, conducted by the Stigler Committee, supports my point of view regarding forced uptrading – despite the fact that the Stigler Committee (like the Boskin Commission) recommended the COLI framework for the CPI. The Stigler Committee was concerned about the problems of price measurement during wartime when many goods are rationed or become completely unavailable. The Committee argued (quoted from Reinsdorf and Triplett 2004: 5):

> In periods of wartime . . . price quotations on the virtually unobtainable commodities may not show much increase, or even be rigidly fixed by price controls. Consumers are driven to available substitutes, which are more expensive relative to desired performance (forced uptrading) or

> rise rapidly in response to expanding demands. Few economists or consumers come to the defense of the rigidly fixed market basket approach under these circumstances. This suggests strongly that what is in fact being measured is not the cost of a fixed set of consumer goods and services, but rather the cost of maintaining a constant level of utility.

In other words, if a consumer is forced to buy a higher-priced substitute, he should be compensated for the extra expense even if the substitute is of a higher quality. This recommendation seems to run against the COLI concept: forced uptrading is still uptrading, implying higher consumers' utilities.

The point I want to make here is this. From the point of view of the benefit-receiving consumer, increases in the level of prices, even if they are accompanied by higher quality, remain price increases if the consumer is compelled to purchase the higher-quality products. There are a variety of reasons why a consumer may be obliged to buy better goods: the cheaper variety is rationed or otherwise unavailable; companies substitute a good with a qualitatively improved variant; an older variety is crowded out because everybody else prefers the new variety, and so on. In order to achieve the same (base-period) standard of living in the changed world, the consumer needs the extra funds that buy the available goods *even if the new goods make him better off* in terms of the 'utility' he or she receives from the goods. This is why a constant-utility approach cannot be appropriate for the CPI.

So far I have argued that a constant-utility framework is inadequate for the CPI because there are important situations in which it seems right to compensate benefit recipients for quality-induced price increases even though the higher quality of the goods increases their utility. There is also the reverse problem: there are situations in which it seems appropriate *not* to compensate benefit recipients even if they incur utility losses. Suppose, unlike the previous examples, that the uptrading is in no way forced but rather a result of a change in tastes. Suppose that over time benefit recipients acquire a taste for the higher-quality varieties of goods at higher prices – given a genuine choice between the two alternatives. This is akin to the expensive-tastes problem for welfarist egalitarianism. These recipients will suffer genuine utility losses if they are not enabled to purchase the better variety but most people would argue that to compensate for such losses isn't a problem for society.

To go back to the quote from the Stigler report, the Committee's other remark is correct: a rigidly fixed-basket approach is not appropriate either. A fixed-basket approach is only adequate in a static world in which nothing but the price vector changes. Now, is there anything positive we can say about what concept is likely to be appropriate?

From the preceding considerations it follows that a trailing Laspeyres index will probably serve the indexation purpose best. In the base year, a basket of goods is defined either by the target group's actual choices or by selecting goods that are regarded as appropriate. This decision, to repeat it, is political. The basket is then regularly updated with goods, which constitute the current substitutes for the base-level goods. The frequency of updating depends on the dynamics of the economy. At one extreme lies a totally static world in which the basket of goods remains fixed. At the other extreme there may be periods of crisis such as wars, where the basket may have to be updated several times a year. Under usual circumstances, in a modern capitalist economy, an adequate period of updating will probably be a small number of years.

It may come as some surprise that the BLS practice *prior* to some of the recently introduced changes is more consistent with the purpose of escalating federal programmes than the recent practice. The CPI used to be a trailing Laspeyres index, its weights being updated every decade or so. Given the dynamics of the US economy, the updating period seems a bit long but the framework is correct. Further, new goods used to be introduced into the index years after their appearance on the market – for example automobiles in 1935, air conditioners in 1964, VCRs in 1987 and mobile phones in 1998. But, as I have argued, this is just how it should be. When the indexation of federal spending programmes is the chosen concern, the old CPI used to be the more appropriate index.

4 Measurement between the absolute and the arbitrary

I

In a famous paper, Jim Bogen and Jim Woodward claim that 'data provide evidence for phenomena' (Bogen and Woodward 1988). The point they want to make is that theories usually make predictions about unobservable *phenomena* – stable and repeatable features of the world that are of theoretical interest – rather than observable *data* – the idiosyncratic outcomes of specific measurement procedures. Phenomena are not there waiting for us to be picked up, we rather *infer* a phenomenon on the basis of data by means of more or less involved procedures. In economics, index numbers play a vital role in this process. But under what conditions is a datum evidence for a hypothesis about some phenomenon? What are the right aggregation procedures? Under what conditions is prima facie evidence for a hypothesis that some economic quantity has such and such a value valid and/or sound evidence?

The aim of this chapter is to discuss these measurement issues at a somewhat more general level. For the sake of continuity with Chapters 2 and 3 I take the so-called index-number problem as the starting point. The index-number problem addresses the issue of combining a set of data on individuals (such as goods, quantities, unemployment, household incomes) such that a single number that represents the aggregate *level* of the pertinent variable results (for an application to price indices, see Diewert 1987). There is an indefinite number of ways to aggregate the data on individuals. Thus, the question is: Which way is the right way?

Various approaches have been offered in the history of economic measurement. In what follows, I will discuss the major contenders and find each of them wanting in one or more respects. Next, I will turn to theories of measurement *in philosophy* and examine whether they can provide the required resources. After rejecting both the set-theoretic account of measurement as well as operationalism I will discuss Hasok Chang's coherentist theory of measurement and develop and apply it to the economic context.

II

In a typical modern economy innumerable market transactions are realised at any given point in time. For policy and planning, we have to disregard the countless details of the particular transactions and try to use one or more indicators that adequately summarise the required information. The index-number problem can be regarded as the challenge posed by the fact that there is an indefinite number of ways to aggregate individual data into a single index.

Often (though not always) the index-number problem is discussed in the context of price indices, which aggregate data on prices and quantities of traded goods into a single number that represents the price level. One reason why I look at that debate here is that it constitutes the only systematic discussion of measurement issues in economics that I am aware of. Another is that the reader is already acquainted with a concrete case from the previous two chapters.

In the history of economic measurement, three major strategies have been offered to solve the (price) index-number problem: the *stochastic* (aka 'atomistic') approach, the *test* (aka 'axiomatic') approach and the *economic* (aka 'functional') approach (Diewert 1993 further mentions a so-called 'fixed-basket approach' and a 'Divisia index approach' but they are less prominent in the literature and discussing them would carry no additional insight).

The *stochastic* approach goes back to William Stanley Jevons's attempts to measure the loss in value of gold after the mid-nineteenth-century gold discoveries in California and Australia (Jevons 1884 [1863], 1884 [1869]). It is therefore a very specific approach to index numbers: not only is it limited to a price index, it also specifies the purpose – which in the case at hand is a particular causal inquiry (for a history, see Aldrich 1992).

According to Jevons, the causes of all price changes could be separated into two kinds of factors: changes in the money (that is, gold) supply and random disturbances caused by what he called the 'conditions of supply and demand'. Thus, with a large number of independent observations, averaging over individual price changes will eliminate the random influences and thereby reveal the effect of the change in the money supply. Jevons advocated taking an unweighted geometric average of price relatives as the correct index number.

The problem with the main idea of Jevons's approach is that it relies on the assumption that the unsystematic influences – those not due to changes in the money supply – are independent. But we know that they are not. When two goods are substitutes for each other (for instance, butter and margarine), their prices will tend to move in opposite directions. By contrast, when two goods are complements (for instance, cars and their spare parts), their prices will tend to move in the same direction. Thus, unless we know *how* the prices (and quantities) of the traded goods bear on each other, we cannot measure the effect of the systematic influence without being likely to encounter a bias. While others have made this criticism before him, John Maynard Keynes's discussion of it appears to have been most influential (Keynes 1909, 1930: 76f.; for a brief account of the history, see Diewert 1993). Keynes in fact attacked the whole idea quite fundamentally by pointing out that there is no *one systematic* influence on all price relatives to begin with. In his view, there are only the prices of various 'composite goods', that is, the purchases of well-defined groups of households. Thus the stochastic approach is at best incomplete. I say 'at best' because, even if Keynes is wrong in saying that there is no systematic influence on all prices, still one has to solve the problem of how to account for relative price changes. But if Keynes is right, the whole idea seems flawed. Modern successors of Jevons (for instance, Clements and Izan 1987; Selvanathan and Prasada Rao 1994) cannot avoid these problems either. For example, Selvanathan and Prasada Rao include a term to account for relative price changes. However, including it renders their problem underidentified and hence they have to make identifying assumptions. Such assumptions will always be to some extent arbitrary, and in particular the choice these authors make seems to contradict the facts.

The *test* approach to index numbers was first systematically explored by Irving Fisher (Fisher 1911, 1922) and later developed into the so-called axiomatic approach (see Vogt and Janos 1997). Its main idea is that index numbers should, by their very nature, satisfy a set of formal tests. For example, when the economy remains totally static – that is, neither prices nor quantities change – the price index should remain unchanged (Fisher's 'Identity Test'). When the prices of all goods change proportionally, the index should grow by the same proportion (Fisher's 'Proportionality Test'). The index should be identical to its reciprocal when the periods are exchanged for one another (Fisher's 'Time-Reversal Test'). The index for period 2 relative to period 1 multiplied by the index for period 3 relative to period 2 should be identical to the index for period 3 relative to period 1 (Fisher's 'Circularity Test'). And so on.

The main problem with Fisher's approach is that it yields too much and too little information about the design of an index number at the same time. On the one hand already in the 1930s Ragnar Frisch proved that no index number could satisfy all tests that seem desirable *a priori* (Frisch 1930, 1936). On the other hand, the test approach is silent on a number of very important aspects of the design of an index number, most saliently the choice of weights (see Reinsdorf and Triplett 2004).

The latter problem of incompleteness can be regarded as the more fundamental of the two. One can always withdraw one or more of the tests and thereby make the remaining set consistent. But since the approach is not informative about which of the tests are more important than others it is unclear which tests should be withdrawn and which should be retained and hence it is incomplete.

The standard response is to analyse the weaknesses of the two approaches as a failure to link index-number design with *theory* – on the basis of which such open questions could be settled. For instance, Keynes (1909) argued that an index number, rather than trying to extract a signal from noisy data as did Jevons's, should attempt to measure a *concrete aggregate*. Usually this has been interpreted to mean 'a quantity given by economic theory', and indeed this is what the *economic* approach to index numbers aims at.

The economic approach regards the problem of finding the best index number as a consumer choice problem. It defines the 'exact' index number as the ratio of the expenditure consumers would have made had they chosen utility-maximising budget weights at the price vector of the current period to the actual expenditure in the base period, holding utility constant. In this way, it allows a number of issues to be addressed that the other approaches leave open. For instance, it does not regard relative price changes as random deviations from a central tendency like the stochastic approach (recall that Keynes pointed out that the deviations are not random) but rather as systematic. How they relate to each other, in turn, can be determined by solving the choice problem. Moreover, it has an answer to choosing the weights, which are left unspecified in the test approach: the actual weights consumers choose (and the counterfactual weights they would choose at the current price vector had utility been constant) are relevant. It also gives some hints about which of Fisher's tests are important and which can be neglected. For instance, it is a well-known fact that, when preferences are not homothetic, income and substitution effects calculated with the initial indifference curve as the starting point will not be equal to income and substitution effects calculated the other way – and hence we know that Fisher's time-reversal test does not need to be fulfilled.

Consequently, the economic approach to index numbers is widely regarded as successful – and indeed imperative (Frisch 1936: 1):

> The problem of how to construct an index number is as much one of economic theory as of statistical technique. Indeed, all discussions about the 'best' index formula, the 'most correct' weights, etc., must be vague and indeterminate so long as the meaning of the index is not exactly defined. Such a definition cannot be given on empirical grounds only but requires theoretical considerations. It seems fitting, therefore, to include a survey of this subject in the ECONOMETRICA surveys of *general economic theory*.

I find this judgement largely unwarranted. True, the economic approach addresses a number of issues that its alternative leave unspecified. But of course, providing *an* answer to a question of interest does not imply that it is *the right* answer even if the obvious alternatives provide no answer at all. Justifying the results of the economic approach to index numbers on the basis of economic theory is question-begging. What is needed, therefore, is a meta-approach that allows us to ask and answer whether the particular solution provided by the economic approach is appropriate. Philosophers tend to pride themselves with having the ability to provide a bird's eye (that is, meta) view on many issues. Let us therefore turn to philosophy and see whether we find any resources to address our question.

III

The index-number problem is an instance of a predicament one can refer to as the 'fundamental problem of measurement'. In most general terms, we can state it as follows. In order to know the value of a variable, we need to know that the measurement procedure associated with it is veridical (that is, that the procedure gives the correct result). But in order to be able to check whether the procedure is veridical, we need to know the value of the variable. Since we have no independent access to either the value of the variable or the accuracy of the procedure, we can never know whether the measurement procedure is veridical or what the value of the variable is (see Figure 4.1).

One can easily see that the index-number problem is an instance of this more general problem. If we want to know what the value of the change of the price level in a given period is, we need to measure it with the right (or in economists' parlour, the 'best' or 'ideal' or 'exact') index number. But in order to know whether any given index number is correct, we need to compare the value it yields with the value of the variable measured. Since we have no independent access to the value of the variable or to the correctness of the index number, we can neither know whether our index number is correct nor what the value of the variable of interest is.

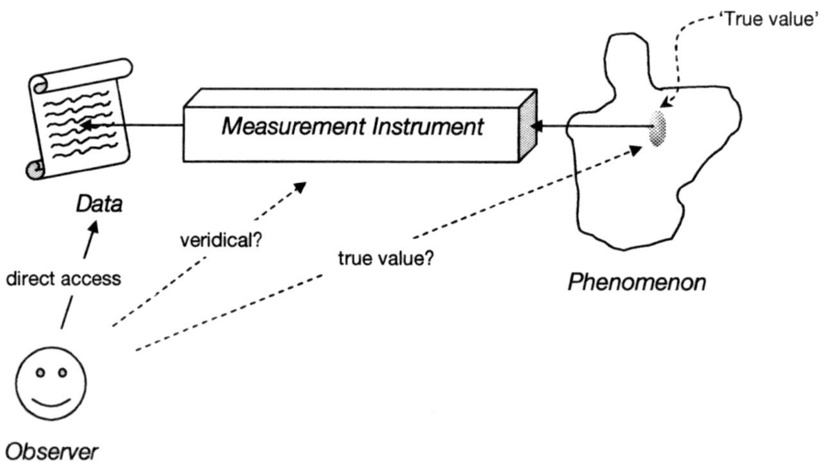

Figure 4.1 The fundamental problem of measurement.

Three solution strategies have been offered in the literature, which I'd like to call the *absolute*, the *arbitrary* and the *equilibrating*, to use Catherine Elgin's apt terms (Elgin 1996, 1997). The first strategy denies the impossibility of independent access to the phenomena of interest. It claims that certain aspects of certain phenomena are independently accessible and tries to build up knowledge from this secure foundation. The second strategy regards certain procedures as reliable by fiat. The third strategy accepts both sides of the epistemic dilemma but asserts that we can gain genuine knowledge about the world by an iterative process that starts with the given but refines (or self-corrects) and enriches the admittedly imperfect initial claims to knowledge. In the measurement literature, the first strategy is exemplified in the set-theoretic account measurement (under *one* interpretation); the second, by a naïve version of conventionalist operationalism; and the third by Hasok Chang's pluralist coherentism. Let us consider each of them in turn.

The set-theoretic account of measurement Measurement can be regarded as the assignment of numbers to attributes of phenomena (for instance, the length of a metre stick; the boiling point of water; the average unemployment rate in the United Kingdom in 2006) in such a way that numerical properties accurately represent these attributes. For example, if we have two rigid rods A and B and we assign them the numbers 100 and 200, respectively, then these numbers accurately represent an attribute, say their length, only if B is indeed twice as long as A. That is, if we produce a synthetic stick 2A by laying two identical copies of A end to end in a straight line, and then place B side by side with 2A such that they coincide at one end, then they coincide at the other end as well. So-called 'fundamental measurement' differs from 'derived measurement' in that it does not require prior measurement of other attributes. Contrast length with density. Density is defined as mass divided by volume and thus requires prior measurement of these attributes.

The set-theoretic account of measurement asks what structural properties a phenomenon must have such that numbers can represent one or more of its attributes accurately (my discussion partly follows the account given in Krantz *et al.* 1971, Ch. 1). The basic strategy is to find a set of axioms, which represent some qualitative laws the phenomenon of interest is supposed to obey, and then to prove two theorems from these axioms. The representation theorem establishes a formal similarity between an empirical and a numerical structure; the uniqueness theorem establishes what kinds of transformations are permissible on the mapping between empirical and numerical structure.

Suppose we have a set of objects S such as stones of different materials. A scratch test reveals which of any given pair of stones is harder and thus defines a relationship 'harder as', $>$. We then call a *relational structure* a set together with one or more relationships defined on that set, for example

$\langle S, \succ \rangle$, which is an *empirical* relational structure. An example for a *numerical* relational structure is $\langle R, > \rangle$, where R is the set of real numbers and $>$ the relationship 'greater than'. With this terminology in place, we can say that a representation theorem asserts that if an empirical relational structure satisfies certain axioms, then a homomorphism can be constructed into a certain numerical relational structure; that is, we can prove that if $\langle S, \succ \rangle$ is a total order, then there exists a real-valued function ϕ on S such that for all $s, t \in S$,

$$s \succ t \text{ if and only if } \phi(s) > \phi(t).$$

We can further prove a uniqueness theorem, which defines the scale on which the attribute is measurable. In this case, for example, one can show that ϕ' is another real-valued function on S with the same property if and only if there is a strictly increasing function f, with domain and range equal to R, such that for all $s \in S$, $\phi'(s) = f[\phi(s)]$, which means that ϕ is an *ordinal* scale.

If an attribute is measurable on an ordinal scale the assignment of numbers is arbitrary as long as it preserves the order among the objects. Two other important kinds of scales are interval and ratio scales. An interval scale is unique under affine transformations, that is, all transformations of the form $\phi'(s) = \alpha\phi(s) + \beta$, where $\alpha > 0$, are permissible. Temperature is measurable on an interval scale. It requires arbitrary fixation of both a unit and an interval (for instance, melting point of water = 0°C, boiling point of water = 100°C). A ratio scale is unique under the transformations of the form $\phi'(s) = \alpha\phi(s)$, $\alpha > 0$. Length, mass and time are measurable on a ratio scale. They require the arbitrary fixation of a unit (the length of some standard rod = 1 m).

Some simple considerations show that the justification of measurement procedures in this foundational sense requires both a great deal of background knowledge as well as stable and potent laws of nature. To establish a scale such as Moh's hardness scale requires at least the knowledge that the harder material will reliably scratch softer material and stable laws governing this behaviour. We could not use it even for a given sample if the orders established by a series of tests did not coincide. Moreover, if the scale is supposed to indicate the relative hardness of substances such as diamond, topaz and quartz (which Moh's scale is aiming at), it is further required that the sample on which the order is established is representative for other specimens of the same substance. That this is not just the usual problem of induction will be plain once we look at economic cases.

Knowledge and stability of the required kind are not always available, even in the measurement of physical attributes. Temperature is a case in point. It is sometimes said that the measurement of temperature depends on an expansion law of a certain form (Krantz 1971: 1428): 'In some cases, physical measurement is based on quantitative laws and their importance for measurement is generally recognised. For example, interval-scale measurement of temperature is based on the law of linear expansion of a thermometric substance.' But how do we know that a thermometric substance expands linearly unless we already know we can reliably measure temperature? (Chang [2004: 59] calls this the problem of nomic measurement. I will discuss Chang's views in more detail below.) Simply *assuming* that a substance expands linearly clearly won't do if there are alternative substances whose expansion behaviour differs – as was observed in the early history of thermometry.

So this is why I call the literature in the foundations of measurement an example of an *absolute* epistemological strategy. It presupposes that we have prior well-established knowledge of certain determinate kinds. In the case of the simple hardness scale it was the scratch test we had to know to be reliable as well as the existence (and knowledge) of a number of laws governing the behaviour of this attribute. But ordinal measurement is the simplest possible case. In other cases we have to know much more about the structure of the attribute under consideration. Take length as another example. Length is extensively measurable; that is, we can define a so-called concatenation operation, which allows us to create synthetic objects by 'adding' individual objects to one another in certain ways. The measurement of length thus not only requires that we can tell reliably which of two rods is longer by simple inspection (that is, without using a measuring device!) but also that we can make perfect copies of some standard rod and that we can compare concatenated 'synthetic' rods reliably and by simple inspection.

For attributes such as length, mass, time and so forth it may make sense to assert that knowledge and stability of the requisite kind are available. But even in these paradigmatic cases of measurement this may not always have been true. Metre sticks, balances and clocks are just as much inventions as are scratch tests or thermometers. Science is a dynamic process, and the amount of reliable background knowledge changes gradually. The theory of measurement is helpful in that it makes explicit conditions that are sufficient for asserting that an attribute is measurable. But it provides little guidance for cases in which none of the typical axioms are known to be fulfilled.

One way to express the problem is this. The set-theoretic account of measurement tells us what structure an attribute of a phenomenon must have in order to be measurable *given we have a reliable measurement instrument* but it does not tell us where and how to look for a reliable instrument in the first place. Measurement in economics provides an excellent case in point. Since our empirical knowledge is so poorly developed, there are few tests available which would tell us whether any axioms of the theory of measurement are fulfilled.

Consider price measurement. At the very least, the one condition that always has to be met when we want to call an attribute measurable is that the objects (or phenomena) that have the attribute can be ordered. But in the absence of an index number, it is hard to tell which of two economies has a higher price level. Consider Table 4.1, first focusing on the left-hand side.

Table 4.1 Two toy 2 × 2 economies and associated price indices

	P_{cocoa}	Q_{cocoa}	P_{cloves}	Q_{cloves}	$I_{arithmetic}$	$I_{geometric}$	$I_{harmonic}$	$I_{Laspeyres}$	$I_{Paasche}$
ES 1	100	3	50	2					
ES 2	50	2	100	3	25%	0%	–20%	–13%	14%

ES = economic structure

In economic structure 1, the price of cocoa is 100 and that of cloves 50; in economic structure 2, it is the other way around. Which structure is, on average, more expensive?

Imagining tests which do not require index numbers is hard but not impossible. Simply laying the structures side by side, as we did in the case of length measurement, is not an option. But we can conceive of laws that connect the price level to some more readily observable attribute. For example, if the two structures are two different countries or regions within a country (rather than the same country or region at two different points of time) there could be a law that prescribes that the trade balance of structure 1 relative to structure 2 is negative if and only if $P_1 > P_2$, that is, the price level in structure 1 is greater than the price level in structure 2 (this assumes that the trade balance is known to be reliably measurable). Alternatively, and perhaps more realistically, we can imagine that we know the quantity theory to be true and we can reliably measure the growth of the money stock in each structure, which allows us to order the two structures at least with respect to the growth rates of their price levels.

Unfortunately, we have very little reliable knowledge of this kind, and, to make matters worse, those attributes with which we imagine the price level to be related usually manifest the same, if not more profound, measurement problems as the price level itself. Two of the founding fathers of modern price measurement, Jevons and Fisher, both encountered the index-number problem in the course of their investigations into the validity of the quantity theory. Surely they would not assume the truth of the theory for measurement purposes. And the history of the quantity theory shows well enough that the concept of money is just as controversial as that of the price level, not to mention the difficulties associated with attempts to measure the velocity of money in Fisher's equation of exchange. The set-theoretic account of measurement therefore cannot be of help in this context because:

> Little seems possible in the way of a careful analysis of an attribute until means are devised to say which of two objects or events exhibits more of the attribute. Once we are able to order the objects in an acceptable way, we need to examine them for additional structure, for example, by

> selecting two or more factors that affect the ordering. Then begins the search of the qualitative laws satisfied by the ordering and the additional structure.
>
> (Krantz *et al.* 1971: 32)

In other words, one has to revert to indices if one wants to make the price level measurable. But as we see from the right-hand side of Table 4.1, different indices give different results. Certainly, the numbers were chosen in this case such that the divergence of the indices is dramatic in order to make a point. Moreover, the large disagreement is an artefact of the small number of goods in the example. But a larger basket and more realistic numbers won't reduce variance to zero. The choice of an index matters.

Operationalism is another theory frequently mentioned in debates about measurement procedures. Does it suffer from the same deficiencies as the set-theoretic account of measurement?

Operationalism By itself operationalism is a non-starter for justifying measurement procedures because it is first and foremost a theory of concept legitimisation. It asserts that a concept can be applied meaningfully if, and only if (and only in the range where), there are measurement operations defined in the concept.

The founding father of operationalism, Percy Bridgman, was deeply impressed by the Einsteinian revolution but at the same time professed that Einstein's discoveries would not have had such a dramatic impact had we been more careful in analysing our pre-relativistic concepts (Bridgman 1927, Ch. 1). Einstein had shown that Newtonian physics leads to inaccurate predictions when objects at high velocities are concerned and moreover that the classical notions of absolute space and time are untenable. But a vigilant – operational – analysis of the concepts of Newtonian physics would have proved just as much. On the one hand, all operations used to establish Newton's theory require low velocities compared to the speed of light. It is then little surprising if the use of different operations, operations that work for higher velocities, leads to incompatible results – even if the concepts associated with the two distinct sets of operations carry the same names. On the other hand, any operation used to measure 'absolute space' or 'absolute time' will necessarily be relative. Hence, Bridgman argues, the terms are meaningless.

Bridgman concludes that such considerations show us that '*the concept is synonymous with the corresponding set of operations*' (ibid.: 5, original emphasis). But it is now generally accepted that he overshot the target. If the intention was to be alert when extending the domain of applicability of a concept from a region where it has been thoroughly tested to a hitherto unexplored region, then the operational definition of concept is certainly a sufficient means towards that end but by no means necessary, and it will often lead to epistemologically adverse consequences (for a historical discussion, see Moyer 1991a, 1991b; for a general account, Walter 1990).

An immediate problem concerns the identity conditions for a set of operations. It is plausible to say that length as measured by a ruler and length as measured by the transit of Venus method are two different concepts. But how similar do rulers have to be in order to play a part in the same operation? Does it matter whether they're made of plastic or platinum? What about apparently irrelevant details such as the hair colour of the person taking the measure? If we argue that neither the ruler's material (as long as it is rigid enough) nor the measurer's hair colour matter because they do not influence the measurement result, we already depart from strict operationalism because we presuppose that these operations measure the same concept.

The best-known problem of operationalism is, however, that of 'concept proliferation'. Many scientific concepts can be and are as a matter of practice measured by a variety of methods. Demanding that each method defines its own concept would lead to an abundance of mutually unrelated concepts, a situation we neither observe in science nor would we wish to.

In order to turn operationalism into a theory of measurement, one has to pair it with a version of conventionalism. Return to Table 4.1, now focusing on the right-hand side. Which of the five indices given here (which are themselves selected from an indefinite number of index-number formulae) measures the price level correctly? One way to decide is via convention. Some consensus emerges either naturally or one votes or a dictator decides by fiat, but no matter which procedure is used, it is important that the decision about which index is correct is socially, and only socially, validated.

This naïve and extreme version of 'conventionalist operationalism' has obvious flaws. The most damaging one from an empiricist's perspective is that which forecloses attempts to find more empirical justifications for measurement procedures, and this in a domain where there is no reason to believe that empirical knowledge enabling such a justification is unavailable. Whereas the set-theoretic account of measurement is defective because it demands *too much* empirical background knowledge for the justification of a specific procedure, the conventionalist account is defective because it demands *too little* (namely none).

Historically, various versions of conventionalism have been put forward in response to a difficulty with the empirical testing of certain kinds of propositions regarding, say, the rules of classical logic and the structure of space. According to some conventionalist positions such statements are analytically true because the terms they describe are implicitly defined by these statements. For example, one can regard the Euclidean geometry to be analytically true because concepts such as 'straight line' and 'point' are implicitly defined by its postulates. In describing physical space we can use any geometry in principle, and the actual choice will be determined by considerations regarding (for example) the simplicity of the resulting laws.

This version of conventionalism has been criticised on the basis of arguments to the effect that even our definitions contain empirical elements (see Quine 1953). But for our purposes it is not necessary to criticise conventionalism fundamentally. It is enough to provide reasons to believe that some choices of measurement procedures are better than others. The remainder of this chapter aims at just that. I will first discuss Hasok Chang's perspective on measurement in the remainder of this section and then proceed to my own views on index numbers, which I regard as an application to the economics context and extension of Chang's approach, in the next.

One last word on operationalism though. Even if it is deficient as a full-fledged theory of measurement, it contains an important grain of truth relevant to the index-number problem. Different measurement methods tend to have idiosyncrasies each of their own, and it is a fallacy to think different methods measure the same concept just because we attach the same name to them. Although, when pressed, most economists would agree that inflation as measured by a cost-of-living index or COLI (which, as we have seen, is close to the concept used in the United States) is a different concept from inflation as measured by a harmonised index of consumer prices or HICP (which is used in the EU). In both academic and non-academic contexts one can frequently find comparisons of 'inflation rates' across countries or time periods, pretending that such differences do not exist. From the perspective I'm trying to advance here, saying that annual inflation in January 2006 was 4.1 per cent in the United States and 2.4 per cent in the Euro zone *a priori* does not tell us anything about their relative values – US inflation may be higher, lower or identical to European inflation. We may, of course, investigate the empirical behaviour of COLI and HICP measures and find that they do not systematically differ. Or we may find that they do differ but not enough to matter in the context of a specific inquiry. But this is a question regarding a contingent fact about the world and hence requires empirical investigation. Operationalism overshoots its target because it tells us to regard concepts associated with different measurement procedures as different independently of whether or not the different procedures yield the same results. But it is right to warn us not to unwittingly use conflicting procedures unless we have investigated the behaviour of these procedures.

Hasok Chang: Henry Victor Regnault and the criterion of comparability In his explorations of early thermometry, Hasok Chang accepts both sides of our inferential predicament – that we cannot know the value of a variable of interest unless we know that our measurement procedure is veridical, and that we cannot know whether a measurement procedure is veridical unless we can compare its results with the actual values of the variable (Chang 2004). But unlike the absolute and arbitrary alternatives, he suggests ampliative principles which lead us out of the quandary – for all practical purposes. Of course, if we accept the fundamental problem of measurement, we can never have foundational knowledge of the phenomena of interest.

However, with effort, ingenuity and a fair deal of luck we can find results that *cohere* with each other.

Here is, in brief, Chang's account. It is commonly thought that temperature is measurable because it is nomically related to an observable quantity, length, by a law of linear expansion (see the earlier quote from Krantz 1971). But as I said above we cannot simply presuppose that a given substance expands linearly with temperature. Furthermore, we have good reason to believe that not all substances expand linearly because different types of thermometers (those, for instance, which use air, alcohol and mercury as thermometric fluid) disagree in their readings except at the calibration points. So how does one pick among the various options the type of thermometer whose fluid expands most closely linearly?

Chang discusses two unsuccessful attempts to solve that problem in the early history of thermometry (Chang 2004, Ch. 2). The first was the 'method of mixtures'. The idea, simplified, was the following. Mix one quantity of boiling water (at 100°C) and one quantity of freezing water (at 0°C), the combination of which should yield two quantities of water at the average temperature of 50°C. The thermometer whose reading agrees with this value most closely is the most accurate.

The method was based on the assumption that the specific heat of water is constant, that it does not depend on temperature. While a convenient and seemingly innocuous assumption at first, it was later disputed by proponents of the caloric theory of heat. According to this theory, heat is an elastic substance, which is possessed by a body to a greater or lesser quantity. The second attempt, then, was made using caloric theory. It was argued that a gaseous thermometric substance should give the most accurate reading because since the particles in gases are more widely separated all significant action in gases would be due to the caloric that fills the space between the particles. The main problem with this suggestion was that, even if the argument is correct, it fails to establish that gases expand *linearly*: even if expansion is due to only one force, this does not entail that the force operates linearly.

Henry Victor Regnault later tried to solve that problem by removing all theoretical assumptions in the interpretation of the results of a measurement procedure. He argued that, if a thermometer is to give us the correct temperature, it must at least give the same reading under the same circumstances; further, if a type of thermometer is to be an accurate instrument, all exemplars of the same type should agree in their reading. Chang calls this idea 'comparability' (ibid.: 77). Using the idea of comparability, Regnault observed the behaviour of various types of thermometer under various conditions relating, for instance, to pressure and make of the thermometer tube and found that a number of gas thermometers performed best. He eventually judged the air thermometer to provide the best standard, probably for practical reasons (atmospheric air is the easiest and cheapest to acquire, preserve and control; ibid.: 82).

It is important to point out that the comparability test does not prove that air expands linearly. It is conceivable, for instance, that another substance such as mercury expands linearly, and that differences among different token thermometers are due to impurities, which we can control to a lesser degree than we can control air impurities. Consequently, Chang concludes: 'He never strayed from the recognition that comparability did not imply truth. In the end, what Regnault managed to secure was only a rather grim judgment that everything else was worse than the air thermometer' (ibid.: 83). Regnault's achievement consisted in providing us with an instrument that reliably measures temperature – that is, whose results can be trusted not to be artefacts of the specific token instrument and context in which the measurement was taken – without the use of untested background theory.

In Chang's view, comparability is a virtue only against an ontological principle he calls the *principle of single-valuedness*, which says that a real physical property can have no more than one definite value in a given situation (ibid.: 90). This principle itself is neither a mere principle of logic, nor an empirical hypothesis whose truth can be established by scientific means. According to Chang it is rather more like a condition for the intelligibility of specific empirical hypotheses. Although the principle may be false, a statement in which someone contradicts it (say, by claiming that a cup of water has a uniform temperature of 5°C and 10°C at the same point in time) would be met with incomprehension.

The biggest advantage of Regnault's comparability criterion can be appreciated best when one sees it as an answer to the holist challenge posed by Pierre Duhem and others. According to Duhem, we can never test a single scientific hypothesis in isolation; rather, a test is always of a whole theoretical group. If we understand any test as an attempt to 'overdetermine' the value for a quantity of interest – for instance, by deriving one value from a theory and various auxiliary assumptions, and another from an empirical test – we see that in most cases various untested assumptions are needed for the determination of the value. For example, we saw above that the method of mixing presupposed (among other things) that the specific heat of water is constant. By contrast, Regnault got rid of all theoretical background assumptions – save the ontological conjecture of single-valuedness of temperature. Therefore, both praise and blame could be attributed more directly. A thermometer that didn't satisfy the comparability test could immediately be discarded (or else either the ontological hypothesis had to go or the ability of the experimenter to read the gauge – options no one felt comfortable with). On the other hand, a successful test is more instructive when fewer hypotheses are involved. If there are no auxiliary hypotheses it cannot be argued that the error from various false hypotheses cancel out each other in a given case.

Of course, comparability is only one possible response to the difficulty raised by the fundamental problem of measurement. But it avoids the criticisms raised against operationalism and the set-theoretic account of measurement. Neither does it admit any measurement procedure or give an arbitrary criterion as operationalism does; nor does it demand an unrealistically high amount of background knowledge as the set-theoretic account. Rather, it constitutes an ampliative principle, which has in this case been successful at breaking out of the circle. Before examining whether we can find a similar solution for the index-number problem, we have to look at another aspect of Chang's work.

IV

Apart from his detailed work on temperature measurement, Chang provides a more general account of justification and progress in physical science (see Chang 2004, Ch. 5). He starts out with a recognition of the circularity inherent in what I call the fundamental problem of measurement. Going through potential responses to the problem, he rejects empiricist foundationalism. The foundationalist requires that there be a set of epistemically privileged beliefs whose justification is self-evident and that other beliefs are appropriately supported by the self-justifying basic beliefs. But there simply are no self-justifying beliefs in science (and even if we think that unarticulated immediate experience is self-justifying in the right way, it has been shown to be impossible to erect edifices of scientific knowledge on it).

Nor can we give up justification altogether. Operationalism and conventionalism are no satisfactory options. The only way out of this stalemate is to seek justification not in secure foundations but in a system of mutually supporting beliefs. There is no Archimedean point to which the system is anchored. Rather, the different parts of the system cohere and thus justify each other mutually.

In the historical example described above, coherence was indeed minimal: all Regnault demanded was that the different tokens of the same type of thermometer give the same reading in the same circumstance. But we can progress from the given by a method Chang calls 'epistemic iteration', which is characterised as (ibid.: 226):

> a process in which successive stages of knowledge, each building on the preceding one, are created in order to enhance the achievement of certain epistemic goals . . . In each step, the later stage is based on the earlier stage, but cannot be deduced from it in any straightforward sense. Each link is based on the principle of respect and the imperative of progress, and the whole chain exhibits innovative progress within a continuous tradition.

Three terminological clarifications are in order. The 'principle of respect' demands that the researcher affirm an existing system of knowledge (ibid.: 225). We cannot start completely without presuppositions. Even if in the course of the inquiry the original system is modified, we should begin the inquiry from what we know. (As an aside, the principle of respect makes this epistemology Baconian rather than Cartesian.) The 'imperative of progress' is simply the driving force behind scientific inquiry – the motivation to improve upon the state of affairs (ibid.: 44). 'Epistemic virtues' are the usual ones of, for example, simplicity, fruitfulness, accuracy, consistency, scope and precision. Science, then, progresses by enhancing an epistemic virtue. Examples for such progress are given throughout the book: temperature evolved from a purely qualitative concept to an ordinal quantity and then to a cardinal quantity. That is, the epistemic virtue of 'precision' was augmented. Moreover, the temperature concept was extended from a narrow band to more extreme conditions by means of new types of thermometers. That is, the virtue of 'scope' was augmented.

In this account, truth plays no significant role. The choice of which set of epistemic virtues to pursue is a decision that is up to the community of inquirers. There is no principle hierarchy among the different virtues. Moreover, it is possible that different virtues conflict – strengthening one will diminish the other and vice versa. But there is no reason to decide *a priori* which path science should take.

V

Chang's epistemology thus suggests a way out of the quandary posed by the fundamental problem of measurement: reduce theoretical commitments to a minimum and find measurement procedures that give us reliable – stable – results. On the basis of these, employ the strategy of epistemic iteration. Finally, progress can be measured in terms of the degree to which the chosen set of epistemic virtues is enhanced. In the remainder of this chapter I want to explore whether one can apply an analogous strategy to economic matters.

There is no doubt that economics, or more specifically the theory and practice of economic measurement, sometimes progresses in Chang's sense. Certainly we know more about economic cost-of-living indices than we did at the time of Konüs, if only because the treatment has been extended from a single household to any number *n* of households (Pollak 1980), because now environmental or demographic variables can be included (Pollak 1989) and because we know how to approximate an exact, theoretical index by means of empirical indices (Diewert 1976). Within the economic approach we have thus enhanced the epistemic virtues of scope and precision. Similarly, means have been found to ameliorate the problem regarding the systematicity of relative price changes within the stochastic approach and to derive standard errors (see Clements and Izan 1987). The epistemic virtue of accuracy could thereby be enhanced.

On the other hand, it is not quite as clear whether index-number theory as a whole has progressed. Even though the economic approach is widely accepted among economists today, there remain serious doubts about its epistemic and practical merits (see Section II of this chapter as well as the two previous chapters). Nor can we say with good reason that the transition from the fixed-basket approach of William Fleetwood and Joseph Lowe (cf. Diewert 1993) to Fisher's test approach (cf. Boumans 2001) or that from the statistical approach of Jevons (cf. Reiss 2001) to the economic approach (cf. Diewert 2004) unequivocally strengthened the epistemic virtues pursued by economists. It seems rather that the different approaches provide more or less (usually, less) satisfactory answers to different kinds of questions, asked on the basis of very different theoretical presuppositions.

Recall that the fixed-basket approach answers how the cost for a given basket of goods develops over time. If this question is supposed to have any *practical* value, the basket of goods that is taken as given must be representative of something; for instance, people's actual purchases. But which purchases? Those of the base period (which yields the Laspeyres index) or those of the current period (which yields the Paasche index) or a weighted mix (which yields the Walsh index among others)? At some point it was discovered that some fixed-basket indices have undesirable properties. For instance, an index for periods 1 and 2 multiplied by the same index for periods 2 and 3, and in turn multiplied by the index for periods 3 and 1, should yield unity. The Laspeyres index fails this test.

Fisher designed his tests in the context of his search for an ideal index number for the purpose of validating the quantity theory of money. He simply wasn't concerned with the *consumer* price level. Thus, even if the test approach constitutes progress over the fixed-basket approach in *some* sense, it hard to see whether any epistemic virtue in relationship to the former question was advanced. Surely Fisher's ideal index (the geometric mean between the Laspeyres and Paasche indices) is no more precise than either the Laspeyres or the Paasche index? Perhaps it's more accurate. But accurate with respect to what variable? And how would we tell?

As we have seen, Ragnar Frisch criticised the test approach by demonstrating that no index number can satisfy all reasonable tests simultaneously, and there is no obviously preferable set of tests among the consistent tests. As an alternative he endorsed the economic approach, but he could do so only by changing the question again. Similarly, Keynes (1930) criticised the statistical approach advocated by Jevons (also in the context of the quantity theory). He, too, endorsed the economic approach but, again, this makes sense only given a change in the question.

Progress, it seems, is often hard to define because economists work on a problem (the 'index-number problem'), but they approach it from radically different backgrounds (for instance, a macro-economic versus a micro-economic background), and in so doing they redefine the question addressed. The problems, then, are only the same by name; Lowe, Jevons, Keynes, Fisher, Konüs and the other pioneers of index-number theory all worked on different problems – and consequently provided different solutions.

According to the stance taken in this book progress should and can only be assessed relative to a problem or purpose. Applying Chang's strategy, thus, entails that we begin with a practical or scientific problem such as examining the causes of changes in the value of money, economic fluctuations, poverty, wealth and income distribution and so forth. It is important to note that most more or less technical economic concepts have a pre-theoretical counterpart that is often relevant in the context of a given problem. Inflation isn't only what is measured by a price index. It is also the feeling of 'the dollar ain't worth what it used to be!' we often experience when we go shopping, particularly of course in times when prices change rapidly. Many other concepts – think of growth, unemployment, poverty and productivity – have the same dual meaning. One purpose of index numbers is to make such pre-theoretical concepts sharper, to quantify a qualitative idea.

Even if the numerical concept corrects the qualitative idea in some respects, the two should not completely disagree. A good recent example of a disagreement of the kind I have in mind happened after the introduction of the Euro in many countries of the European Union. Almost everyone I know who lives in the Euro zone has at some point complained about the enormous price increases introduced when the currency changed. And yet, official inflation rates remained modest and rather below average for most countries. This shows either that there is something wrong with the way inflation is measured in the relevant countries or that we must make some effort to explain away the mistaken impressions many people have had. Perhaps statistical agencies in the Euro area use outdated baskets of goods that are not representative of what people actually buy these days and price increases have been much lower in the old than in the new categories. But perhaps people were just more attentive to price changes when the new currency was introduced. Prices increased at the usual rate – but unlike before people now noticed the rises. The point is, we should get official inflation figures and pre-theoretical experiences in line.

An index number, thus, makes a prior, qualitative idea more precise. But how? Which of an infinite ways to quantify a quality is the correct way? That, as I've pointed out various times in Chapters 2 and 3, crucially depends on the purpose of the inquiry. We will quantify the notion of 'price inflation' differently if we aim at, say,

- escalating social security benefits;
- the indexation of private contracts;
- the indexation of tax brackets;
- providing an output deflator for separating changes in the GDP into price changes and changes in 'real' output;
- providing a target for central banks; or
- testing the quantity theory.

For indexation purposes we should measure the change in the general level of prices for the part of the population concerned (for instance, benefit recipients or waged employees with a salary between \$*X* and \$*Y*). For these purposes, for example, it is completely immaterial how the change in the price level was brought about. Not so for testing the quantity theory. Here we need to find out how much (if any) of a given change in the price level was due to changes in the money stock. We therefore have to look not only at consumer prices for specific groups of consumers but rather at all prices that can be affected by money. Further, we need to disentangle the putative influence of money from other influences.

As we have seen in the previous two chapters, a heavily circumscribed purpose will get us a long way towards a complete index-number design. Implementing such indices, then, will sometimes allow us to test their empirical relevance. If insulating benefit recipients from changes in the general level of consumer prices is the purpose of a given index and social security payments are indeed escalated by that index, we can test whether the index was successful. If the living conditions of benefit recipients over some period dramatically change (controlling for other causes of the living conditions), there must be something wrong with the index – and we can improve it and test it again and so forth.

Sometimes causal inference will have to proceed at the same time as concept formation. We neither know whether money causes prices nor, if money causes prices, which of the various aggregates is relevant. If this is the case, the strategy is complicated but in principle the method of epistemic iteration is applicable in the same way. We start with one notion of the price level, one notion of money and run tests for causality (which will be discussed in Part II of this book). If that does not yield satisfactory results, we change an associated measurement procedure and run the tests again. We stop if we get satisfactory results this time around, otherwise review the measurement procedures again, run more tests and so on. Often the process will be simplified by the nature of the purpose of the inquiry. We don't really care whether money causes *any* level of prices whatsoever. Rather, because we can control money more immediately, we would like to use it as an instrument to control the price level in so far as it is relevant for society – for example because high inflation can cause poverty and reductions in productivity because businesses cannot plan well. If this is so, the notion of 'price level' that is used in our tests for causality is already fairly constrained.

The different 'evidence' concepts of Chapter 1 can be straightforwardly applied to measurement procedures. The result of any index number that aggregates prices and quantities into a single number is prima facie evidence for a hypothesis; say, the hypothesis that the change in the cost-of-living index measured for the US urban population over a certain period was such-and-such. We turn prima facie evidence into valid evidence by ruling out error in the inference from (price and quantity) data to (hypothesis about) the value of the variable. Have we collected the right data? Are the weights the ones required by the index at hand? Is the formula correct? How do we deal with the various kinds of change? Trying to measure a cost-of-living index we could aggregate, say, the wrong set of prices. Thus we'd have prima facie but invalid evidence. Detailed answers to these questions have been given in the context of a specific case in the previous two chapters. The difference between valid and sound evidence lies on a different level. We can correctly measure a cost-of-living index but the result will still not be sound evidence for the hypothesis that relates to our purpose; say, the indexation of contracts or the escalation of payments. The result will thus be valid evidence for some hypothesis but not sound evidence for the policy hypothesis at stake.

How do we judge whether we have made progress in this process of epistemic iteration? Chang characterises progress as follows (Chang 2004: 227–28):

> Whether and to what extent an iterative procedure has resulted in progress can be judged by seeing whether the system of knowledge has improved in any of its epistemic virtues. Here I am defining progress in a pluralistic way: the enhancement of any feature that is generally recognized as an epistemic virtue constitutes progress.

I agree to a large extent but want to point out that Chang leaves out pragmatic or political values. Most inquiries in economics have such a pragmatic or political component apart from their epistemic component. We want to understand the causes of inflation not primarily out of curiosity but because we want to control it. We try to understand unemployment in order to reduce it. We aim at a comprehension of the processes that lead to poverty because we want to eliminate it. Progress, therefore, consists in the enhancement of *any* of these values. (Some philosophers such as Heather Douglas and Jesús Zamora argue that epistemic virtues are in fact secondary virtues and themselves instruments for achieving the primary pragmatic or political values. We try to understand in order to change. While I would tend to agree, in the context of this book I am content with pointing out that pragmatic or political virtues exist alongside epistemic ones. That is, here I am outlining a more pluralistic standpoint without an obvious ranking between the two kinds of virtues.)

VI

The pluralist outlook in Chang's account comes at a price: it is overly permissive. Chang explicitly rejects commitment to a ranking between the different virtues theoretical systems can possess. Scientists advance whichever virtue or virtues they consider most valuable, and it is not up to the methodologists to recommend any of a number of possible paths as superior.

Once political and pragmatic virtues form a part of the story it seems harder to abstain from commitment. Suppose there are two scientific traditions working in a given society. One values, say, the epistemic virtue of simplicity. This tradition considers change in theories and experimental methods as progressive whenever the new set of tools gives a simpler, more unified image of the socio-economic systems studied. Suppose also that the set of tools provided by this tradition is deficient in terms of application – it provides simple and unifying theories and models but these theories and models cannot readily be applied for economic policy. The alternative tradition values success at practical objectives such as the joint achievement of full employment, monetary stability and sustainable growth. It regards change as progressive whenever the new tools provide better strategies for reaching these goals. Suppose further that the stated goals are shared by a majority in society, even by proponents of the first tradition. The latter, however, regard application as falling in the domain of policy makers. According to them, failure at achieving objectives is due to policy failure, not scientific failure.

It seems difficult to argue that the choice between the two traditions is a matter of mere personal taste. One advances the values held by the society the scientific tradition is a part of, the other advances values held primarily by scientists. On what basis would we be justified in choosing one tradition over another one?

This question hints at a very general problem for philosophers of science. As the discussions about consumer-price measurement of Chapters 2 and 3 as well as that of Chang's account of measurement have shown, values pervade all scientific activity, be they the political values on the basis of which we choose between different notions of 'cost of living' or the epistemic values that define progress in Chang's work. As long as we content ourselves with purely descriptive reconstructions of science, we can hold back comments on the adequacy of the value system chosen. But as soon as we aim at giving a more ambitious account of what constitutes *good* science, we cannot stop short of an explicit discussion of the adequacy of the values promoted by this or that practice.

There is a perspective on values that is congenial to the stance taken in this book, namely Philip Kitcher's: scientific practice should reflect the goals and values of the population affected by the results of science – science should be 'well-ordered' (Kitcher 2001). My reason for endorsing Kitcher's position has to do with the general empiricist outlook I propose. According to this point of view, good science is a science that reduces the prejudices and preconceptions of the individual scientist to a minimum. In as much as this is possible, an empirical inquiry takes its cues from the world it is supposed to describe rather than from the hopes, wishes and speculations of the scientist.

But it would be mistaken to suggest that we could do without any perspective whatsoever: that science provides a 'view from nowhere'. Science, as we have seen, is necessarily perspectival – it takes the point of view of the value commitments implicit in scientific practice or explicitly endorsed by the scientific community. Demanding that science should reflect the goals and values of the people this science is made for extends the empiricist's outlook from the domain of 'pure facts' to that of 'value-laden facts' (such as the price level). Just like a purely factual inquiry should be driven by the facts rather than the researcher's views about them, when values matter it should be the values of the people concerned rather than the researcher's.

Admittedly, this construal opens a pandora's box of new problems and questions: How do we aggregate individual people's goals and values? How do we protect minority views? If Chapter 3's distinction between 'brute' and 'reflective' preferences was correct, how do we elicit people's reflective preferences? How, in a deeper sense, can we justify that the proposed is the right way to go about values? And so forth. But as important as these issues are, they go far beyond the scope of this book, so I'll leave them for another time.

Part II

Error in experiment

5 For a new experimentalism in experimental economics

I

According to standard wisdom, economics is not and will never be an experimental science. Unlike particles or model rats in the laboratory, whole economies can never be controlled to a sufficient extent that reliable inferences can be drawn. Moreover, passive modes of observation are also likely to produce uninformative results because economies never 'naturally' come in pairs that differ with respect to one factor only and thereby allow reliable inferences. Therefore, economics has to be a deductive science: conjecture hypotheses about the laws of human behaviour, derive observable consequences from them and compare the consequences with market results.

Methodology, too, has followed this deductive model, by and large. But economics has changed over the years. I take it that it is still an accepted pillar of truth that experiments *with whole economies* are impractical. But this does not mean that the observation of human behaviour in a controlled – laboratory – environment cannot yield useful results. Indeed since Maurice Allais first asked real people to choose among lotteries under relatively controlled conditions in the 1950s, the new field of experimental economics has grown prodigiously.

Experimentalism, it seems, has finally reached the *philosophy* of economics too. Just like our colleagues in the philosophy of natural science, we have come to realise that science has not only a speculative dimension – one that is dominated by 'thinking' – but also an applied dimension – one that is dominated by 'doing'. Consequently, reflections on general equilibrium theory, game theory and rational choice theory are more and more supplemented by accounts of measurement, statistical and causal inference, policy analysis and, most recently, economic experiments. Does this mean that deductivism in economic methodology has yielded to more inductive methodologies?

Unfortunately not, I will argue in this chapter. By and large (as with everything, there are exceptions), experiments in economics are regarded primarily as powerful vehicles to test theories. This has some adverse consequences. First, by digressing via theories researchers forgo the ability to achieve the usual scientific goals of prediction, explanation and control more directly. Second, and more importantly, by framing policy issues in terms of economic theory (which are then tested in the laboratory) economists often change the question from a broad policy question to a much narrower economic question and thereby leave out aspects that at least at first glance seem very important. I will discuss these two problems of theory-centredness of economic experiments in what follows and end with a sketch of an alternative that, or so I hope, avoids the discussed problems.

II

This chapter takes its starting point from the conviction that, despite some recent efforts to the contrary, experimental economics is still very theory-centred. The huge majority of economic experiments I know of either directly tests a prediction of theory or explores a phenomenon whose existence is due to the fact that it deviates from a theory's prediction. Some methodologists explicitly place theory testing at the core of the experimental endeavour:

> One major goal [of experimentation in economics] is to test theory by which is meant statements of conditional expectation, e.g. if condition *x* holds, effect *y* is more likely to occur.
>
> (Hogarth 2005: 263)

> In understanding how and why experimental economics has generated controversy, it is useful to look at the first sustained research programmes in this field. Two such programmes – the programmes in which, respectively, the two Nobel Prize winners worked – have been especially influential. [. . .] Methodologically, these two programmes share important common features. In each case, there is a pre-existing theory (the theory of competitive equilibrium, the theory of rational choice) which claims to explain economic behaviour in the field. [. . .] On an apparently natural interpretation of the methodology of these programmes, an experiment is a test of a pre-existing theory.
>
> (Sugden 2005a: 178ff.)

And most strongly:

> Laboratory methodology involves a shift from a focus on particular economies as they are found in the wild to a focus on general theories, models and principles that govern the behavior of economies.
>
> (Plott 1991: 902)

True, others don't. Alvin Roth, for one, distinguishes three uses: 'Speaking to Theorists', 'Searching for Facts' and 'Whispering in the Ears of Princes' (Roth 1995, section II). 'Speaking to Theorists' is the usual theory testing and search for regularities that can be brought under a theoretical framework. 'Searching for Facts' is what some 'new experimentalists' call 'tinkering with phenomena' – relatively theory-free establishing of robust phenomena and investigating what happens when parameters are varied. 'Whispering in the Ears of Princes' is motivated by the demands of policy makers and attempts to test the consequences of policy changes. Vernon Smith, for another, mentions seven purposes of economic experiments, only some of which deal with theory (Smith 1994).

But in my view, practice (both printed and orally presented) gives a strong indication that even in these other uses theory plays a significant role. Consider the first two of Roth's three functions for experiments: theory testing and tinkering with phenomena. He presents it as if theory plays a role only in the former. Indeed, it is now standard to distinguish at least these two uses of experimentation (see Morgan 2005; Sugden 2005b). But let us not be fooled: theories play an important role even in the second tradition. One property Ian Hacking ascribes to 'phenomena', as he understands the term, is that of 'noteworthiness'. When you see a dustbin toppling over in Chinatown, you don't witness a phenomenon. When you observe blackbody radiation, you do. Interestingly, the reason why many experimentally created phenomena count as noteworthy in economics is that they constitute violations of theory. Robert Sugden's term 'exhibit' is closely related to that of a phenomenon (ibid.: 291f.):

> An exhibit is an experimental design which reliably induces some specific regularity (or 'effect', or 'phenomenon') in human behaviour.
>
> Typically, an exhibit is of interest because the regularity it captures contravenes – or at least, is not adequately explained by – some received theory of decision-making behaviour. The Allais and Ellsberg paradoxes are violations of the independence axiom or sure-thing principle of expected utility theory. The endowment effect is a violation of a fundamental principle of Hicksian consumer theory, that a person's preferences between given consumption bundles are independent of her current endowment. Individuals' ability to use focal points to solve coordination games is not explained by standard game theory. The rejection of positive offers in ultimatum games is contrary to conventional game theory, given the background assumption that players prefer more money to less.

Sugden also points out that exhibits are often much less noteworthy if considered independently of their relationship with theory. After all, who would not have predicted that, when asked to split a pie between him- or herself and a second person, a subject would divide it roughly evenly? (This alludes to experimentally established violations of game theory predictions in dictator games; for this and other technical terms, see the Glossary.) It is thus important to point out that theories play a dominant role in the writings even of those commentators who accept a plurality of purposes for economic experiments. Francesco Guala, for example, mentions the possibility that a 'phenomenon . . . can be "freestanding" for a long time, detached from any or even informal explanation of its occurrence' (Guala 2005: 46). In fact, much of his book seems to be aimed at reducing the over-reliance on theory in experimental economics. Nevertheless, my point regarding the *practice* in experimental economics is proved because every experiment mentioned in Guala's book is either a test of theory or it concerns an exhibit in Sugden's sense.

What are the reasons for such theory-centred experimental practice? Of course, there are likely historical or sociological reasons. Many of the pioneers in experimental economics were driven by theoretical concerns. Vernon Smith (Nobel Prize 2002 for his contributions to experimental economics), for example, ran his first experiment after encountering difficulties teaching the theory of the competitive equilibrium to undergraduates (see Smith 2003). Maurice Allais (Nobel Prize 1988 'for his pioneering contributions to the theory of markets and efficient utilization of resources'!) is chiefly a mathematical – theoretical – economist (even if in the Anglo-Saxon world he is best known for his experimental demonstration of the 'Allais paradox'). All of Charles Plott's (another pioneer of experimental economics) early publications are contributions to economic theory. And so forth. But this does not mean that there are good epistemological or methodological reasons for theory-centredness. Are there any?

In the earlier quote, Plott points towards two contrasting couples of notions. On the one hand, we may seek 'explanations about *particular* economies and *particular* situations in those economies' but such economies found 'in the wild' are 'extremely complicated' (Plott 1991: 902, emphasis added). On the other hand, '*general* theories must apply to *simple* special cases' (ibid., emphasis added). We cannot study particular economies in the laboratory because they are too complicated – too many factors are responsible for bringing about an outcome. But since theory focuses on a few salient factors, we can study it in the laboratory, and since it is general, it applies (at least in principle) outside the laboratory too (ibid.: 902):

> These simple [laboratory] economies can then be used to test and evaluate the predictive capability of the general theories when they are applied to the special cases. In this way, a joining of the general theories with data is accomplished.

and (ibid.: 903):

> It is important to note that it makes no difference where the economy is found. The economy could have been found evolving in nature or it could have been a home-grown, laboratory variety; as long as the parameters are known, the theory will produce a prediction. It is this

general property of theory that is important for laboratory experimental work.

This shift in focus from actual economies to theories, then, brings with it the ability to study questions that can actually be answered. Theory focuses on a small number of factors that can be controlled or manipulated in the laboratory. Instead of studying complex economies 'in the wild' directly, we thus concentrate on a manageable set of factors and worry about application later.

At this point we seem to have two options. First, we can try to mimic other laboratory sciences, which according to Ian Hacking (Hacking 1992: 33):

> are those whose claims to truth answer primarily to work done in the laboratory. They study phenomena that seldom or ever occur in a pure state before people have brought them under surveillance. Exaggerating a little, I say that the phenomena under study are created in the laboratory.

We study phenomena created in the laboratory in order to learn about these phenomena and (at least initially) nothing else. In this strategy, theory plays the role of providing the initial set of phenomena of interest. Economies 'in the wild' as Plott says are characterised by their complexity in the sense that zillions of factors have to cooperate in order to bring about a result. In the laboratory, we can study only a small set. Theory indicates which ones. Of course, theory provides only an *initial* selection. The phenomena we create in the laboratory will often be defined by a violation of a theory – such as Sugden's 'exhibits'. Such a violation calls for explanation, and in seeking it we may uncover some new causal factor that will from now on be included in laboratory investigations.

In this perspective, then, there is a strict divide between 'pure' science and 'applied' science. Phenomena are created in the laboratory in order to learn what happens under laboratory conditions. Engineers may try to apply the fundamental knowledge outside the laboratory using typical engineering techniques. But, undoubtedly, application is a by-product, not a characteristic effect of laboratory science.

This view would be unusual for an experimental economist, however. I don't think knowing the validity of theories is ever an end in itself in experimental economics. While many theorists seem to think that pure and applied economics are independent enterprises, and that that's good for the discipline (Carl Menger was a clear proponent of this view; see Menger 1963), experimental economists ultimately tend to be motivated by more practical concerns. Ultimately, in their view, the purpose of economic experiments is to address policy questions such as:

- How do we match medical residents and hospitals such that no resident–hospital couple would prefer a different allocation (Kagel and Roth 2000; Roth and Peranson 1999)?
- How do we change water systems 'smartly' (Murphy *et al.* 2000)?
- How should the Federal Communications Commission (FCC) auction licences for personal communication systems (PCS) (Plott 1997)?
- How do we prevent the winner's curse phenomenon in outer continental shelf (OCS) oil lease sales (Cox *et al.* 1999; Kagel and Levin 1986)?

Economic experiments provide 'testbeds' for policies (Plott 1997; see also his brief autobiographical sketch on his website as well as Croson 2002), that is, they evaluate policy proposals (Smith 1994). But I do not have to commit to the view that providing testbeds for policy is the ultimate or only aim of experimental economics. Here I try to answer the conditional question: *if* the aim of experimental economics is to gather evidence for policy hypotheses, then why is its methodology (by and large) one of theory testing? And what are the consequences?

One reason that immediately springs to mind has to do with external validity. It is now standard in the experimentalist literature to distinguish between 'internal' and 'external' validity. In order to use the terminology of Chapter 1, let us first distinguish between 'experimental hypotheses' and 'policy hypotheses'. An experimental hypothesis h_t is a hypothesis that some phenomenon obtains in a test population *T*. For instance, 'In *T*, a percentage between *x* and *y* of players cooperate when playing the prisoner's dilemma game.' A policy hypothesis h_p is, analogously, a hypothesis that the very same phenomenon obtains in a target population *P*, that is, 'In *P*, a percentage between *x* and *y* of players cooperate when playing the prisoner's dilemma game.' We can then define:

Internal validity. An experimental hypothesis h_t is said to be *internally valid* for *T* if there is valid evidence that h_t holds.

External validity. A policy hypothesis h_p is said to be *externally valid* for *P* if there is sound evidence that h_p holds.

In other words, if we have good reason to believe that a hypothesis is true of our experimental or test population, that hypothesis is internally valid. By contrast, if we have good reason to believe that the very same hypothesis is true of some other, yet untested population of interest, then the hypothesis is externally valid.

An idea related to that of external validity is that of parallelism. Vernon Smith defines it as follows (Smith 1987):

> Propositions about behaviour and/or the performance of institutions that have been tested in one microeconomy (laboratory or field) apply

also to other microeconomies (laboratory or field) where similar *ceteris paribus* conditions hold.

But there are two differences. First, 'external validity' is a property of hypotheses while 'parallelism' is a thesis. We can believe that some hypothesis is externally valid for some target population of interest without subscribing to the general thesis of parallelism. Furthermore, I think it is useful always to qualify for which population a hypothesis is supposed to be true. A hypothesis can always be true of one but not another experimental population, and even if we can export it to *some* target population of interest, there is no guarantee and it should not be presupposed that it can be exported to other potential target populations.

The quick answer to our question regarding the role of theories is that theories – by virtue of being general – ensure the external validity of the experimental hypotheses. Suppose that a certain hypothesis is internally valid for some experimental population. But since this hypothesis is derived from theory (the theory of rational choice, say), it confirms the theory, and since the theory is general it applies (in principle) everywhere.

This would, of course, be a tremendously naïve reading. Few if any theories are genuinely universally quantified. Rather, they apply (where they apply) subject to the condition that no relevant factor interferes (or '*ceteris paribus*'). This seems to lead us into a dilemma. We either find situations outside the laboratory ('in the wild') that are relevantly similar to the population studied in the laboratory. But if that is so, the initial motivation for running experiments directed at studying theory seems mistaken. Recall that we study simple laboratory economies for learning about theory only because economies found 'in the wild' are too complex to study directly. But if we don't find situations in which the appropriate conditions are met in natural circumstances, what do we learn from experimental results?

The answer therefore must be: *economic experiments (when used to test theory) teach us something about non-laboratory settings even when relevant factors interfere* (that is, when *ceteris paribus* conditions are *not* fulfilled).

The strategy, then, might be the following. Experimental economists run experiments in order to investigate the purely economic aspect of human behaviour (see Hausman 1992 for a discussion of the thesis that an economic aspect is separable from other aspects of social phenomena). Their findings continue to hold (with qualifications) in natural settings, when other aspects contribute. For a reliable prediction, we need to know these contributions from other sciences (say, social psychology, criminology, anthropology). But studying the economic aspect by itself is worthwhile because what people do when motivated by purely economic considerations continues to play a role in more complex situations.

Unfortunately, this does not quite seem to work. Experimental results in economics seem to be extremely sensitive to variations in the setup. And this even concerns factors economists usually regard as falling under the 'economic aspect'. Here are some examples.

Monetary incentives It is very reasonable to expect that human behaviour is responsive to what is at stake. If I am asked to give my opinion on the next general election the care I take in deriving the prediction and the motivation I act on is likely to depend on whether I make it over a drink among a group of friends (meaning that nothing or very little is at stake), in front of a large audience of peers (meaning that my reputation is at stake), if I'm a political advisor to my client (meaning that my professional career is at stake), if I'm offered money for a correct prediction or if my own life or the life of a loved one is threatened in case my prediction turns out to be false.

But it is in no way clear whether there is a general story to be told how exactly *monetary* incentives (that is, incentives of the kind economists should know best how to handle) influence results (for overviews, see Read 2005 and Guala 2005, Ch. 11). One can distinguish three mechanisms by which monetary mechanisms work (Read 2005: 266):

- *cognitive exertion*: the incentive increases the amount of thought put into the task;
- *motivational focus*: the incentive changes the agent's goals; and
- *emotional triggers*: the incentive is a prerequisite for the agent to predict or emit their response.

There is some evidence that a switch from non-monetary to monetary incentives makes people think harder about the situation they are in (Wilcox 1993). But this does not mean that such incentives make them more rational in the economists' sense. For example, monetary incentives appear to increase the frequencies of preference reversals (Grether and Plott 1979). While money incentives appear to reduce the frequency of the Allais paradox, the implications for rationality are less clear cut (Read 2005: 268). Higher monetary incentives reduce offers in the dictator game but do not influence ultimatum games (within the limits provided by experimental constraints: Forsythe *et al.* 1994; Hoffmann *et al.* 1996). Especially when the third mechanism operates it is often very hard to generalise from what happens under an incentive at level \$*x* to what happens when the level of incentive is changed to \$*y*. Suppose, for instance, we want to test under what conditions a bequest of a certain size induces feud among a group of heirs. While it is easy to imagine that there is *some* size of the bequest that will produce quarrels, it is very hard to predict what the size will be from people's behaviour from experiments with hypothetical or small money sums.

The effect of monetary incentives on experimental outcomes is not stable. While there appear to be some regularities (e.g. *on average* people take decisions with more care when the stakes are higher), it is very hard to predict what direction the effect will take in a new context. Incidentally, this is just what experimental economists say about the matter (Forsythe *et al.* 1994: 347):

> The need for an examination of the effect of increased stakes on ultimatum bargaining is suggested by a literature survey of the effect of varying the stakes in a wide variety of decision making and market experiments over the last 33 years (Smith and Walker 1993). Many cases were found in which the predictions of theory were improved when the monetary rewards were increased. There were also cases in which the level of monetary rewards had no effect on the results. Consequently, it is necessary to examine the stakes question on a case by case basis.

Information Ultimatum games share interesting structural properties with a host of real-life situations. Whenever a single supplier of a good (a monopolist) sets a price or a single employer (a monopsonist) sets a wage, the situation resembles an ultimatum game: the monopolist or monopsonist divides the share, and the buyer or employee may take it or leave it. Typical ultimatum-game experiments, however, leave out an important feature of these more realistic situations: often the size of the pie is not known to the responder. As can be expected, when experiments are run such that responders are uninformed about the total amount to be distributed, proposers make significantly smaller offers and rejection rates decrease (Croson 1996).

In sequential dictator games, too, information influences the decisions made by proposers. Interestingly, offers decrease when irrelevant information is supplied (in this case, about another player's birthday) but when relevant information is supplied (about other proposers' decisions) offers are not affected (Cason and Mui 1998).

For another example, suppose a community plans the provision of some threshold public good, say a dam or an environmental programme. The cost of the good is to be met by voluntary contributions of the members of the community. If the sum of the individual contributions meets or exceeds the cost of the good (the 'threshold'), it will be provided. Otherwise the contributions are paid back to the members. An efficient Nash equilibrium in such a situation occurs when the sum of contributions is exactly equal to the cost of providing the good and when no individual pays more than he or she benefits. The problem is one of coordination: will the group find an efficient Nash equilibrium? That is, will the members group contribute enough so that the public good will be provided but not more?

Information plays a surprising role here. It appears to make no difference whether subjects know the *aggregate contribution* or nothing at all (Sell and Wilson 1991). Moving from a situation where only the aggregate contributions are communicated to a situation where also individual contributions (albeit unidentified) are made known *reduces* the ability of the group to converge to an efficient equilibrium: group contributions are significantly lower and farther from the efficient equilibrium level when individual contributions are known than when only the aggregate volume is known. However, moving from announcing unidentified to identified individual contributions improves coordination (Croson and Marks 1998). When subjects are told how their contributions rank in comparison to other subjects' contributions, cooperation decreases (Andreoni 1995).

Experience The endowment effect is one of many anomalies studied by behavioural economists. Against the prediction from economic theory, agents appear to value a good higher once they own it – once it is part of their endowment. Indeed, the endowment effect seems to be robust across a variety of different goods and traders.

One disadvantage of laboratory experiments is that they are almost always conducted with university students as experimental subjects. This may in some cases make the laboratory situation unrealistic for more naturally occurring settings. The endowment effect seems to be such a case. When studied by means of a field experiment rather than a laboratory experiment, the phenomenon seems to obtain only for inexperienced traders. Once subjects have sufficient market experience, trading behaviour is consistent with the predictions from economic theory (List 2003). Similarly, field experiments testing the generalised axiom of revealed preference find that violations decrease with increasing market experience (List and Millimet 2005). However, this does not mean that a market in which all participants are experienced is most efficient. Rather, markets where inexperienced and experienced traders mix seem more efficient than homogenous markets (List 2002).

Culture and environment Another limitation of laboratory experiments is that they are typically conducted in universities in the Western world, most notably in the United States. It is therefore interesting to see whether varying the cultural background influences the outcomes in games such as the ultimatum game. This seems to be the case. Whereas the overwhelming majority of American students appear to be 'monotonically rational', that is, responders in a dictator game reject offers below a certain threshold and accept above (while the threshold can vary among subjects), other cultures display more complicated patterns. In two multi-ethnic republics in Russia, for instance, about half of the subjects behave monotonically rational but the other half follow a strategy of 'hyper fairness': they reject offers that are either too low or too high (Bahry and Wilson 2006). There is a great variety in the mean offer made among non-Western societies, ranging from about a quarter (for instance, 27 per cent among the Hadza in Tanzania, with very high rejection rates) to over a half (for instance, 58 per cent among the Lamelara in Indonesia, with rejection rates near zero). Group-level differences in economic organisation and the degree of market integration explain a substantial portion of this variation but individual differences do not (Henrich *et al.* 2001). Proposers made more generous offers in two experiments in Kansas City than in an identical experiment in Vermont. Students in a Kansas City community college offered more than workers in a nearby warehouse. Interestingly, students in either location offered more in the ultimatum game than in the dictator game – as should be expected – but workers made on average identical offers (Carpenter *et al.* 2005).

It is thus clear that the social norms prevailing in a society strongly influence behaviour in games. Perhaps it is also the *perception* of these rules that influences behaviour. Subjects in a laboratory environment are aware of the fact that their behaviour is being monitored, recorded and analysed. Therefore, they may behave more the way they think is expected from them, trying more to do the 'right thing', than in other settings where they feel unobserved. It is an undeniable robust empirical regularity that a large proportion of dictators in a dictator game give a non-zero amount of money to the other player. But maybe they do so merely because they think this is what is expected of them. If their option set is enlarged to include the possibility of *taking* money from the second player, contributions disappear. Giving unsolicited money to a complete stranger with no ulterior motive is seldom observed in non-experimental conditions. The usual dictator game results are therefore sometimes regarded as artefactual (Bardsley 2005a; List 2005; Schram 2005).

The lesson to be drawn from this discussion is twofold. First, any factor can matter in any conceivable way. Experimental research in physics is often made easy by the fact that we have theories that specify in advance the kinds of intervening factors that one needs to control in an investigation. For instance, there is a law that tells us that only forces produce motion. If that is so, we know that, if we want to investigate the influence of a particular kind of force on the motion of a body, we have to control for other kinds of forces, and we know what other kinds there are. The socio-economic world is not as neatly conceptualised. Economic theory provides few clues if any as to which factors we have to control. All relevant factors I have seen described in the literature are results from experimental studies.

Theory provides little guidance about what we should expect the intervening factors to do once they are identified. Sometimes they behave in a way that is consistent with theory – for instance, by and large, higher incentives make people think harder about their decisions – but often they don't – for instance, we'd expect information about the aggregate contribution in a threshold public goods game to decrease contributions but this does not happen.

Second, it is hard to think of factors in these experiments *in general* to constitute persistent factors that continue operating whether or not other factors intervene (such factors are usually called factors exhibiting causal capacities; see the detailed discussion in Chapter 9). Some factors, without doubt, exhibit a certain degree of stability. We can say that three motives operate in ultimatum games: greed, fairness and reciprocity. Let us assume that people tend to be greedy in the sense that, other things being equal, they prefer more money to less. It is sometimes said that people also have a preference for fairness, and therefore they offer a greater share than game theory predicts in ultimatum games. But fairness isn't the only greed-checking motive in games of this kind. People also fear retaliation and therefore don't make offers they expect the responder to regard as unfair – since the responder can (against his own benefit) reject and thereby deny the proposer's profit. In dictator games reciprocity is controlled because the responder has no say. Therefore, the motive of greed is less constrained. But fairness is still there: subjects offer persistently non-zero shares. Both fairness and greed are factors that persist over a variety of situations and continue to contribute even when other factors impede their action.

But other cases don't follow this model. When incentives are high enough, greed can completely crowd out other motives. It's not that other motives contribute very little – they are just not there any more. Other factors such as information, learning, framing, experience, upbringing and culture can all completely change the outcome of a game and it does normally not make sense to regard an outcome as a 'vector product' of individual contributions. What a factor does depends on the whole situation (recall the earlier quote by Forsythe *et al.*; the effect of monetary incentives must be studied on a case-by-case basis).

It is therefore reasonable to question the efficiency of the 'bottom-up' approach pursued by experimental economists if addressing policy questions is the ultimate aim. The bottom-up approach studies the behaviour of the constituents of a complex situation individually (individuals rather than groups; simple rather than compound motivations; shielded from rather than including outside influences, and so forth) and derives predictions about realistic – complex – situations on the basis of what is known about the behaviour of the constituents. But, by and large, the behaviour of those individual factors studied in experimental economics seems to depend on the *whole setting* in which they operate. They don't usually bring stable characteristic effects with them that can be transferred from situation to situation. What is known about the behaviour of the parts therefore gives little indication of what happens in the complex situation (for a discussion of a special case of the context-dependence problem, see Bardsley 2005b). The lesson is therefore: having valid evidence for some hypothesis in experimental economics does not get us a long way towards sound evidence for the hypothesis of interest (alternatively, knowing a hypothesis is internally valid gives us little reason to believe it is externally valid, too).

III

Perhaps, then, the focus on theory makes economic experimentation an inefficient practice. There is a further problem with theory, one that is outright harmful for achieving the goals set by experimentalists: because the focus is on theory, research questions are often changed such that they fit into the framework provided by the theory. This may change the goals of the investigation, and in some adverse ways.

The case I want to discuss here is that of the Federal Communications Commission (FCC) auctions in the United States. Not only does it illustrate the point I want to make exceedingly clearly, it is also well documented and widely discussed in the literature on experimental economics (for explicit methodological discussions, see Alexandrova 2006; Callon and Muniesa 2007; Guala 2001, 2005, Ch. 8; Mirowski and Nik-Khah 2007; Nik-Khah 2005, 2006). In fact, even the point I want to make seems to be well known in at least part of the literature – though, to my mind, no methodological consequences have been drawn in the previous accounts.

So here is the story. Generally speaking, there are four ways to allocate licences for the use of the electromagnetic spectrum (McMillan 1995):

- administrative process
- lottery
- first come, first served
- auction.

Each of these has advantages and drawbacks. The greatest advantage of an administrative process is the flexibility in its implementation: the administration can impose any criteria it sees fit in order to promote chosen policy objectives. But the process is usually slow, costly and not always transparent to companies applying for licences as criteria may be vague and their interpretation and weighting unclear. Lotteries and 'first come, first served' are fast and frugal procedures. But particular lotteries may attract, and in the United States have attracted, opportunists seeking windfall gains, as companies without genuine interest in the licences can apply and, in case of success, sell licences on a secondary market. Auctions, lastly, are also relatively fast, they generate revenue for the state and economists argue that they put licences in the hands of those who value them most.

In the United States, licences for wireless personal communication systems (PCS) used to be assigned through an administrative hearing process. Applications had to be made to the FCC and a commission would decide to what company to grant a licence. The process – aka 'beauty contest' – was often criticised as cumbersome. One former member of the FCC described it as 'the FCC equivalent of the Medieval trial by ordeal' (quoted from ibid.: 192). In 1982 it was replaced by a system of lotteries. But the secondary market that was thereby created generated huge profits for freeloaders: it was estimated that over $45bn changed hands from telecommunication companies to lottery winners. Such windfall gains are often considered unjust because the winners have done little to deserve the profits. A more suitable alternative allocation mechanism was therefore sought.

In August 1993, the US Congress passed legislation giving the FCC the authority to auction licences. The FCC was commissioned to design and test alternative methods of competitive bidding and auctioning was to begin in May 1994. The political goals of the auctions were stated as follows (US Congress 1993, section 309 (j)(3)):

> In particular, the Commission is required to develop methodologies that promote the development and rapid deployment of new technologies; promote economic opportunity and competition and ensure that new and innovative technologies are available to the American people by avoiding excessive concentration and by disseminating licenses among a wide variety of applicants, including small business and businesses owned by members of minority groups and women; recover for the public a portion of the value of the public spectrum resource made available to the licensee and the avoidance of unjust enrichment; and promote the efficient and intensive use of the spectrum.

Auctioning spectrum licences wasn't a new idea, and indeed some commentators wonder why it was established *so late* in the United States (Hazlett 1998). In fact, Congress had held hearings about the possibility as early as 1958, and Nobel laureate Ronald Coase had advocated auctioning in an article at about the same time (Coase 1959). But establishing an auction-based allocation procedure successfully is not a trivial task. Earlier experiences in New Zealand and Australia were less than encouraging. In New Zealand, following advice of a US–UK consulting firm, a second-price auction was used. Second-price auctions are advantageous from a theoretical point of view: bidding one's true value is a dominant strategy. But they have obvious disadvantages if bidders collude or markets are thin: in New Zealand receipts from the licence sales were far below expectations because many second-highest bids were exceedingly small. For instance, in an extreme case a firm that bid NZ$100,000 paid only NZ$6 for the licence. In Australia, where first-price auctions were used, bidders frequently defaulted on their excessive bids (which they could do without cost to themselves because no deposits were required); this delayed the process and also resulted in lower revenues (McMillan 1994).

These difficulties in mind, the FCC surveyed a number of possible auction-design mechanisms, made some preliminary recommendations in the 'Notice of Proposed Rule Making' of October 1993 and called for comments from the industry. More than 220 firms and lobby groups submitted recommendations, some of which were written by academics.

In March 1994, the FCC announced the chosen auction structure, which was essentially simultaneous multiple-round bidding (for high-value licences) where bidders could withdraw their bids, albeit with penalties. In order to make sure that bidders were serious, large upfront payments had to be made. In addition, bidders from certain supported groups (small businesses, rural telephone companies, businesses owned by women and minorities) were granted special rights such as payments in instalments and bidding credits. Finally, to prevent unjust profit making by auction winners and to deter participation by speculators who did not intend to provide a service to the public, the transfer disclosure requirements were established.

How did the FCC arrive at the conclusion that this structure would effectively serve the goals set by Congress? In the eyes of one commentator (McMillan 1994: 147):

> Although pork-barrel politics had shaped the debate on whether to use auctions, the auction-design process was driven not by politics, but by economics.

That is, economists not only helped with details of the design of the auctions, they dominated the design process. But these experts weren't economists of just any denomination: they were microeconomists and specialised in auction theory. Prima facie, choosing auction theorists as consultants in this process seems an odd decision. Auction theory is a subfield of microeconomics that is concerned with the design of 'optimal auctions'. An 'optimal auction' is one that maximises the expected revenue for the seller (see Klemperer 2004). But maximising expected revenue for the government was emphatically *not* the aim of the licence auctions. Nonetheless, most of the aspects of the design were justified on the basis of promoting this objective, not the objectives set by Congress (for what follows, see McMillan 1994).

Open versus sealed-bid auctions An open auction is best at providing information because participants can observe other participants' bids. For this reason, open auctions are said to reduce the likelihood of the winner's curse phenomenon. Rational bidders bid low in order to avoid the winner's curse. The discount can be very large when estimates range widely around a true value. Making more information available should therefore increase government receipts because bidders have less reason to be cautious.

However, there are countervailing tendencies. First, when bidders are risk averse, sealed-bid auctions can generate higher revenues than open auctions. Because of the sums at stake, it was very likely that bidders in fact were risk averse. Second, collusion is less likely in a sealed-bid auction. Eventually, the information effect was thought to dominate these two other effects. In fact, a system of multiple rounds of sealed bidding was chosen which allowed the government to control the amount of information to be released in between rounds.

Simultaneous versus sequential auctions Items sold in auctions are often related (such as different patches of land, stamps, pieces of art), and spectrum licences are no exception. The more telecoms can aggregate (adjacent) licences, the more value each single licence has. Sequential auctions (items are sold one after another) have the advantage of simplicity. But they eliminate the possibility of back-up strategies should the bidder not be able to acquire his first choice. Simultaneous auctions allow for back-up strategies but they can be very complex and have high information-processing demands on bidders.

Although the FCC left itself the option of choosing from a variety of auction forms, it recommended the use of simultaneous multiple-round auctions for high value–high interdependence licences.

Combinatorial versus continuous ascending auctions When the values of items are interdependent, some auctions allow bids for *bundles* of items. Should the licences be sold as bundles or item-by-item? The FCC initially further suggested a hybrid form according to which sealed bids would be made for the bundle in a first round, and in a second round the licences would be auctioned one-by-one. If the sum of bids for the individual items exceeded the highest bid from the first round, they'd be sold separately, otherwise the first-round winner would be chosen.

There are some theoretical arguments against combinatorial bidding that would allow the buying of licences that together cover the whole nation because there are situations in which free-rider problems can obtain and thus the sum of the individual valuations may exceed that of the bundle (Palfrey 1983). Still, sub-nationwide combinatorial bidding may be efficient (Banks *et al.* 1989). However, combinatorial auctions seemed to raise too many practical problems to be solved within the time framework provided by the FCC (Guala 2005: 170ff.). Most licences were therefore sold using a continuous ascending design almost entirely due to Stanford economists Paul Milgrom and Robert Wilson (see Milgrom 2004).

For a simultaneous auction a stopping rule has to be designed. It should be relatively simple, end the auction in a reasonable time and close on the different items almost simultaneously. The implemented auctions had various rules for eligibility, activity and withdrawal. In order to be *eligible*, a bidder had to make a deposit proportional to the number of licences he intended to compete for. A bidder is said to be *active* if he either has the standing high bid from the previous round or is submitting an eligible bid. If a bidder is not active, his eligibility is reduced. Bidders could also *withdraw* a bid but with the possible consequence of paying the difference between the selling price and the withdrawn bid if the latter exceeded the former (the withdrawal rule was due to Preston McAfee of Caltech).

Most of these arguments, then, were made with maximising the government's revenue in view. How possibly could the original Congress commission be interpreted in this way? The auctions were designed such that those who were willing to pay most for a licence were likely to be awarded the licence. This would not only guarantee maximum expected government revenue but would also be 'assigning the licenses to the bidders who value them most'. The latter, in turn, meant that the allocation was likely to be efficient from an economic point of view: no participant would prefer (in the sense of being willing to pay for) a different allocation.

At first glance, this goal was vindicated by the requirement of Congress 'to promote the efficient and intensive use of the spectrum'. But interpreting this passage in terms of the economic efficiency of the licence allocation is only one possible interpretation and not one that is likely to be correct. The aim to be promoted was probably *spectral* efficiency – the best use of the spectrum relative to the level and variety of services offered.

Prima facie, then, it seems that consulting auction theorists and experimental economists were asked to give advice on one problem but ended up addressing another (to my knowledge, Edward Nik-Khah and Phil Mirowski were the first to make this point in the methodological literature; cf. Mirowski and Nik-Khah 2007; Nik-Khah 2005). It is as if a government asks a group of epidemiologists to design an effective strategy to combat AIDS, and they come up with a strategy designed to fight obesity (because they happen to be obesity experts!). How could such a change in goals be justified? A few reasons spring to mind: one could argue that Congress was confused about its aims; or that its aims are unattainable and therefore had to be substituted by attainable second-best aims; perhaps the goals of Congress were abstract and those of the economists concretisations. All these reasons are implausible, and I haven't seen them used anywhere in the literature. The only slightly plausible reason, and the one given in the literature, is that economists' goals are in fact means to achieve the more ultimate goals of Congress. Economic efficiency is a valid aim to pursue because it helps to 'promote development and rapid deployment of new technologies', to 'ensure that new and innovative technologies are available to the American people' and so forth.

This argument was effectively made by Paul Milgrom and his colleague Robert Wilson (Milgrom and Wilson 1993, quoted from Nik-Khah 2005: 123):

> Since a bidder's abilities to introduce valuable new services and to deploy them quickly, intensively and efficiently increase the value of a license to a bidder, an auction design that awards licenses to those bidders with the highest willingness to pay tends to promote the development and rapid deployment of new services in each area and the efficient and intensive use of the spectrum. In addition, in view of the expected intense competition during the auction, the prices paid by this group of what we shall call the 'highest value bidders' are likely to constitute a significant fraction of the societal value of the licenses, consistent with another of the Act's objectives.

But without a lot of further – empirical – substantiation, the argument is highly dubious. The subjectively expected value of a licence may be far off the true value for the winning licensee; the highest bidder may not be the company with the highest valuation because of capital-market constraints; the highest economic-value use of a set of licences may exclude rural areas; the best *economic* allocation of licences may not 'avoid . . . excessive concentration' and 'disseminat[e] licenses among a wide variety of applicants' (the preferential treatment of women and minorities was stopped after two auctions because of a Supreme Court ruling; see McAfee and McMillan 1996: 167f.); economically *efficient* use of the spectrum in no way guarantees its *intensive* use; and so forth.

In fact, none of the goals outlined by Congress appeared to have been met adequately up until about ten years after the auctions (see Nik-Khah 2005, Ch. 5):

- *Develop and deploy new (PCS) technologies rapidly*: while licence assignment probably has sped up the process, considerable delays occurred due to licences being returned to the FCC for reassignment, especially in later auctions.
- *Ensure that new and innovative (PCS) technologies are available to the American people, including rural populations*: great disparities remain between urban and rural areas; in 2000, almost 86 per cent of the most populous urban areas had PCS compared to 56 per cent in rural areas.
- *Disseminate licences among a wide variety of applicants*: many of the licences initially awarded to so-called 'designated entities' (e.g. small or minority-owned businesses) went to large companies later on because of defaults on licence payments (which also delayed the process) and partnerships where the junior partner's only function was to win a licence for the senior partner.
- *Recover for the public a portion of the value of the public spectrum resource*: the earnings made on the sale of the licences were certainly high (about $20bn; see Cramton 1998) but perhaps not as high as they could have been because of collusion and other anti-competitive behaviour on the part of the bidders (a fact which seems to indicate that the aims of generating revenue for the seller and allocating sold items efficiently might not always pull in the same direction).
- *Ensure efficient and intensive use of the spectrum*: if by 'efficiency' spectral efficiency is meant, the goal is probably not achieved because of spectrum under-utilisation problems and the neglect of better technologies to relieve spectrum congestion.

No doubt, this analysis is to be read with caveats. Most of the facts described may be momentary and initial results of the auctions, which over the course of time will change in order to meet the desired goals. Furthermore, economic efficiency is a concept notoriously difficult to measure (for an attempt, see Cramton 1998). Perhaps the auctions simply failed at this immediate goal and therefore the more ultimate goals could not be reached. But what is nonetheless striking is the vehemence and intensity with which the results of the auctions were praised – and praised, in particular, as a success for auction theory and experimental economics – given that the performance relative to the aims stated by Congress is relatively meagre.

IV

It is hard to blame (only?) the consulting economists for the performance of the auctions for a variety of reasons. Most notably, an economist consultant is a specialised expert, and a specialist will always frame a problem in terms of his discipline. But, and now I come back to the topic of this chapter, namely economic experiments, there is no reason to restrict the domain of economic experiments to the domain of economic theory. Let me therefore suggest an alternative.

If the aim of economic experiments is to provide policy advice, it should accept as given the goals set by the polity seeking the advice. Policy recommendations are to be evaluated against these goals and no others. Of course this cannot mean that economists could or should not play a role in the initial process of setting political goals. Perhaps Congress (or whatever client is seeking advice) can be convinced that extending coverage to rural areas or a high degree of competition among companies or intense use of the spectrum are not goals that are worth pursuing. But it is certainly wrong to replace one set of goals with another, perhaps conflicting set in the name of 'scientificness'.

Once the goals are set, strategies can be conjectured and their likely success at reaching the goals experimentally tested: How do licences have to be bundled in order to maximise the likelihood that rural areas are and continue to be served? How can we provide incentives such as to encourage the participation of businesses run by women and minorities (as an alternative to positive discrimination, say)? How do we encourage small, that is, above average, innovative companies to participate and how do we ensure they are able to afford licences without backup from a large company? Which are suitable institutions for maximising customer benefit from personal communications services (as opposed to shareholder value, say)? And so forth.

In order to avoid the problems discussed in Section II (problems regarding the sensitivity of results to the exact make-up of the experimental setting), the way these questions are to be addressed is top-down rather than bottom-up. Let us call the orthodox bottom-up method the 'Lego-model' view of experimental inference. As described in detail above, according to the Lego model complex phenomena are first analysed into simple parts (which are as a matter of fact defined by economic theory but do not have to be). The behaviour of the simple parts is then investigated severally in experiments. For a policy prediction, a complex model is built from the knowledge about the simple parts in the same way a complex Lego model is built from individual pieces.

As I have argued above, the Lego-model view of experimental inference is mistaken because – unlike in a real Lego model – the parts are unlikely to remain the same when conjoined with other parts: what an individual factor does depends on the whole setting of which it is a part. It is overwhelmingly *un*likely that what is learned about the behaviour of a factor in one setting can be exported to another setting without significant modification.

The economic experiments run in the advent of the FCC auctions are, in fact, a nice example for *this* aspect of experimental design. Charles Plott points out exactly the point I have just made (Plott 1997: 629):

> The concepts of withdrawals, eligibility, increments, and announcement of stage changes all involve reasonable-sounding concepts when considered alone, but there remain questions about how they might interact with each other, with other policies, and with the realities of software performance. Can one waive and bid at the same time? What happens if you withdraw at the end of the auction: should the auction remain open so the withdrawal can be cleared? How shall a withdrawal be priced? How is eligibility of everyone influenced by withdrawals? Should it go up so anyone can buy the item released to the market? How is eligibility influenced by increments: should eligibility be lost if increments are reduced because of lack of bids? As these interactions become discovered, there is a tendency to change the policy.

Hypotheses about the effectiveness of strategies should therefore be studied in settings that are as realistic as possible. While there remains a (heuristic) role for experiments testing simpler hypotheses – namely, to generate hypotheses about which factors *could* make a difference – the litmus test of a strategy hypothesis is an experiment under as 'natural' conditions as possible. Being aware of these issues, the experimental economists in the FCC case may have followed the top-down strategy (this has been argued convincingly by Anna Alexandrova; see Alexandrova 2006). Nevertheless they too relied too much on economic theory and thus misinterpreted the goals set by Congress.

In my view, the FCC story is a beautiful case study for showing that the distinction between 'valid' and 'sound' evidence is hugely important for evidence-based economics. The hypothesis that should have been tested is of the kind 'an auction of form *x* maximises the attainment of the goals of Congress, namely the rapid development and deployment of new technologies, the wide dispersion of PCS technologies, the dissemination of licences to a wide variety of applicants and so forth'. But the hypothesis for which eventually evidence was gathered was 'an auction of form *x* maximises revenue for the government'. Since this is the wrong hypothesis, evidence in its favour can at best be valid but never sound.

Certainly, I do not want to suggest that policy advice is the only possible function for economic experiments. Perhaps economists are interested in the validity of economic theory out of pure curiosity; perhaps, the aim is indeed to mimic other 'laboratory sciences' that create phenomena in and for the laboratory with no immediate and little indirect concern for the outside world; perhaps, economic experiments constitute a new kind of activity altogether. But as long as policy advice is the aim, what we need is a new experimentalism in experimental economics.

6 The role of theory in evidence-based economics

Models, mechanisms and thought experiments

I

In an enormously influential article Milton Friedman and Anna Schwartz tried to establish money as the principal cause of economic fluctuations, in particular as measured by nominal income (Friedman and Schwartz 1963). Following the tradition of NBER-empiricism, the proof was to be empirical: it had to be 'evidence based', based on a detailed analysis of patterns in the data. Friedman and Schwartz present a great variety of evidence, not just evidence of one kind. They note, first, that the correlation between changes in the money stock and nominal income is persistently high over nine decades, and that that result is robust to various specifications of 'correlation'. Importantly, perhaps, the correlation between money and nominal income is higher than that between autonomous expenditure – the cause of economic fluctuations according to the alternative hypothesis – and nominal income. Moreover, money screens off autonomous expenditure and income, but expenditure does not screen off money and income. Second, the relationship between money and nominal income hasn't changed across changes in the monetary constitution (for example, from a gold standard to a paper standard with floating exchange rates). Third, changes in autonomous causes of money (such as wars) have produced changes in nominal income. Statistical arguments in favour of a causal hypothesis are the topic of Chapter 7. In this chapter, I want to focus on a final argument given by Friedman and Schwartz (p. 59, emphasis added):

> However consistent may be the relation between monetary change and economic change, and however strong the evidence for the autonomy of the monetary changes, we shall not be persuaded that the monetary changes are the source of the economic changes unless we can specify in some detail the *mechanism* that connects the one with the other.

Accordingly, the specification of a mechanism that connects a putative (aggregate) cause with a putative (aggregate) effect is an indispensable element of sound causal inference. The purpose of this chapter is to clarify and discuss a number of versions of this claim. There is indeed some prima facie plausibility in it. Causal inference in the social sciences is hard, especially when 'social' or 'aggregate' or 'macro' variables are concerned. Situations of interest to the social researcher tend to be complex in the sense that a great number of causal factors operate jointly in bringing about an effect. This can be read as a material as well as a modal statement: many factors happen to act together in a given situation; but also, causal factors in the social domain (as a rule) cannot produce anything by themselves. They require a complex setting of other conditions in order to function. Related to this is a second point: causal factors do not only require a composite set of background circumstances to produce anything at all; how they behave frequently also depends on the precise composition of those background circumstances. We have seen examples of this interactive characteristic of some social factors in the context of economic experiments in the previous chapter. Moreover, the relationship between causes and effects is typically many–many. That is, any given effect can be brought about by what John Stuart Mill called a plurality of causes (Mill 1872, bk III, Ch. 10), but also, vice versa, most causes are able to bring about a plurality of effects. Further complications arise from the fact that social (macro or aggregate) phenomena cannot always be controlled to an extent necessary for reliable inference and that researchers often lack adequate causal background knowledge that could alleviate other problems.

Because of these circumstances it seems very plausible to require that statistical evidence about the relationship between aggregate variables be substantiated by micro evidence about the precise nature of the link between the variables. In the sections that follow I will first clarify the notion of a mechanism and then discuss various versions of the claim that mechanisms aid causal inference concerning aggregate variables.

II

Thinking about mechanisms has become increasingly popular in relatively recent philosophy of science and methodology. Almost all discussions about mechanisms I know of are motivated by the attempt to provide an adequate account of scientific *explanation* (see Elster 1989, 1999; Glennan 2002; Little 1991, 1998; Machamer *et al.* 2000; Woodward 2002, 2003). Here, by contrast, I am concerned with whether mechanisms can help in causal *inference* (as was Dan Steel in Steel 2004).

What is a mechanism? As often in debates regarding relatively novel (or newly rediscovered) ideas, there are about as many characterisations of key terms as there are contributors to the discussion. Many regard a mechanism as a process or a set of entities *in the world* (for example, all of the above-mentioned). Others, mostly social scientists, regard a mechanism as an entity of language or thought (see Hedström and Swedberg 1999b; Schelling 1999; Stinchcombe 1993 [1991]). Still others equivocate (see the two definitions of mechanism on p. 866 of Mas-Colell *et al.* 1995, as noted by Guala

2005: 163). For our purposes it is, of course, important to distinguish the two uses.

Let us first focus on the first meaning, a mechanism as something in the world. Now, since we are concerned with inference about causal relationships, we want to qualify that a mechanism is always a mechanism *for* a specific causal relationship. Causal relationships can be singular or generic. An event such as the decision of the Federal Reserve Bank board to raise interest rates on a particular day can be the cause of another event such as the collapse of the Tiger economies. On the other hand, a variable such as changes in the money stock can be the cause of another variable such as nominal income. What are mechanisms mechanisms for? Single or generic causal relationships? I think they can be for both but yet another qualification is due. Consider the following rhyme usually ascribed to Benjamin Franklin (I owe this example to Anne Fagot-Largeault):

> For want of a nail the shoe was lost.
> For want of a shoe the horse was lost.
> For want of a horse the rider was lost.
> For want of a rider the battle was lost.
> For want of a battle the kingdom was lost.
> And all for the want of a horseshoe nail.

Although the rhyme describes a causal sequence from one event (say, lack of care about a horseshoe nail) to another (say, the defeat of a kingdom), we would hardly say that a mechanism from the former to the latter was present. Some authors flesh out this intuition by requiring that the sequence of events is governed by regularities (again, all of the above-mentioned philosophers). Indeed, although *in this particular case* (say) the missing nail caused the loss of the horseshoe, the loss of the horseshoe caused the loss of the horse and so forth, it would be hard to uphold a claim to the effect that there is a lawlike generalisation from missing nails to royal defeats.

But the arguments against regularity accounts of causation are overwhelming. An account of a mechanism based on regularities, too, is implausible. Although in the case described by Franklin's rhyme we would deny the existence of a connecting mechanism, calling the sequence of events from the Federal Reserve Bank's decision to raise interest rates to the collapse of the Tiger economies a mechanism is perhaps more credible – even if this particular sequence of events occurs only once. Whether or not a mechanism operates depends on whether or not there is a system or structure in place that has the right properties such that, if it *were* to persist, it could operate undisturbedly and, if the sequence was triggered repeatedly, then a regularity *would* ensue (cf. Nancy Cartwright's definition of a nomological machine in Cartwright 1999a: 50). Without such a setup, no mechanism can operate.

We can therefore define:

CM. A causal mechanism for a causal relationship between (aggregate, macro or social variables) *X* and *Y* is a set of entities and properties that are such that, if they were embedded in a stable structure, could operate unimpededly and, if *X* fired regularly, then *Y* would follow regularly.

A mechanism in the second, linguistic or mental sense is a representation of a causal mechanism in the sense of CM. In order not to conflate the two meanings, let us call this latter kind of mechanism a *model* for a causal mechanism:

MCM. A model for a causal mechanism is a representation of a causal mechanism according to CM.

These definitions share important aspects of previous accounts but differ in others. Consider the following quotations, starting with:

> A causal mechanism, then, is a series of events governed by lawlike regularities that lead from the explanans to the explanandum.
>
> (Little 1991: 15)

There are a number of differences between CM and Little's definition. First, according to CM a mechanism is a set of entities together with their properties rather than a sequence of events. Consider a vending machine (quoted from Wikipedia Online Encyclopedia):

> Certain vending machines use a spiral kind of mechanism to separate and to hold the products. When the machine vends, the spiral turns, thus pushing the product forward and falling down to be vended.

The customer throws a coin in the slot, the coin falls down and through its momentum pushes a lever. The lever is connected to the spiral, which turns and thereby pushes the product forward. The product falls into a compartment from where the customer can take it. The sequence of events happens on or through or because of the mechanism, it does not constitute the mechanism. Second, a representation of a mechanism together with other statements constitutes an explanans for a statement about a causal relationship, the explanandum; the mechanism does not 'run from' explanans to explanandum. The vending-machine equivalent of the kinds of social relationships this chapter is concerned with would be, say, the observable relationship between inserting a coin and receiving a soda: regularly, when a coin is inserted, a can of soda appears. Never, when a can of soda is inserted, does a coin appear. Why does this relationship hold? The explanans cites a description of a mechanism perhaps with assertions that it operates inside a machine which shields it from outside influences and so forth. Third, as mentioned above, it is possible that a mechanism exists without a regularity to follow; for instance, because it is frequently disturbed or not often enough triggered.

> Mechanisms are entities and activities organized such that they are productive of regular changes from start or set-up to finish or termination conditions.
>
> (Machamer *et al.* 2000: 3)

This definition is very similar to CM but it leaves out the structure in which the mechanism is embedded. Furthermore, as before, a mechanism can be a mechanism without producing a regularity.

> (MECH) A necessary condition for a representation to be an acceptable model of a mechanism is that the representation (i) describe an organized or structured set of parts or components, where (ii) the behavior of each component is described by a generalization that is invariant under interventions, and where (iii) the generalizations governing each component are also independently changeable, and where (iv) the representation allows us to see how, in virtue of (i), (ii) and (iii), the overall output of the mechanism will vary under manipulation of the input to each component and changes in the components themselves.
>
> (Woodward 2002: S375)

In Woodward's definition, 'invariance under intervention' plays the same role as 'regularity' in other philosophers' definitions. I don't see a strong reason why the causal relationships a mechanism supports always have to be invariant under intervention. Of course, we would like to be able to intervene and exploit the money–income relationship for policy. But if we can't (even in principle), this does not entail that there is no mechanism from one variable to the other. More importantly, the fact that mechanisms are always embedded in a structure without which they cannot operate gives a strong reason to believe that their components are not always independently changeable (for a discussion of this aspect of Woodward's definition, see Cartwright 2001).

> A mechanism for a behavior is a complex system that produces that behavior by the interaction of a number of parts, where the interactions between parts can be characterized by direct, invariant, change-relating generalizations.
>
> (Glennan 2002: S344)

Glennan conflates a mechanism with the structure or machine in which it is embedded. A vending machine contains and enables the operation of one or several mechanisms. Likewise, a mechanism for the causal relationship between money and income – if there is such – operates within a complex socio-economic machine (and might not thus operate were it not for a socio-economic machine of a certain kind) but doesn't constitute it. Mechanisms can also overlap and interfere. Whole structures or machines, typically, cannot.

Let us now turn to mechanisms as representations.

> I propose . . . that a social mechanism is a plausible hypothesis, or set of plausible hypotheses, that could be the explanation of some social phenomenon, the explanation being in terms of interactions between individuals and other individuals, or between individuals and some social aggregate.
>
> (Schelling 1999: 32f.)

On the view proposed here, a model for a causal mechanism (MCM) is not a hypothesis but a representation. Hypotheses are required in order to make the representation relevant to the world. For instance, a hypothesis could state 'Our model *xyz* is a correct representation of the mechanism through which money causes income'. Moreover, I speak about entities and properties, not about individuals. The mechanism from the Federal Reserve Bank's decision to raise interest rates to the collapse of the Tiger economies may involve no single individual. Many models will refer to individuals but that should not be a necessary condition.

In the ellipsis Schelling says that he is paraphrasing Hedström and Swedberg, who define:

> a mechanism . . . as a systematic set of statements that provide a plausible account of how I and O [two social entities, usually thought of as cause and effect] are linked to one another.
>
> (Hedström and Swedberg 1999b: 7)

Nor does the above definition contain the requirement that a model be 'plausible'. However, as we shall see, economists standardly do require this, so I will discuss this point in detail below.

Finally, a definition by leading sociologist Arthur Stinchcombe:

> . . . mechanism means (1) a piece of scientific reasoning which is independently verifiable and independently gives rise to theoretical reasoning, which (2) gives knowledge about a component process (generally one with units of analysis at a 'lower level') of another theory (ordinarily a theory with units at a different 'higher' level), thereby (3) increasing the suppleness, precisions, complexity, elegance, or believability of the higher-level theory without excessive 'multiplication of entities' in it, (4) without doing too much violence (in the necessary

simplification at the lower level to make the higher-level theory go) to what we know as the main facts at the lower level.

(Stinchcombe 1993 [1991]: 25)

Verifiability, too, will be discussed in detail below. The view proposed here follows Stinchcombe in that the entities (social aggregates) 'for which' the mechanism is a mechanism are of a higher level than the entities of the mechanism. But the terminology used in the social sciences is not uniform. According to Herbert Simon, and following him Kevin Hoover, a network of relationships among aggregate variables can be a mechanism provided these relationships are causal and not merely associational. An explanation in terms of a causal mechanism does deepen our understanding of an aggregate phenomenon. In this respect I follow Stinchcombe, too.

III

With these concepts in place, we can formulate a first thesis:

Thesis 1. Knowledge about a causal mechanism for *X* and *Y* is indispensable for inferring the causal relationship between *X* and *Y*.

Given the results of the huge amount of work spent on developing econometric techniques for causal inference over the past twenty years or so, Thesis 1 is probably false. The main players in these developments are Bayes'-nets techniques (see Glymour and Cooper 1999; Pearl 2000; Spirtes *et al.* 2001) and invariance methods (see Hendry 2004; Hoover 2001; Woodward 2003). Both seek to identify causal relationships from data without explicit knowledge about the mechanisms connecting causes and effects. Certainly, a great deal of causal structure has to be assumed to get these techniques off the ground. But the required kind of background knowledge is not mechanistic in character (arguments to this effect have already been made by Harold Kincaid and endorsed by Steel; see Kincaid 1996: 179–82; Steel 2004). If knowledge about mechanisms is not required, it seems we don't need *models* about these mechanisms either. Thesis 1 is therefore false on both possible readings of the term used by Friedman and Schwartz.

But one point just made indicates that perhaps something else is meant. Statistical methods of causal inference do require a great deal of background knowledge; for instance about possible confounders and the relationship between causality and probability. Moreover, depending on the number of and causal relationships between the variables involved, statistical techniques cannot always distinguish between competing causal accounts for a given set of correlations. Perhaps, then, Friedman and Schwartz are saying that, *in a situation in which the presuppositions for the reliable use of statistical techniques aren't met*, mechanistic knowledge is essential:

Thesis 2. Knowledge about a causal mechanism for *X* and *Y* can be necessary in the circumstances for inferring the causal relationship between *X* and *Y*.

Thesis 2 is true if we read it as saying that for a given inferential problem all alternative methods suffer from a lack of reliable background knowledge (which is needed to apply such methods with success), and thus inferring a causal connection on the basis of knowledge about the connecting mechanism is the only remaining option.

But if this thesis is supposed say anything *positive* about knowledge about mechanisms, it has to be demonstrated that, in such situations, knowledge about a mechanism for a causal relationship between *X* and *Y* can be inferred more reliably than the causal relationship between *X* and *Y* directly. That is to say, can claims about a mechanism for a causal relationship between *X* and *Y* be established more reliably than claims about a causal relationship between *X* and *Y* (in certain situations, or, perhaps, more generally)?

IV

Let us digress for a moment and examine a more up-to-date method of tackling the problem. Today academic journals are replete with mathematical models whose apparent aim is to provide an explanation for aggregate social phenomena. Thomas Schelling's checkerboard model of racial segregation (see Schelling 1978) and George Akerlof's lemons model of the second-hand car market (see Akerlof 1970) are stock examples that are widely used in methodological debates. Many such models have the following four characteristics, which we might term 'explanatory virtues':

- *Mathematisation*. The assumptions idealise such that the mode of deriving the representation of the phenomenon is mathematical proof. The derivation makes use of the tools and techniques of recent developments in mathematical economics such as non-cooperative game theory, rational expectations modelling and so forth.
- *Rationality*. The representation concerns individuals (or institutions such as banks, households, firms, etc.) that maximise their utility under the given information and budgetary constraints.
- *Equilibrium*. Individuals (and/or institutions) interact such that an equilibrium results.
- *Empirical adequacy*. The model is consistent with patterns observed in aggregate data.

Here I want to discuss an example that concerns the transmission mechanism (from changes in the money stock to nominal variables). In Friedman and Schwartz's original sketch of the transmission mechanism, roughly the following happens. The initial change in the growth rate of the money stock (implemented by, for example, an increase in the rate of open market purchases) causes an imbalance in the portfolios of the market participants: they hold too much liquidity relative to their preferences. They thus seek to adjust their portfolios and demand assets. Initially they buy assets that are similar to those sold to the Federal Reserve Bank (that is, relatively risk-free titles); later they seek further and also buy riskier securities. Increased demand will drive up the prices for these assets and, correspondingly, lower interest rates. Higher asset prices will make people feel wealthier and hence increase demand for non-financial goods and services. Increased aggregate demand will, in turn, increase income, employment and output. After a while, however, the prices of goods and services, too, will react to the higher demand and increase. The increased rate of inflation will, finally, reverse the initial wealth effects of the liquidity shock because it reduces the real value of the assets. In the long run, thus, the effect of the increased rate of monetary growth is mainly on prices, while in the short run there are also real effects.

In a recent paper Jess Benhabib and Roger Farmer provide an alternative model of the transmission mechanism (Benhabib and Farmer 2000). The problem with Friedman and Schwartz's sketch according to Benhabib and Farmer (as well as many other economists) is that it assumes that people suffer from money illusion, which means that it lacks the second explanatory virtue (in Friedman and Schwartz's presentation it also lacked the first virtue but that defect was easily fixed later on). If they were fully rational, they would predict the eventual increase in prices and thus never change demand for goods and services. Like a self-fulfilling prophecy prices would immediately react to the monetary shock; thus there would be no real effects and the short run would be identical with the long run. However, this neoclassical alternative potential explanation is inconsistent with the observed patterns in the data, violating the fourth virtue. A number of writers have now attributed the real initial effects of money – the effects on variables such as income and employment – to an imperfection that prevents markets from clearing. This, however, violates the third virtue: equilibrium. Benhabib and Farmer's aim is to sketch a model that realises all virtues: the first three theoretical explanatory virtues as well as the fourth empirical virtue.

Their model is too complex to reproduce it fully. Thus, instead, I focus on a number of details demonstrating that the model indeed exhibits all four virtues. (Impatient readers, or readers with some experience with mathematical models in economics, are welcome to skip the technical details that follow – they are given for purely illustrative purposes.)

Mathematisation Benhabib and Farmer's model contains a number of standard assumptions that allow the derivation by mathematical proof; for example, that the economy contains a large number of identical representative households. Key economic quantities are represented by time-indexed variables such as y_t, c_t, m_t and b_t, defined as the ratio of output, consumption, real balances (money) and bonds to a growing trend, respectively. The variables are functionally related to each other by equalities such as the CES production function $y_t^\lambda = (1 - a)L_t^{\alpha\lambda} + am_t^\lambda$ (where L denotes labour and a, α and λ are parameters) and the utility function $u(C, L, S, \bar{L})$ (where S is technological progress and $\bar{L}$ the average labour supply of other members of society).

Rationality Households maximise the utility function

$$U = E_0\left\{\sum_{t=0}^{\infty}\delta^t\left[\frac{c_t^{1-r}}{1-r} - \frac{1}{1+\chi_1}\frac{L_t^{1+\chi_1}}{\bar{L}_t^{\chi+\chi_1}}\right]\right\},\quad \delta^0 = 1,\quad \delta^t = \left(\frac{1}{1+\rho}\right)^t\prod_{v=1}^{t-1}\gamma_v^{1-r}, t>0 \quad (1)$$

with respect to $c_t \equiv C_t/S_t$, where E is the expectation operator (in this case expectation at time zero), ρ is the rate of time preference, r is the elasticity of intertemporal substitution, χ_1 is the inverse private elasticity of individual labour supply, and χ measures the external effect of other people's labour on individual utility. The budget constraints are as follows:

$$m_t + b_t = r_t^m m_{t-1} + r_t^b b_{t-1} + f(L_t, r_t^m m_{t-1} + \tau_t) - c_t + \tau_t, \text{ for } t = 1, 2, \ldots \quad (2)$$

$$r_t^m \equiv \frac{p_{t-1}}{p_t\gamma_t}, \qquad r_t^b \equiv \frac{p_{t-1}}{p_t\gamma_t}(1 + i_{t-1}), \quad (3)$$

$$b_0 = 0, \qquad M_0 = m_0 \quad (4)$$

$$\text{Lim}_{s\to\infty} Q_t^s\delta_s(m_s + b_s) \geq 0, \qquad Q_t^s = \frac{P_s}{P_t}\prod_{v=1}^{s}\frac{1}{(1+i_v)}, \quad (5)$$

where p is the money price of a commodity and τ_t is defined as T_t/p_tS_t, the real value of the lump sum nominal transfer T_t households receive in each period relative to the growing productivity trend.

Equilibrium There are a number of equilibrium relationships in the model, which can be separated into intratemporal equations, that is, relationships between variables at a single date, and intertemporal equations, that is, relationships between variables at consecutive dates. The intratemporal equations are the following:

$y_t = f(L_t, m_t)$, the production function, and (6)

$$\frac{-u_L(L_t, \bar{L}_t)}{u_c(c_t)} = f_L(L_t, m_t), \text{ labour demand and supply.} \quad (7)$$

Empirical adequacy A number of Benhabib and Farmer's modelling decisions are guided by previous empirical findings. Consider the following three:

1 A CES rather than a Cobb–Douglas production function is chosen because choosing the latter would imply an interest rate elasticity of money demand equal to –1 while empirical studies estimated it to be closer to –0.5.
2 The result that money affects output in the short run could be modelled by making it a productive factor with great importance. However, since the elasticity of money in production is equal to the opportunity cost of holding money, and the latter quantity is relatively small, this approach is empirically implausible. Benhabib and Farmer achieve the same result by modelling a downward sloping supply curve. Assuming a negative wage elasticity of labour supply is non-standard but in line with empirical estimations of that elasticity.
3 The third empirical consideration concerns the utility function. First, technological progress directly affects consumers' utility. In the authors' eyes, this reflects the fact that technological progress has created household appliances such as microwave ovens, toasters and washing machines, which increase the time available to the household for market-based activities as well as leisure. Second, household utility is affected by average labour, which according to the authors reflects the fact that we are more prone to put in more hours of work when everybody does the same. This is the assumption that leads to a negatively sloping labour supply curve at the aggregate level.

The mechanism represented by this model can be described as follows (Benhabib and Farmer 2000: 531):

> An increase in money has two effects on employment. The first occurs as an increase in real balances causes firms to increase their demand for labor. [At any given wage rate, firms are willing to employ more labour, i.e.] the labor demand curve shifts to the right. The second occurs as increased production leads to increased consumption. [At any given rate of employment, employers demand a higher wage, i.e.] the labor supply curve shifts up.

In other words, an exogenously created monetary shock first increases production (and labour demand) – since money is considered a productive factor – and then increased production affects employment because labour and consumption are functionally related through consumers' utility functions.

Why is this story an advance over Friedman and Schwartz's original story? The fact that it is considered an advance by many economists suggests a third thesis:

Thesis 3. Knowledge of a causal mechanism for the causal relationship between *X* and *Y* can be necessary in the circumstances for inferring the causal relationship between *X* and *Y*. Constructing a *model* for a causal mechanism for *X* and *Y* is sufficient for this inference only if the model has the right kinds of explanatory virtues.

Thesis 3 in my view is quite consistent with much of economic practice. Building models of the described kind is a standard activity. Importantly, providing a deeper, mechanistic explanation of an already established causal relationship is not always the purpose of this activity. Rather, the mathematical model is itself regarded as evidence for the existence of the causal link represented by the model. Even policies are frequently tested in the laboratory of the mind rather than in an economic laboratory or in the field. Moreover, a number of leading theoretical economists have vindicated this practice in their methodological writings. Consider the oft-cited passage from Nobel laureate Robert Lucas (Lucas 1982: 271):

> One of the functions of theoretical economics is to provide fully articulated, artificial economic systems that can serve as laboratories in which policies that would be prohibitively expensive to experiment with in actual economies can be tested out at much lower cost.

If I am correct, the mode of inference used by these theoretical economists is a type of *inference to the best explanation*. Simply put, any model that can reproduce a phenomenon of interest constitutes a *potential* explanation of that phenomenon. Of all potential explanations the one that maximises the explanatory virtues required by the profession is the 'best' and hence there is reason to believe in its correctness.

Whatever the virtues of inference to the best explanation as an inductive scheme for science in general (for a defence, see Lipton 2004), in the context of causal inference it is utterly implausible. In general, inference to the best explanation relies on a strong rationalistic intuition that the world is such as we would like it to be: simple, unified, precise, mechanistic or what have you. While there is no space to discuss this intuition in any detail here, this book tries to defend a pragmatist, goal-oriented stance against rationalism of this kind. According to this point of view, a good explanation is one that helps us realise our practical goals – whatever they may be. Of course, we won't realise any given goal if the strategy pursued does not take into account the realities of the world in which the goal is to be reached. If this world as it behaves towards us appears pied rather than planned (even if, deep down, it is well ordered), then so be it.

But more to the point, in the context of causal analysis, inference to the best explanation seems entirely misplaced. Suppose, for the sake of the argument, that we have relatively clear ideas on how to test whether a model really has a given explanatory virtue, and on how to rank the different virtues in case of conflict. Suppose further that only one model maximises explanatory virtues or that all models that maximise explanatory virtues result in the same causal order. Shall we trust this model?

The first three explanatory virtues, in particular, require an extreme degree of idealisation in the resulting model. Now, while all models idealise to some degree, typical models that manifest the said virtues are often unusual in that standard defences of the use of idealisation in science do not apply.

One defence is based on convergent sequences of approximations (see Laymon 1985). Take the inclined plane, which is often represented as frictionless in models. Of course, there doesn't exist a literally frictionless plane. But we can approximate the model results in the laboratory by making planes smoother and smoother, and we then observe that the experimental results converge with the model result.

Quite obviously, this defence of using idealised assumption does not apply to the case at hand. If it were possible to run a converging sequence of experiments, there would be no need to construct a model for we could experimentally test the causal claim in the first place.

The reverse defence has been made by Robert Sugden (Sugden 2000: 23ff.). If in a very simple model *X* causes *Y*, and this result persists when assumptions are relaxed, more causal factors are allowed to play a role and the model becomes more realistic, then we are justified in believing that *X* causes *Y* in the world too. For isn't the world just an enormously complex model? More formally, Sugden endorses the following form of inference:

In an extremely simple model M_1, *X* causes *Y*.
In a slightly more complex model M_2, in which assumptions made in M_1 have been changed to somewhat more realistic assumptions, *X* causes *Y*.
In an even more complex model M_3, in which the initial assumptions have been further relaxed, *X* causes *Y*.
Etc. . . .
. . .
In M_n (the real world), *X* causes *Y*.

While I think that this schema is a plausible model of inference in general, I doubt that it is applicable to the case at hand. The previous chapter has described how sensitive to the precise setting many results in economic experiments are. An analogous fact is true, and known to be true, about results derived from certain kinds of economic models: they are, by and large, extremely sensitive to the precise set of assumptions made. Just change the transportation cost function slightly, change the setting from static to dynamic, introduce risk aversion, take out money illusion and so forth; all these factors will often make a dramatic difference to the derived result. Worse, because of the difficulty of constructing *any* model that manifests all four explanatory virtues, very often it will not be possible to relax a model's assumption. Moreover, we often do not know which of any of the assumptions made is true of a given population (*in the relevant population*. Are relevant people risk averse or neutral? Are their transportation cost functions linear or quadratic? etc.). Therefore, if X causes Y in M_1, little can be said about the behaviour of X for a different model let alone a real socio-economic system.

A third line of defence is also due to Sugden – and also inapplicable to the case at hand. A good model, says Sugden, represents a credible world (op. cit.). That is, it represents the world not how it is but how, for all we know, it *could* have been. Because in the model world we can prove a causal relationship and our intuitions tell us that the model world could have been the real world, we have reason to believe that in the real world the same causal relationship holds. Sugden's epistemology seems to be one of casual empiricism. The experience gained by living in this world shapes our intuitions, which in turn provide a reliable guide for what is possible. If we judge a model to be realistic in this sense, we have reason to believe in the truth of its consequences. This way he justifies both Schelling's checkerboard model of racial segregation and Akerlof's lemons model of the second-hand market for automobiles (for more detail on Akerlof's model, see below and Chapter 9). *We all know* that most people don't like to be in an absolute minority; we all know that cities are racially segregated and that borders between relatively homogenous areas move. If, then, in a simple model the minutely racist preference reproduces the known phenomena, we have reason to believe that this slight preference – rather than, say, outright racism – is a cause also in the real world. Similarly, since we know that Akerlof's model is a realistic depiction of how a second-hand car market could look, there is reason to believe that in the real world, too, asymmetric information lowers trade volumes.

My intuitions differ. I don't see why we would call a model in which people are motivated by greed alone, where cars have but one – abstract – property, 'quality' and where people receive an infallible quality signal the second they buy a car particularly realistic. Nor will the most realistic model reliably pick out the true causal story. But more importantly, credibility is yet another explanatory virtue, one that will not always pick out the same model as the above-mentioned virtues. In my experience, in case of conflict economists tend to give preference to the other virtues. If given the choice, say between a credible model that isn't mathematically expressible and a less credible one that is, of course the latter one will be chosen. Just consider one characteristic of Benhabib and Farmer's model, the downward-sloping labour supply curve. If asked to state 'what we all know' about supply curves, any economist will reply that it is an upward-sloping schedule. But Benhabib and Farmer use the non-standard curve anyway in order to reproduce the patterns in the data – and to build a model with other virtues.

No other defence of idealisation I know of works in this case either. But since the realisation of the said explanatory virtues requires such idealisations to be made, we should not infer from explanatoriness to truth.

Moreover, it looks rather as if the Benhabib–Farmer model buys explanatory virtues *at the expense* of truth. Consider again the downward-sloping labour supply schedule. The evidence the authors provide is that a downward-sloping curve 'is consistent with estimates of labor supply in aggregate data, in the work of Mankiw *et al.* (1985) and Farmer and Guo (1995)'. Interestingly, the first study does not claim that the aggregate supply curve is downward-sloping. Rather, the authors conclude that 'observed economic fluctuations do not easily admit of a neoclassical interpretation'. The neoclassical (market-clearing) model is of course that which is at the heart of Benhabib and Farmer's study. Further, just before concluding Mankiw *et al.* say that 'the parameter estimates are usually highly implausible. The estimated utility function is often not concave, which implies that the representative individual is not at a maximum of utility, but at a saddle-point or at a minimum. In addition, when the utility function is concave, the estimates imply that either consumption or leisure is an inferior good' (p. 226). Thus, at best, aggregate labour supply may sometimes be downward-sloping but there is no evidence that it is. Only when the utility curve is concave, as it should be, it is either consumption or leisure that is an inferior good, not that it must be leisure. They conclude (pp. 243ff.):

> This result provides powerful evidence against the hypothesis that observed labor supply behavior can be described as resulting from continuous maximization of a stable additively separable intertemporal utility function [i.e. the kind of function Benhabib and Farmer assume]. The estimated utility function is extremely implausible . . . [S]ince consumption and leisure move in opposite directions for any given real wage, one must be inferior if the movements represent voluntary maximizing behavior. These results probably emerge because over the business cycle consumption and leisure move in opposite directions. At the same time, we simply do not observe at the aggregate level the procyclical movements in the real wage that would rationalize this behavior.

Likewise, the later study by Farmer and Guo has been plausibly criticised. For example, if both supply and demand curves slope downward, the implied correlation between productivity and employment is negative. However, the empirical value for the correlation is about zero (see Aiyagari 1995).

V

But now we seem to have run into an impasse: if knowledge of a causal mechanism can be necessary in the circumstances for causal inference but the orthodox methodology does not yield such knowledge, does that mean that in such circumstances causal inference is impossible? In the already cited paper, Steel describes an alternative method for inference to mechanisms, a method he calls 'process tracing'. He illustrates it with an example from the anthropologist Boris Malinowski and defines (Steel 2004: 67):

> Process tracing consists in presenting evidence for the existence of several prevalent social practices that, when linked together, produce a chain of causation from one variable to another. A successful instance of process tracing, then, demonstrates the existence of a social mechanism connecting the variables of interest. For instance, in the case just described, the social practices are (1) that brothers are required to contribute a substantial store of yams to the households of their sisters and (2) that yams are the primary means used by chiefs to finance their various endeavors. Supposing that Malinowski was right about (1) and (2), the conclusion that the number of wives had an influence on wealth among Trobriand chiefs is unavoidable.

Steel, of course, does not fail to notice that the crux of this method is to provide convincing evidence that the social practices mentioned in the argument actually exist. Doesn't that mean that the problem isn't just shifted one level down? Isn't causal inference at the level of the individual stages of the mechanism just as difficult as causal inference for relationships between aggregate variables?

In my view it all depends on the specifics of the case at hand. Perhaps we don't have enough causal background knowledge to reliably infer the causal direction between money and income. But perhaps we do have enough background knowledge to be able to estimate the 'liquidity effect' – the first step in the chain from money to income (for a detailed discussion, see the following chapter). In some cases we may be able to run experiments to test whether people in the appropriate context behave in the way required by the mechanism. In other cases measurement error – a serious problem for causal inference – may be alleviated at the lower level. In still other cases, uncertainty about the time lag between cause and effect – another serious problem for causal inference, especially regarding aggregate money (see for instance Tobin 1970) – may be reduced.

But these case-by-case advantages face other case-by-case difficulties. While experiments are very good at establishing a causal claim that is true of the test population, results are often hard to export to other situations (see Chapter 5). One can always run statistical analyses of past data. But we can never run an experiment with people living in the past. While moving to the level of the mechanism may take the edge out of measurement problems, afterwards we will have the opposite problem of aggregating data. And so forth.

Furthermore, process tracing has one serious defect relative to the problem at hand. As Steel notices (Steel 2004: 71), it can at best establish qualitative causal claims. Many disagreements in economics, however, are of a quantitative nature. Friedman and Schwartz don't deny that there is a 'feedback loop' from economic activity to money. The whole discussion revolves around the relative strengths of the influences. Therefore, even if we can establish by means of mechanistic knowledge that there is a causal relationship between two aggregate variables, relatively little advance is made.

It is therefore hard to draw a general conclusion about the usefulness of moving to the level of the mechanism for causal inference regarding aggregate variables. It is true that it may at times be necessary in the circumstances. But the fact that something is required doesn't entail that it can also be had. In many situations, reliable causal inference may just be something very hard to get.

VI

Nancy Cartwright distinguishes between what she calls 'clinchers' and 'vouchers' among methods of causal inference (Cartwright 2007). The former 'clinch' their results: under specific, very strong background assumptions, one can demonstrate deductively that the results must hold. Examples are randomised clinical trials, Bayes'-nets methods and various econometric techniques such as the method of causal instrumental variables (see Chapter 7). The latter merely 'vouch' for their results: they make them likely – or they provide reason to believe them – but they are not certain. Examples are comparative methods and ethnographic methods.

There is an obvious trade-off between the two kinds of methods. Clinchers make their results certain but only under very restrictive conditions that are rarely met. It is often not known how to interpret results when reached in a situation where the conditions were not met. Vouchers have wider applicability. But they introduce uncertainty about the results they vouch for.

There are analogues of these two types of methods in theoretical economics. Mathematical models of the kind described here 'clinch' their results. The causal knowledge thus achieved is certain. But we can model only highly idealised, plainly unrealistic situations in this way. There is an alternative, less formal method that also gets inspiration from economic theory: thought experimentation. Consider Akerlof's lemons model. Akerlof, in fact, provides two arguments in favour of his conclusion, not just one as usually supposed. Apart from the mathematical model with which he derives the conclusion by way of mathematical proof and which (more or less) manifests the above explanatory virtues, he also supplies a less formal argument to the same effect: a thought experiment (Akerlof 1970: 429):

> Suppose . . . that there are just four kinds of cars. There are new cars and used cars. There are good cars and bad cars (which in America are known as 'lemons'). A new car may be a good car or a lemon, and of course the same is true of used cars.

> The individuals in this market buy a new automobile without knowing whether the car they buy will be good or a lemon. But they do know that with probability q it is a good car and with probability $(1 - q)$ it is a lemon; by assumption, q is the proportion of good cars produced and $(1 - q)$ is the proportion of lemons.
>
> After owning a specific car, however, for a length of time, the car owner can form a good idea of the quality of this machine; i.e. the owner assigns a new probability to the event that his car is a lemon. This estimate is more accurate than the original estimate. An asymmetry in available information has developed: for the sellers now have more knowledge about the quality of a car than the buyers. But good cars and bad cars must still sell at the same price – since it is impossible for a buyer to tell the difference between a good car and a bad car. It is apparent that a used car cannot have the same valuation, it would clearly be advantageous to trade a lemon at the price of a new car, and buy another new car, at a higher probability q of being good . . . Thus the owner of a good machine must be locked in. Not only is it true that he cannot receive the true value of his car, but he cannot even obtain the expected value of a new car.

A mathematical model differs from a thought experiment in its level of explicitness and logical stringency. A model is a fully articulated system in the sense that all claims it makes follow deductively from a set of assumptions. A thought experiment, by contrast, leaves many details unspecified. For example, in Akerlof's scenario, there are four types of cars, good and bad, new and old. But nothing is said about any other properties they might have. In a mathematical model, cars have nothing but these properties. This is made sure by making quality and nothing else an argument in the agents' utility function and by defining 'new' as 'agents know about the quality' (that is, the car's quality rather than an expected value is an argument in their decision function) and 'old' as 'agents do not know about the quality'. As a consequence, the way we derive results from models and from thought experiments differs. A model proves a conditional of the form $A \rightarrow R$; that is, for systems in which the model's assumptions A hold true, the results R must be true. The inference proceeds much more informally in thought experiments. Thought experiments make a result plausible in the light of our intuitions about an economic situation. But reverse results are always possible. Nothing forces us to 'lock in the owners of good cars'. Owners may reveal the quality of their cars, and buyers may believe them. People may give away the cars because they suddenly prefer biking. Or owners of bad cars may not notice the arbitrage opportunity that arises when they learn about the inferior quality of their cars. The result follows on account of our intuitions about what economic behaviour consists of. But outside the more formal mathematical model, nothing necessitates it.

Another way of putting the issue is as follows. Modelling proceeds hypothetico-deductively while thought experiments reason in a way which closely resembles Mill's method (Mill 1844) *a priori*. For Mill, truths in political economy cannot be found by induction from specific phenomena as there is no experimentum crucis. Rather, we need to establish the fundamental tendency laws on the basis of introspection. In my view, thought experiments can help us to establish such fundamental laws. They answer questions of the form, 'Had I been in situation *S* and acted on the economic motive alone, what would I have done?' The answer to that is obviously hypothetical but it is not arbitrary: it is based on my experience with situations similar to *S* and with being greedy. The result of the mathematical model is more or less certain at the same time. It is more certain in that the conclusion must follow from the premisses, given of course we make no mistakes in the calculation. But it is less certain in that the initial premisses are more arbitrary, more purely hypothetical (I take, say, the assignment of a definite utility function to an agent to be more arbitrary than the ascription of an economic motive). Two final remarks. First, the difference between the thought experiment and mathematical model is one of degree, not one of kind. The assumptions of a model may well be very plausible, and in many cases even consist of well-established laws. The other way round, we may design thought experiments so tightly such that our results follow as if by deduction.

VII

The title of this chapter is 'The role of theory in evidence-based economics'. Let us therefore conclude with some musings about the role of economic theory given what has been established regarding mechanisms, models and thought experiments. Models and thought experiments are representational devices, which sketch mechanisms that may be operative in an economy. Economic theory provides resources – principles, concepts, ideas, solution techniques – that can be used in the construction of models and thought experiments. Economic theory makes a modeller or thought experimenter regard humans as rational maximisers of utility; it suggests factors such as information, preferences, costs and profits as salient explanatory factors in a given situation; it supplies equilibrium concepts as tools to solve problem situations, and so forth. Using these ideas a model or thought experiment can be built, which itself provides a hypothesis for a mechanism that may or may not be responsible for some aggregate phenomenon.

The antirealism towards theory suggested here is thus quite robust. Not only are abstract theories themselves not to be regarded as literally true descriptions of economic phenomena; also the more concrete models built using the concepts and principles from theories are mere tools. In terms of our definitions from Chapter 1: models and thought experiments provide prima facie evidence in favour of a causal hypothesis. They invite further investigation into whether the causal mechanism they represent is operative in the phenomenon under investigation.

The usefulness of this method of creating prima facie evidence for a causal hypothesis depends on the context. I don't think we need a mathematical model to see that money either causes income or it does not. In a different context having prima facie evidence can be of genuine epistemic value. Take Schelling's checkerboard model. As I understand it, at the time Schelling first published the model in the early 1970s (Schelling 1971), most people were convinced that racism was responsible for the patterns of racial segregation in cities. Schelling demonstrated that the same patterns at the aggregate level could be produced by a very mild preference not to be in the absolute minority. Without Schelling's demonstration of the model, the idea that strong segregation patterns should be created by very mildly racist preferences seemed implausible. But with it, everybody could check for him or herself that the causal relationship is possible. Of course, this does not say anything about whether in any given city segregation patterns are indeed produced in the way represented by the model. Whether or not they are has to be settled by further empirical investigation.

A similar story can be told about Akerlof's model. The phenomenon he sought to explain was an immense difference between the prices of a new car and one that has just been sold. Received wisdom at the time was that a preference for novelty explains the phenomenon. Akerlof demonstrated that an alternative explanation is also possible. The same phenomenon arises from an asymmetry in the information distribution: sellers have an informational advantage and, without institutions that can reduce the skewness in the information distribution, prices for second-hand cars drop. Such possibility results may be invaluable in many contexts. But they create prima facie, not valid (or sound), evidence.

7 Practice ahead of theory

Natural experiments and causal instrumental variables

> We comfortably divide ourselves into a celibate priesthood
> of statistical theorists, on the one hand,
> and a legion of inveterate sinner-data analysts, on the other.
> The priests are empowered to draw up lists of sins
> and are revered for the special talents they display.
> Sinners are not expected to avoid sins;
> they need only confess their errors openly.
>
> Edward Leamer (in Leamer 1978: vi)

I

The aim of this chapter is twofold. First, I argue that John Stuart Mill's scepticism of using inductive methods in the investigation of social phenomena is ill-founded. Mill maintained that, since there is no 'crucial experiment' in the moral sciences (in the sense of having two situations that are identical except for some causal factor of interest), scientific investigation could not proceed bottom-up from experimental facts to more general truths (Mill 1872, bk VI, Ch. 7). Rather, it had to proceed top-down from general laws of human nature and boundary conditions to predictions about concrete phenomena. I claim that the major premiss of this argument is false: there are situations that given the right kind of causal background knowledge can mimic Mill's crucial experiments. If that is so, the principal reason for deductivism in economic methodology is shown to be false and we might as well become inductivists.

The second aim relates to the details of the econometricians' stand-ins for experiments. As the above quote from Edward Leamer illustrates, econometric methodology divides into a set of official dogmas that together constitute the saintly textbook scriptures and an implicit methodology found in sinful practice. Here I invert the usual hierarchy: I suggest that we revere the sinners and damn the priests. Until not very long ago, it was part of the official doctrine to identify parameters of interest on the basis of knowledge about correlations only. In practical applications, however, free use of institutional, historical and in particular causal knowledge is made. I want to argue that, if the official methodology was followed, a particular technique in econometrics would yield misleading conclusions. In practical applications, by contrast, econometricians do not follow the official line but exploit the right kind of non-correlational knowledge to identify their parameters correctly (cf. Lawson 1997, Ch. 1, who notes a similar tension between theory and practice).

The two seemingly disparate claims are in fact connected. This is due to a second sin theoretical econometricians tell us not to commit: to estimate parameters that have no theoretical significance. At least since the heyday of the econometrics of the Cowles Commission, it has been received wisdom that econometrics is the junior partner of economic theory and that its function is to test implications of this theory and to estimate theoretically identified economic parameters. In the case studies I examine here, little respect is paid to theory; right to the contrary, the parameters that are estimated are hardly related to theoretical claims at all. This is, then, a second way in which practice is ahead of theory: practice implicitly commits to an inductive methodology similar to the kind I am trying to defend in this book.

Before going into the details of all this, I will provide some background in Section II by reviewing Mill's argument against inductivism in political economy and why it is still relevant. Sections III and IV provide the main discussion regarding the saints and sinners story. Section V wraps up the discussion by projecting an inductive methodology based on the mimicked econometric experiments of Sections III and IV.

II

In the view of many economists and methodologists, economics is an abstract and deductive science. It is abstract in a twofold sense. First, its basic principles do not describe actual states of affairs but 'pure' states of affairs that would obtain if it were not for the operation of disturbing factors. Second, the basic principles are unspecific and stand in need of fitting in for concrete results. Take as a basic principle the desire to seek wealth or the rule to maximise utility. In order to derive anything from these principles, it must be specified what the object in the concrete case consists of and what the alternative means are towards the object. Further, economics is deductive in that concrete or, at any rate, more concrete results are derived from the basic principles in conjunction with assumptions about the structure of an economic system of interest deductively. Evidence at best plays the role of testing whether in one's deductions a disturbing factor has been left out.

This image of economics dates back to at least the writings of John Stuart Mill. He constructed it because he thought economics could not be an inductive science, building up from particular items of evidence to general knowledge. His argument against induction in economics makes two claims. First, Mill says, the economic world is too complex to make inductive inferences. This claim is based on his method of difference which presupposes there being two situations which differ only with respect to presence of the one causal factor of interest. He then claimed that to find these situations in a political economy would be excessively rare because of the complexity involved.

The second claim is that experimental control is hardly ever possible in the social world. In natural phenomena, even if their natural occurrence is complex, single causal factors can be isolated experimentally and hypotheses tested on the basis of the experimental setup. Now given the social world is complex and it does not allow of experiments, the prospects for the inductive method are dire. However, Mill further claims that the basic principles of economics are known *a priori*. This has to do with the fact that economics is the science of an aspect of human conduct with which we all have first-hand acquaintance. The only difficulty that remains is to find all the disturbing factors that will get us from the basic principles to the concrete circumstance (see Mill 1844; 1872, bk VI).

A glance at modern economics shows that economists still follow Mill's precepts to some extent. To be fair, his 'fundamental laws of behaviour' – the desires to seek wealth and avoid work – have been replaced by the principle of utility maximisation, and his demand to deduce more concrete results from the abstract principles has been made more precise by the demand to provide a mathematical model of the concrete situation, but the general outlook remains the same.

Mill's argument is mistaken. While it is hard to disagree with the truism that the social world is complex and that conducting controlled experiments with whole economies is seldom an option, inductive methods have improved since his day, and nowadays there are substitutes for controlled experiments, which enable inductive causal inference even in complex situations where no control is possible. The premiss in his argument that I am attacking is thus the implicit premiss that inductive inference presupposes either natural or experimental isolation of a single causal mechanism.

The case studies I use to make the point about inductive inference are drawn from the natural experiments movement in econometrics. This movement can be regarded exactly as an answer to the challenge Mill posed. Suppose we would like to know whether military service causes earnings later in life. Finding a correlation between the two variables would not suffice even if we can assume that earnings do not cause military service because of the temporal order. This is due to the reasons Mill gives. There is simply a myriad of factors that could be responsible for earnings, some of which may be related to military service too. Suppose that, on average, fitter people both tend to join the army and tend to have higher wages. A positive correlation, then, would be indicative of this common cause rather than of a direct causal connection.

Ideally, hence, we would divide up (a representative sample of) the male population into two groups such that all other causes of earnings are identically distributed and send one group to serve and one group not to serve.

But, as Mill noticed, such a social experiment is, for whatever reason, impossible. Proponents of natural experiments now aim at finding situations that resemble a genuine controlled experiment without explicit control. For example, the draft for the Vietnam War was organised by assigning numbers from 1 to 365 at random to every day of a given birth year of potential recruits. The men were potential draftees up to a certain threshold number, for instance 195 for men born in 1950 and 125 in 1951. Assignment to draft status, thus, can be regarded as independent of other causes of the effect (the precise day someone was born should not directly affect earnings in life, or so current views regarding astrology have it). Now if there remains a correlation between draft status and earnings after stratifying with respect to a random sequence number, there is reason to interpret the correlation causally.

Natural experiments are a species of a broader approach in econometrics, called instrumental variables estimation. This approach is used when a relationship between two variables, say X and Y, is potentially confounded by other variables. The instrument is defined as a third variable Z which has two characteristics: it is correlated with X but uncorrelated with the error term of Y. In the following section I want to demonstrate that the instrumental variables approach makes valid causal inference only under a set of very strong assumptions about the socio-economic system studied and that it is epistemically preferable to make explicitly causal assumptions.

III

'Correlation is not causation' is a well-rehearsed slogan. In this section I am going to argue that prior knowledge about causal relationships is not only necessary to identify causal parameters from statistics but that it is also often easier to acquire than knowledge about correlations.

The reason to re-rehearse the slogan is that econometrics textbooks tend to avoid explicitly causal language in their descriptions of estimation procedures. For example, in simultaneous equations variables divide into endogenous and exogenous variables, and that means that they are either determined within the model or outside it. Importantly, without qualification, the 'determined' can be read both functionally or causally. Sometimes a model is called 'structural' if its form is given by the underlying theory. But no word is lost on whether the theory specifies functional or causal relationships. To give a third example, the error term in a regression model is often said to represent 'stochastic disturbances' or 'shocks' as well as omitted factors, measurement error and other 'influences'. Again, it is unclear whether these terms carry a causal meaning or not.

The neglect of causality in econometrics has its roots deep in the origins of modern statistics itself. Modern statistics was created in an intellectual climate in which many scientists and philosophers shared Bertrand Russell's famous sentiment (Russell 1913: 1):

> The law of causality, I believe, like much that passes muster among philosophers, is a relic of a bygone age, surviving, like the monarchy, only because it is erroneously supposed to do no harm.

Thus Karl Pearson, one of the founders of modern statistics, is well known for his attacks against causal language and his substitution of the Humean concepts of association and correlation for causal concepts. For him, like Russell, causal language was the language of the past; the language of the new era was that of association and correlation (see Pearson 1911). This sentiment carried over to early econometrics. For example, in one of his volumes on business cycles, Wesley Clair Mitchell muses (Mitchell 1927: 55, quoted from Hammond 1996: 10):

> In the progress of knowledge, causal explanations are commonly an early stage in the advance toward analytic description. The more complete the theory of any subject becomes in content, the more mathematical in form, the less it invokes causation.

Surveying more recent contributions (a growing number of exceptions notwithstanding), one still gets the impression that, in order to be scientific, causal language has to be avoided, while the Humean language of correlation and association counts as scientific (see also Pearl 1997). In particular, many textbooks contain 'recipes' for econometric inference that give the impression that econometrics can proceed without causal background assumptions.

But strangely, a large part of theoretical economics asks questions that are causal in nature. Many historical controversies, for example, can be understood as controversies about the causal role certain aggregates play in the economy. Famous examples include the causal role of money in determining other aggregates such as income or prices or the interest rate or the causal role of aggregate demand. Methods tailored to measure the association between variables only seem ill-suited to bear any light on such controversies.

Suppose, then, we use the standard techniques of econometrics to answer particularly causal questions. Say we are interested in the monetarist question of whether money (X) causes income (Y), as in the previous chapter. We can expect the estimator $\hat{\beta}$ of the causal effect of X on Y in the standard regression model:

$$Y = \alpha + \beta X + \varepsilon \tag{1}$$

to be biased for a number of different reasons. First, it is possible that X is measured with error, and that the measurement error is correlated with Y's error term ε. That X is measured with error is more than likely; it has been a matter of dispute what the 'right' definition of money should be for about as long as economists have thought about the quantity theory. The construction of the money variable has also been one of the major criticisms of Milton Friedman's epic studies of the role of money in the economy. Second, the relationship can be confounded by an unobserved variable. Equation (1) is simplified in so far as the vector of known confounders (for example, a time trend) has been omitted as a regressor on the right-hand side. However, not all potential confounders can be measured, and thus there might always be residual correlation between X and ε. Third, there may be feedback effects from income to money. This is also a point that came up in the debate about Friedman's analysis of the role of money. Critics tended to understand the monetarist position to assert that money is the only cause of economic activity, but Friedman emphasised time and again that he regarded money merely as one cause (the principal cause, however), and that it is well possible, especially in the short run, that causality runs from income to money.

For any of these three reasons, X might be correlated with ε, which biases the estimator for β. A standard technique to solve that problem is instrumental variables estimation. According to many econometrics textbooks, a variable Z is an instrument with respect to (X, Y) if and only if the following conditions are satisfied (see for instance Greene 2000: 370ff.):

IV-1. Z is correlated with X.
IV-2. Z is uncorrelated with the error term for Y, ε.

If such a variable can be found, an estimator of the parameter of interest can be constructed as follows:

$$\hat{\beta} = \rho_{Z,Y}/\rho_{Z,X}, \tag{2}$$

where ρ is the correlation coefficient. If these are the only assumptions made about the system of interest, the definition of an instrumental variable is too weak for a causal interpretation of the estimand. To see that most clearly, let us proceed in three stages with increasingly stronger assumptions made about the relationships between the variables. The basic structure is shown in Figure 7.1. X and Y are the variables of interest, Z is the purported instrument and ε is Y's error term. A dashed line marks correlation between two variables. Y's error term is correlated with X, which is why we need an instrument to estimate ε in the first place.

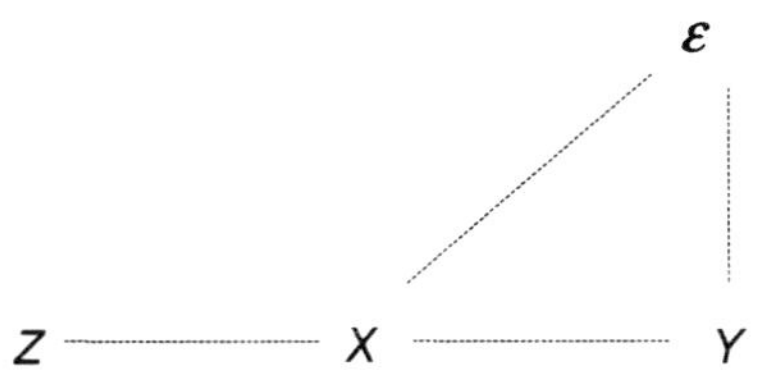

Figure 7.1 Instrumental variables: the basic structure.

There are two steps involved in the inference from correlations to causes. The first is the inference from sample correlations to the probabilities of the underlying populations. The second is from probabilities to causes. In all that follows, I take the first step to be unproblematic. That is, I take all measured correlations to be representing the true population probabilities. Although the two steps may be interrelated in practice and it is disputable whether the step from correlations to probabilities must be taken prior to inferring from probabilities to causes, analytically the two steps can be separated, and discussion of only the second step makes for a much clearer argument.

Now, without any further assumptions, the above pattern of correlations is compatible with any causal structure imaginable. The basic principle one needs for causal inference from correlations is an inductive principle which connects probabilities with causes. This is implicit in all econometric work but it is hardly ever addressed explicitly. The reason is simple: if we allow for 'brute correlations', that is, correlations that cannot be accounted for in terms of causal relationships, then any attempt to infer causal relationships from statistics – no matter how strong the additional assumptions about the system of interest – is bound to be futile. Any residual correlation could then always be 'brute'. An almost identical remark has been made by Daniel Hausman and James Woodward (Hausman and Woodward 2004: 151):

> So when X_j [the putative effect variable] 'wiggles' in response to an intervention with respect to X_i [the putative cause variable] (or in general without any change in its parents) one has a covariation between X_i and X_j that cannot be explained by X_j causing X_i or by a common cause of X_i and X_j [this follows from their definition of an intervention]. If there are no restrictions on the ways that a correlation between X_i and X_j might arise, one could go no further. But if one takes CM1 [their principle which connects causes and correlations] for granted, then one can conclude that X_i causes X_j.

I am going to assume the following 'Reichenbach principle' (after Hans Reichenbach's pioneering work in this area; see Reichenbach 1956):

RP. Any two variables *A* and *B* are correlated if and only if either (a) *A* causes *B*, (b) *B* causes *A*, (c) a common cause *C* causes both *A* and *B* or (d) any combination of (a)–(c).

Let us call two variables that are related by any of the causal structures (a)–(d) causally connected (and causally unconnected in case they fall under none of the structures). I do not want to argue for the truth or plausibility of the particular version of the principle here. But let me stress again that we need some principle of the kind, and since investigations in economics typically face causally complex systems, we cannot, for example, exclude *a priori* the possibility of simultaneous causation or any other combination of the simpler structures (a)–(c).

The second general assumption we must make is the transitivity of causal relationships. Singular causal relationships are not always transitive. The dog bites off my right index finger. Hence I use my left finger to detonate the bomb. The dog bite causes the event 'press button with left index finger', and this event in turn causes the detonation of the bomb. But we would not say that the dog bite causes the detonation (McDermott 1995). But at the generic level, the level I am concerned with here, transitivity seems a safe assumption. Thus:

T. For any three variables A, B and C, if A causes B and B causes C, then A causes C.

I will restrict the analysis to linear equations of the general form $X_j = \alpha_{j1}X_{j1} + \alpha_{j2}X_{j2} + \ldots + \alpha_{jn}X_{jn} + \varepsilon_j$. For these, I assume 'functional correctness':

FC. A structural equation $X_j = f(X_{j1}, X_{j2}, \ldots, X_{jn}, \varepsilon_j)$ is functionally correct if and only if it represents the true functional (but not necessarily causal) relationship among its variables.

T and FC are innocuous. T is assumed for convenience – one could derive very similar results without it but formulations would be much more complicated. FC formalises that I focus on causal inference and take correct statistical inference as given. On the basis of these assumptions, let us examine what further assumptions we must make about the system of interest in order for the instrumental variables technique to yield causally correct conclusions. I will proceed in three stages, each with different causal assumptions added to the general assumptions.

Stage 1: No assumptions added If no causal assumptions are added to RP, T and FC, one can easily show that the instrumental variables technique can yield causally incorrect conclusions. The system consists of two functionally correct equations:

$$Y = \alpha X + \varepsilon \tag{3}$$

$$X = \beta Z + \varepsilon. \tag{4}$$

According to the instrumental variables technique under these assumptions, the claim is that if Y is correlated with Z then X causes Y. However, it is possible that the correlation between X and Y arises from other causal relationships. Consider the structure in Figure 7.2.

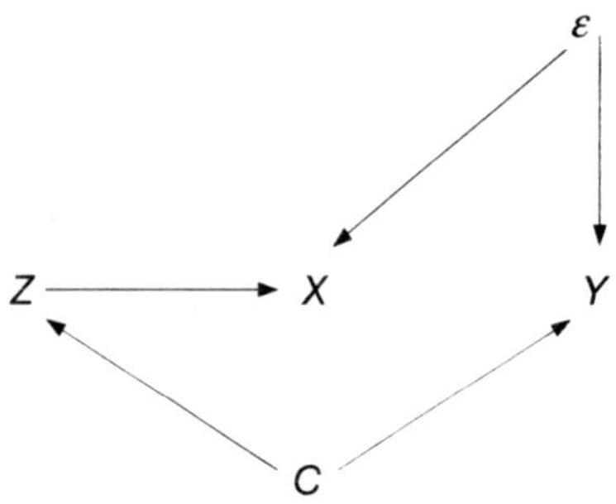

Figure 7.2 A counterexample to IV under RP, T and FC.

Nothing in the assumptions prevents this situation. In addition to (3) and (4), we now have two further functionally correct equations:

$$Z = \gamma C + \mu \text{ and} \tag{5}$$

$$Y = \delta C + \nu. \tag{6}$$

If $\beta > 0$ (which is implied by RP), then Z and X are correlated and thus IV-1 is satisfied. Suppose further that $\gamma > 0$ and $\delta > 0$ (which, too, is implied by RP), which implies that Z and Y are also correlated. This means that the test condition is fulfilled. Now, depending on the various parameters, there are cases in which IV-2 is satisfied: Z and ε may or may not be correlated as can be seen from the following derivation:

$$Z = (\gamma/\delta)Y - \gamma\nu/\delta + \mu \qquad \text{[substitute } C \text{ from (6) into (5)]}$$

$$= (\gamma\alpha\beta/\delta)Z + (\gamma/\delta)(1+\alpha)\varepsilon - \gamma\nu/\delta + \mu \qquad \text{[substitute for } Y \text{ from (3) and (4)]}$$

$$= \zeta(1+\alpha)\varepsilon - \zeta\nu + (\zeta\delta/\gamma)\mu \qquad \text{[define } \zeta = 1/(\delta/\gamma - \alpha\beta) \text{ and rearrange]}$$

$$E(Z\varepsilon) = \zeta(1+\alpha)\,E(\varepsilon^2) - \zeta\,E(\varepsilon\nu) + (\zeta\delta/\gamma)\,E(\varepsilon\mu), \tag{7}$$
[multiply by ε and take expectations]

which may or may not be zero. This means that there are parameterisations under which IV-1, IV-2 and the other assumptions are satisfied, but X does not cause Y.

It seems unlikely that such exact cancellations (which makes (7) equal to zero) should occur but it is not impossible. One way to ensure that exact cancellations do not obtain that has been offered in the literature is to assume that correlations are stable under parameter changes. In this example, we see that the lack of correlation between Z and ε obtains only under a very specific parameterisation.

One assumption that would make the procedure stronger is that the error terms in an equation represent the net effect of all other causes. The above counterexample could not obtain because there could not be a cause of *Y*, *C*, which is not represented by ε. That the technique yields causally correct conclusions in general I proved in Stage 2.

Stage 2: ε represents the net effect of all other causes on Y (except X and any cause that influences Y through X or lies on the causal route from X to Y) If *Z* and *Y* are correlated, RP tells us that they must be causally connected. Since there is a third variable, *X*, I will first show that *Z* and *Y* cannot be causally connected on a route that excludes *X*.

Can *Z* and *Y* be causally connected on a route that excludes *X*? Under the given assumptions, *Z* cannot cause *Y* directly or via a route that excludes *X* because its influence would be represented by ε, which we have excluded. *Y* cannot cause *Z* unmediated by *X* either, since by transitivity ε would cause *Z* and by RP they would be correlated. Nor can there be a common cause (that causes *Z* and *Y* on a route that excludes *X*) because its influence would be represented by ε. Hence, the causal connection between *Z* and *Y* must run through *X*.

Hence there remain three possibilities: *Y* causes *Z* through *X*, *X* is a common cause of *Y* (or a common cause causes *Z* and *Y* through *X*) and *Z* and *Z* causes *Y* through *X*. *Y* cannot cause *Z* through *X* because, as before, that would imply that ε is correlated with *Z*. A common cause now may either be between *X* and *Y* or between *X* and *Z*. If it is between *X* and *Y* (which means that its influence is represented by ε) then *X* must cause *Z* and thus ε causes *Z* by transitivity and would be correlated with it. However, there may be a common cause between *Z* and *X*. In this case *Z* and *Y* would be correlated if and only if *X* causes *Y*, and thus *Z* would be a valid instrument.

The last remaining possibility is that *Z* causes *Y* via *X*. Again, in this case *Z* and *Y* would be correlated if and only if *X* causes *Y*, and *Z* is a valid instrument. The two causal structures in which *Z* is a valid instrument are depicted in Figure 7.3.

Thus, under the above assumptions, the instrumental variables technique makes causally correct inferences. The difficulty with the technique is,

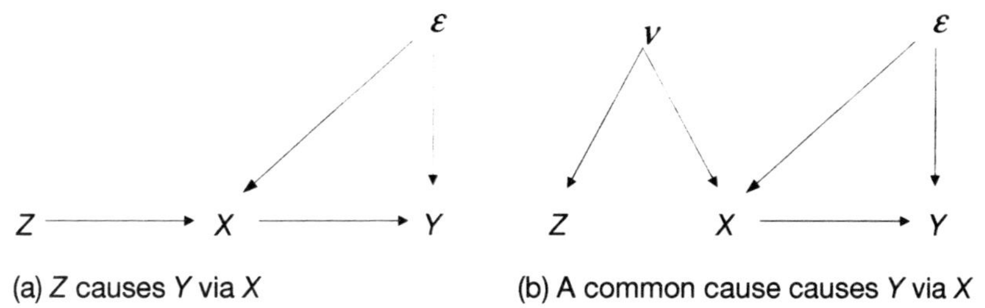

Figure 7.3 Two valid instruments to identify β.

however, that it is, taken literally, unoperationable. By its very nature, the error term is unobservable. Hence it is not possible to test statistically whether *Z* is or is not uncorrelated with the error term. This is a particular problem because even slight correlations can severely bias the estimator (see Pearl 1993 and Bartels 1991).

The irony is that one motivation to use the instrumental variables technique is exactly that there are unobservable common causes between *X* and *Y*. Now, if that is so, it seems hard to see how an instrument in the sense of a variable that satisfies IV-1 and IV-2 should be found (if a variable is not measurable, *a fortiori* its correlation with another variable is not measurable).

Stage 3: Assuming Z is a 'causal instrumental variable' In practice, econometricians identify an instrument on the basis of causal background knowledge, which often derives from an institutional and/or historical analysis of the case at hand. Statisticians sometimes judge background assumptions of this kind inadmissible, 'subjective' (even Judea Pearl once seems to have thought this; see Pearl 1993). But apart from the fact that the whole approach would be ineffective unless these background assumptions (in addition to the general assumptions) are made, there are two further justifications for making the causal assumptions explicit. First, the structure of assumptions shows that the system *Z–X–Y* is equivalent to an experimental setup in which *Z* is used as a 'switch variable' to test the hypothesis whether *X* causes *Y*. Let us call a variable *Z* a 'causal instrumental variable' with respect to (*X*, *Y*) if and only if RP, T and FC as well as the following assumptions are satisfied:

CIV-1. *Z* causes *X*.
CIV-2. *Z* causes *Y* if at all only through *X* (that is, not directly or via some other variable).
CIV-3. *Z* and *Y* do not have causes in common (except those that might cause *Y* via *Z* and *X*).

CIV-1–CIV-3 make the similarity with a controlled experiment very easily visible. A randomised clinical trial (RTC) is a paradigmatic example for a controlled experiment. In an ideal RTC (that is, when problems about compliance, failed randomisation, measurement issues and so forth have been assumed away), the random allocation is the causal instrumental variable *Z*. It (and only it) causes whether or not a subject will receive treatment (*X*). It does not have a causal influence on recovery (*Y*) which is not mediated by *X*. And the allocation itself is not caused by anything that also causes recovery. It is in fact RP which ensures that randomisation is successful (if the random allocation 'happened' to produce biased groups, the resulting correlation of a cause of recovery with the allocation would have to have a causal explanation, which would violate either CIV-2 or CIV-3).

In the literature about scientific experiments, 'switches' or 'handles' are similarly defined. For instance, James Woodward defines an intervention *I*, his equivalent, as follows (Woodward 1997: S30; for a discussion of the differences between his proposal and mine, see Reiss 2005):

1 *I* changes the value of *X* possessed by U_i [the 'experimental unit'] from what it would have been in the absence of the intervention and this change in *X* is entirely due to *I*.
2 *I* changes *Y*, if at all, only through *X* and not directly or through some other route. [. . .]
3 *I* is not correlated with other causes of *Y* besides *X* (either via a common cause of *I* and *Y* or for some other reason) except [those that cause *Y* via *Z* and *X*].

Thus, the instrumental variables approach receives additional credence by identifying it as a species of experimentation. The second justification is that CIV-1–CIV-3 give us a nice algorithm to assess the design of studies using the instrumental variables technique. As I will discuss in detail below, James Heckman criticised Joshua Angrist's study of the causal effect of veteran status on civil earnings on the basis of what he calls a 'behavioural model' that relates random draft lottery numbers (the putative instrument *Z*) with investment in training (a cause of the putative effect *Y*: see Heckman 1996). Such a relationship would clearly invalidate the results of Angrist's study. Using the causal instrumental variable interpretation, we have a simple algorithm to test for potential failures: check all the routes through which *Z* may cause *Y* and whether *Z* and *Y* have causes in common. Importantly, there are more tests available than statistical tests. In particular, causal hypotheses can often be tested without the requirement that variables involved are measurable in the statistician's sense. For example, there may simply be no data on training investments available. But it could still be known by other means whether or not employers typically invest more in people with high draft lottery numbers.

IV

In this section I want to show that, in their applications, many econometricians do not eschew causal language but, right to the contrary, make precisely those causal background assumptions that are needed to turn the 'instrumental variable' into a 'causal instrumental variable' in the sense of the previous section. These assumptions are thus sufficient to identify an instrument in the (theoretical) econometrician's sense but not necessary as many other causal structures would imply the same correlations; and they are both necessary and sufficient for the identification of a causal instrumental variable.

I am going to report three brief case studies. The first is probably most naturally regarded as a 'natural' experiment as there are two populations, which (so the authors assume) can be regarded as identical with respect to the distributions of the causes of the putative effect but which occur naturally, and one of which receives the treatment while the other does not. The second case resembles a 'randomised' experiment because the treatment and control groups are allocated using a random mechanism, in this case a lottery. From the point of view of the econometrician, this still constitutes a natural experiment as he does not influence the allocation mechanism but merely observes allocation and outcome. In the third case the causal instrumental variable is constructed out of observed data. This case of an experiment is probably most remote from the usual reading of a natural experiment because a model is used in order to measure the instrument in the first place. However, due to the nature of the assumptions involved the case can be made that the procedure still constitutes a natural experiment.

Do minimum wages cause unemployment? The standard competitive model of neoclassical economics implies that a minimum imposed on the wage rate will, if higher than the competitive rate, reduce employment. David Card and Alan Krueger challenge this prediction or, to be more precise, the universal character of the prediction. The natural experiment they observe and from which they extract information that in their view conflicts with the competitive model is an increase in New Jersey's minimum wage from $4.25 to $5.05 per hour on April 1, 1992. They attempt to measure the impact of the increase on employment by comparing employment growth at fast-food restaurants in New Jersey and neighbouring eastern Pennsylvania. They conclude that there is no indication in the data that would confirm the standard model.

Relevant for the context of this chapter is Card and Krueger's use of background assumptions for the identification of a causal instrumental variable. Recall that a causal instrumental variable Z has the properties: (i) Z causes X, the putative cause of the effect of interest Y; (ii) Z causes Y if at all only via X; and (iii) Z and Y have no causes in common (except causes of Z that cause Y via Z and X). It must further be assumed that operating the handle does not alter the causal laws that have X, Y or Z as cause or effect. Since the causal relationship of interest here is that between an enforced level of wages and employment, I suggest that the minimum wage legislation is regarded as the instrument or putative causal instrumental variable, actually paid wages as the putative cause and employment as the putative effect.

(a) Does the minimum wage law cause wages? To make sure that the first assumption is fulfilled, Card and Krueger choose the experimental population such that the right causal relationship can be expected. Their population consists of 410 fast-food restaurants in New Jersey and Pennsylvania because: 'fast-food stores are a leading employer of low-wage workers' (thus an increase in the minimum will be relevant), and 'fast-food restaurants comply with minimum-wage regulations and would be expected to raise wages in response to a rise in the minimum wage' (Card and Krueger 1994: 773f.).

(b) Does the legislation cause employment through other channels than the actual wage? The most important confounder in this category would probably be if the minimum wage bill had been passed along with other bills that were likely to affect employment at the same time (for instance, if it had been passed along with a second bill that would change health and safety requirements for employees in low-wage occupations). This was not the case, however.

Another channel through which legislation could affect employment is expectations. Card and Krueger measure the difference in employment growth between the time just before the actual increase and about half a year after the increase. Since the bill was introduced more than two years before the actual increase, however, it is possible that all its employment effects had already occurred before they were measured because employers expected the wage to increase and adjusted payrolls accordingly.

Card and Krueger were helped in this matter by the fact that the minimum wage bill remained contested till almost the time of the actual increase (ibid.: 773):

> The scheduled 1992 increase gave New Jersey the highest state minimum wage in the country and was strongly opposed by business leaders in the state . . .
>
> In the two years between the passage of the $5.05 minimum wage and its effective date, New Jersey's economy slipped into recession. Concerned with the potentially adverse impact of a higher minimum wage, the state legislature voted in March 1992 to phase in the 80-cent increase over two years. The vote fell just short of the margin required to override a gubernatorial veto, and the Governor allowed the $5.05 rate to go into effect on April 1 before vetoing the two-step legislation. Faced with the prospect of having to roll back wages for minimum wage earners, the legislature dropped the issue. Despite a strong last-minute challenge, the $5.05 minimum rate took effect as originally planned.

(c) Does employment have any of its causes in common with the wage legislation? The easiest way to test this is by checking whether any of the causes of the minimum wage legislation also affects employment through a different channel than the actual wage.

Historically, minimum wages have often been raised in times of favourable economic conditions in order to minimise the potentially adverse effects of the increase. Therefore, in these cases results would be confounded by a common cause between legislation and employment, namely 'economic conditions'. Card and Krueger control for this potential confounder by employing the so-called differences-in-differences method. That is, they do not merely compare employment before and after the increase but rather employment growth in New Jersey with employment growth in eastern Pennsylvania. Since, so they assume, economic conditions should affect both states in the same way (they judge this on the basis of observing the socio-economic structure in the two states), differencing should filter out all causes of employment that the two states share, as for instance economic conditions or the season.

Further, Card and Krueger's project was once more assisted by the course of events. Whatever may have been the original rationale for increasing the minimum wage, at the time the final decision was made (just before the actual increase, in March 1992), the economy was in a recession and thus economic conditions, if a cause at all, would rather have prevented the introduction of the new wage law.

Under these assumptions Card and Krueger find that the increase of the minimum wage actually raised rather than lowered employment in New Jersey, both as compared with Pennsylvania as well as with high-wage stores in New Jersey. Far be it from me to pretend that their results are unexception. It has, for example, been claimed that the results are reversed if instead of the employment data from Card and Krueger's telephone survey payroll data are used (Neumark and Wascher 2000).

But the point to make here is not whether or not minimum wages actually cause an increase or a decrease in employment but a methodological point about the nature of the assumptions econometricians make to identify a valid instrument. Very clearly, the assumptions Card and Krueger make are not only sufficient to identify an instrument (that is, wage legislation is correlated with the actual wage increase but uncorrelated with the causes of employment other than the wage increase) but just the right assumptions to identify a causal instrumental variable. And, therefore, the causal conclusions they draw are valid conditional on the correctness of their assumptions.

Does military service cause later civilian earnings? For reasons of social justice, governments aim at compensating veterans for losses they suffer due to serving in the military. One of the potential losses due to military service lies in the lower wages veterans might receive in later civilian life. One cannot measure the impact of serving in the army on civilian earnings by simple regression of earnings on a dummy indicating whether or not someone has served because there are factors that may affect both variables and thus bias the estimator. For example, men may be more inclined to serve in the military because they have fewer job market opportunities, which also affects their future earnings.

Joshua Angrist attempted to solve that problem by exploiting a random lottery that was conducted in order to prioritise draft eligibility for the Vietnam War (Angrist 1990). In particular, each birth date of a cohort of a given year was assigned a random sequence number (RSN) from 1–365. Depending on the Defense Department's manpower needs, a ceiling was determined; that is, a number up to which men were drafted. In this example, the instrument is the RSN, the putative cause is serving in the military and the putative effect civilian earnings.

(a) Does the RSN cause military service? Angrist estimates that draft eligibility raises the probability of veteran status by 10–15 percentage points for whites born 1950–52 (ibid., Table 2: 321). Given it can be assumed that the lottery is truly random and thus veteran status does not cause the RSN nor is there a common cause and assuming the Reichenbach principle, information about the probabilities would already be sufficient to establish that the RSN causes serving in the military.

(b) Does the RSN cause earnings through channels other than serving in the military? As I will discuss momentarily, this is an assumption that actually was contested later on. However, once more the point is not to justify any of these studies but to investigate the kind of assumptions authors make in order to identify the instrument they use. With respect to this assumption, Angrist says (ibid.: 320):

> The justification for estimation of the effects of military service in this manner is clear: it is assumed that nothing other than difference in the probability of being a veteran is responsible for differences in earnings by draft-eligibility status.

(c) Does the RSN have any causes in common with earnings? Due to the random nature of the lottery, this assumption is also particularly easy to defend. If it is truly random, it is not caused either by a factor that also causes earnings nor by a cause that causes it through earnings.

On the basis of these considerations Angrist concludes that (ibid.: 330):

> Estimates based on the draft lottery indicate that as much as ten years after their discharge from service, white veterans who served at the close of the Vietnam era earned substantially less than nonveterans. The annual earnings loss to white veterans is on the order of $3,500 current dollars, or roughly 15 percent of yearly wage and salary earnings in the early 1980s.

James Heckman challenged Angrist's investigation in a way that is also illuminating from our point of view. He argued that the RSN is not a proper instrument because among other things 'persons with high numbers are likely to receive more job training, because their likelihood of being drafted is reduced and firms have less likelihood of losing them' (Heckman 1996: 461). That is, Heckman believes that the RSN causes earnings not only via actual military service but also via the firms' expectations whether employees have to serve in the military and subsequently base their training decisions on their expectations. In both the original article and the criticism it is thus causal background knowledge that identifies the instruments rather than mere information about correlations. But Heckman, in my view mistakenly, bases his criticism on a behavioural – theoretical – model rather than valid evidence to the effect that the RSN causes earnings via a route that does not go through serving in the Vietnam War. As I have argued in the previous chapter, such a model is at best prima facie evidence for a causal claim. In order to provide valid evidence for his criticism, he would need to show empirically that the alleged mechanism is at work.

Does money cause interest rates? The third case differs from the others in two respects. First, confounding in this case is not due to one or more common causes but due to the fact that there is simultaneous causation between the variables of interest. Or more precisely, it is known that the putative effect is a cause of the putative cause, and hence if there is causation in the direction of interest, then there is simultaneous causation. Second, the instrument is not straightforwardly observable but constructed by the econometrician.

James Hamilton attempts to measure the 'liquidity effect'; that is, the effect a change in the money stock has on interest rates (Hamilton 1997). More specifically, the variables of interest are non-borrowed reserves (the putative cause) and the federal funds rate (the putative effect). An ordinary regression of the form

$$i_t = \lambda R_t + \gamma' x_t + v_t^i, \tag{8}$$

where i is the federal funds rate, R reserves and x a vector of 'other causes', will result in a biased estimator λ because the Federal Reserve actively chooses the supply of reserves each day in response to the value of the federal funds rate using a reaction function of the form

$$R_t = \delta i_t + \psi' x_t + v_t^R. \tag{9}$$

Hamilton exploits an institutional detail to solve the simultaneous causation problem. The US Treasury maintains an account with the Federal Reserve system which fluctuates in response to fiscal receipts and expenditures. Cheques drawn on private banks reduce their reserve requirements the moment they are deposited into the Treasury's account. The Federal Reserve, in turn, attempts to take this effect into account and predicts daily fluctuations before announcing reserve requirements. However, it cannot do so perfectly and therefore the prediction error induces variation in the reserves available to banks independently of monetary policy. Hamilton proposes to take these forecast errors as an instrument for measuring λ.

(a) Do the forecast errors cause reserves? As just stated, institutional background knowledge justifies the assumption that the Federal Reserve's forecast errors cause the reserves available to private banks. The Federal Reserve, however, does not publish its forecasts. Hamilton therefore constructs a forecast model whose residuals provide estimates of the actual Federal Reserve forecast errors. Essentially, he estimates a third-order autoregression for the Federal Reserve deposits held by the Treasury, which is allowed to have different coefficients when the previous day's Treasury balance exceeds a certain level. In a regression of non-borrowed reserves on changes in the federal funds rate and other explanatory variables that include the forecast errors, the errors are highly correlated with reserves. Hamilton concludes (ibid.: 88; emphasis added):

> There is no question that the forecast errors of my model of the Treasury balance prove to be an excellent instrument for nonborrowed reserves, in the sense that $\hat{\varepsilon}_t^U$ [the forecast error] *exerts a highly significant effect on* R_t.

(b) Do the forecast errors cause the federal funds rate via channels other than the non-borrowed reserves? Hamilton clearly proceeds on this assumption (ibid.: 82):

> The claim will be that the error the Fed makes in forecasting the Treasury balance matters for the federal funds rate only insofar as it affects the supply of reserves available to private banks.

(c) Are there any causes common to the forecast errors and the federal funds rate? There is a pretty simple argument that there cannot be such common causes. The argument is that, if there were such a cause, the Federal Reserve would make systematic errors in its predictions of the Treasury balance. That, in turn, would imply that Hamilton's model (if the model represents the Federal Reserve's forecasts accurately) is mis-specified. In order to avoid this kind of error, Hamilton tests his specification (ibid.: 86):

> I investigated how good this specification is at describing the dynamics of the Treasury balance by using a battery of Lagrange multiplier tests. [. . .]
>
> Hamilton 1996 reports 43 separate Lagrange multiplier tests of the specification in Table 2, of which three are significant at the 5-percent level and none at the 1-percent level. I conclude that the model of Table 2 provides a good parsimonious description of the series U_t.

And hence he can assume (ibid.: 81):

> However, the Fed is not able to anticipate the end-of-day Treasury balance perfectly, with the result that this variable induces substantial daily fluctuations in the reserves available to private banks for reasons that are completely exogenous with respect to monetary policy.

V

The 'causal instrumental variables' technique is a 'clincher' in Nancy Cartwright's terminology introduced in the previous chapter: *if* the conditions of the method are satisfied, then the causal conclusion must hold. Under the given assumptions, prima facie evidence (in the form of a correlation between two variables) is immediately turned into valid evidence for a causal hypothesis because all alternatives are ruled out in one go. This is an obvious advantage. But it comes at a price: it is very hard to know whether the background assumptions are met – Heckman's criticism of the Angrist study is a case in point.

For Mill, the fundamental laws of political economy are known *a priori* in a particular sense. This sense deviates from the Kantian *a priori*, which means 'prior to all experience'; it means merely 'prior to specific investigations in political economy'. Thus prior to any specific investigation, we know the principal causes of any effect in political economy. These laws, the so-called 'laws of human nature', were established by introspection and casual observation, that is, inductively. Together with what one might call 'general initial conditions' (conditions shared by many cases), one can deduce abstract truths from the laws. The abstract truths are applicable to concrete circumstances only with qualifications; the qualifications concern the operation of 'disturbing causes'. Had we knowledge about disturbing causes, or could we experimentally control for them, political economy would be a science as exact as the best branches of natural science. However, more often than not disturbing causes are not known, and almost never are they known before the event. Specific experience can still play a role, namely that of verifying whether or not the major causes of a phenomenon have been taken into account.

So maybe there is no such thing as a deductivism–inductivism dichotomy. In Mill's 'deductive' scheme, the basic principles are established inductively; in the 'inductive' scheme proposed here, the conclusions follow deductively given the premisses. Does this mean that the whole distinction is a mirage?

I agree that all serious scientific methodologies combine deductive and inductive elements. As we have seen earlier, even the professed champion of inductivism in economics, Gustav Schmoller, argued that 'we need deduction and induction for sound scientific inference like we need the left and the right feet for walking' (for a brief discussion of Schmoller's views, see Chapter 1). Pure deductivism does not allow us to make reasoned guesses about yet unobserved phenomena; pure inductivism doesn't transcend the realm of the immediately observable. The difference between Mill's views and the perspective advanced here consists rather in the kinds of premisses that are allowed to form the core of an inference. Mill limited these principles to the basic laws of human nature. He appeared to think that only these laws are known with a degree of certainty high enough to form the core of what he called the 'method *a priori*'.

But such a restriction to laws of behaviour seems largely unwarranted. As we have seen in the previous chapter, human behaviour appears to be extremely sensitive to the precise setting in which it occurs, and there seem to be few factors that are genuinely stable in order to allow Mill's project to get off the ground. On the other hand, there may well be aggregate relationships that are stable enough to be useful for further inferences.

The point is therefore: it is itself an empirical question whether or not generalisations are stable and knowable. Pace Mill (and Carl Menger), we do not know *a priori* which postulates are 'basic'.

Part III

Error in policy analysis

8 Explanatory mechanisms and the aims of economics

I

Economists pursue a wide variety of different ends with their model-building practices. To name but a few, data models are built for measuring complex social phenomena; forecasting models are built for predicting the future values of target variables of interest; explanatory models are built for gaining a deeper understanding of phenomena of interest; policy models are built for analysing the likely effects of interventions.

Among many philosophers and methodologists of economics and other social sciences, however, there seems to be a tendency to focus on one (or a few) of the variety of different ends to the exclusion of others. For example, positivists in the philosophy of the social sciences tend to emphasise the importance of description and prediction, professing their belief that genuine understanding is impossible, while their opponents think only understanding is important.

Generally speaking, there are four possible reasons for a methodologist to ignore an aim of the science he or she is concerned with. First, one may think that there is a hierarchy among the different aims and focus on that or those which one believes to be the more important, more ultimate end or ends. For instance, one may believe that the major purpose for prediction is the confirmation of explanatory theories and hence focus on explanation while considering prediction only in its relationship to the more ultimate aim. Second, one may think that some aims are unattainable and consequently focus on those that one believes to be attainable. For example, one may regard successful prediction of social phenomena as impossible and therefore concentrate on the more promising explanatory endeavour. Third, one may regard an aim as both important as well as attainable, but as methodologically trivial. For example, one may regard the measurement of inflation as an important purpose of economics but deny that it involves any problems of particular methodological interest. Fourth, one may think that important classes of models serve a variety of different purposes at the same time. For example, if one believes that good models do or ought to represent the laws of nature and one believes that knowledge of the laws of nature allows us to explain past events and predict future events by the same token, one can safely focus on either of the two aims because the other will be served in tandem.

In this chapter I discuss in more detail a relatively recent movement in the philosophy of economics and the philosophy of the social sciences, which emphasises the importance of investigating causal mechanisms. According to this movement, which I am going to call the 'new mechanist perspective' or NMP, theoretical explanation of social phenomena is the only or ultimate aim of the social sciences and causal mechanisms play an essential role in theoretical explanation. Against these claims I argue that causal-mechanistic explanation is neither the only nor the most important or ultimate aim of economics and that investigating causal mechanisms will not usually be the optimal strategy when other aims of economics are concerned.

The next section introduces the movement, derives a more precise statement of the NMP and gives a number of examples of causal-mechanistic explanations for social phenomena of interest. In the two sections that follow I go through the four possible reasons why a number of non-explanatory aims of economics might safely be ignored and demonstrate that neither of the given arguments succeeds. In conclusion, I argue in favour of a tighter fit between methodology and purpose and, since there are a variety of different purposes with more or less equal rights, for a more pluralistic methodology of economics and the social sciences in general.

II

Thinking about mechanisms has become increasingly popular in recent work in economics, economic methodology and social science at large. While the idea that it is necessary to provide a description of a mechanism of a certain kind in order to adequately deal with social events and phenomena has been an item on the neoclassical agenda in economics for quite some time, this basic picture has now been adopted explicitly and in its own way in some heterodox schools of economics and in parts of sociology, social psychology and by a number of philosophers of social science. In particular I am thinking of the critical realism movement in economics, sociology and general social science (see for instance Lawson 1997, 2003 for economics, Brante 2001 for sociology and Sayer 2000 for social science), various accounts of social mechanisms in economics and sociology (see in particular the contributions to the volume Hedström and Swedberg 1999a) as well as contributions to the philosophy of social science (see for instance Elster 1983, 1985, 1989; Little 1991, 1998). While the individual accounts differ in their details, they share a number of fundamental convictions. The first common idea is the emphasis on theoretical explanation as scientific virtue. Many proponents of the NMP appear to claim that theoretical explanation is the only aim of the social sciences. A somewhat weaker form of this claim is that theoretical explanation is the most important or ultimate aim of the social sciences. Consider the following statements:

> Sociology must seek to be an *explanatory* science, implying a deepening of its own theoretical knowledge. [. . .] I propose that the ultimate goal of sociology is *to identify social structures harbouring causal mechanisms that generate empirically observable effects*. [. . .] According to Bhaskar . . . the object of sociology is *social relations*, and the task is to explain the reproduction and transformation of social relations.
>
> (Brante 2001: 168 and 178, original emphasis)

> In addition, the impossibility of engineering, and the absence of spontaneously occurring, closed social systems, necessitates a reliance upon non-predictive, purely explanatory, criteria of theory development and assessment in the social sciences.
>
> (Lawson 1997: 35)

> The main message of this book is that the advancement of social theory calls for an analytical approach that systematically seeks to explicate the social mechanisms that generate and explain observed associations between events.
>
> (Hedström and Swedberg 1999b: 1)

The second common feature is the idea that the social world is structured or layered in the sense that, on the one hand, there are higher-level (macro or aggregate or readily measurable) events and event-patterns, such as the rise of the dot.com industry, German inflation in 1923, the (in)effectiveness of crime prevention programmes and the effects of people's religious beliefs on their economic behaviour, and, on the other hand, there are the lower-level (micro or individual or theoretical) structures and processes that give rise to the higher-level events or phenomena. Let us call social event tokens and types of interest 'phenomena' (basically adopting Ian Hacking's terminology; see Hacking 1983), the higher level the 'empirical layer' and the lower level the 'underlying layer' (bearing in mind that the lower level can itself be structured so that there may be a hierarchy of ever deeper layers within the social world).

The third common feature is the thesis that the only or ultimate aim of economics/social science is fulfilled if and only if the social phenomenon *S* (at the empirical layer) is explained in terms of the causal mechanism(s) (at the underlying layer), which is responsible for *S*. As we have seen in Chapter 6, there exist about as many accounts of 'mechanism' as there are contributors to the debate. To some, a 'mechanism' is the embodiment of the causal powers of a structure and thus something in the world (e.g. the critical realists), to others it is a piece of theory (e.g. Stinchcombe 1993 [1991]). Some are explicit methodological individualists and thus demand that mechanistic explanations cite (only) the interaction of individuals and their constraints (e.g. Little 1998) while others are explicit methodological holists (e.g. Lawson 1997). As much as the details differ, 'mechanism' always refers to that structure or process at the underlying layer which is causally responsible for the event or phenomenon at the empirical level (or, in some accounts, to a representation of the underlying structure or process). Synoptically, we can say that the NMP subscribes to the following theses:

1 Theoretical explanation is the only or ultimate aim of social science.
2 The explananda of interest are empirical phenomena.
3 The desired explanantia consist of or make reference to the underlying causal mechanism(s) that give rise to the empirical phenomena.

Consider the following examples of causal-mechanistic explanations. The empirical phenomenon in our first case is that of bank runs. Robert Merton uses a well-known mechanism pattern in his explanation, the 'self-fulfilling prophecy' (Merton 1968 [1948]). In general terms, a self-fulfilling prophecy is a mechanism by which an expectation induces just that kind of behaviour that is likely to make the expectation come out true. In this case some depositors (possibly, unfoundedly) expect a bank insolvency and withdraw their savings. Observing the first withdrawers, other depositors start sharing the negative expectation, follow them and also withdraw their money. Thus expectation and withdrawing behaviour are mutually re-enforcing. Eventually, the bank can go bankrupt even if it was financially sound when the rumour started.

In the second example the empirical phenomenon is the well-established strong correlation between monetary growth and nominal income growth (for a detailed discussion, see Chapter 6). Milton Friedman and Anna Schwartz try to explain this phenomenon by means of the following mechanism (Friedman and Schwartz 1963: 60ff.). The initial change in the rate of growth of the money stock (produced by, say, a change in the rate of open-market purchases by the Federal Reserve) will induce investors to have more liquidity in their portfolios than they prefer. They will therefore seek alternative investments, initially in assets that are similar to the ones sold to the Federal Reserve; that is, relatively risk-free assets. The increased demand for low-risk assets will bid up their prices, and hence make higher-risk investments relatively more attractive. The initial impulse is thus spread out to various asset categories, including non-financial assets. The general increase in the prices of assets means an increase in wealth relative to income, which makes the purchase of goods and services cheaper (relative to the purchase of the sources of those goods and services, i.e. assets). In this way, demand for goods and services will be increased, and therefore money income will also increase. With this story, of course, Friedman and Schwartz want to argue the monetarist case, namely that the causal direction (at the aggregate level) runs from money to nominal income and prices rather than the other way around (or mainly in this direction).

The third example concerns the relatively poor performance of the UK productivity growth rate in the past one hundred years (Lawson 1997: 255ff.).

Here the relevant underlying structure is the UK collective bargaining system, which is far more highly decentralised than in other countries. This structure 'facilitates mechanisms which inhibit coordinated decision-making and works against quick or smooth responses to changes in production possibilities' (p. 257). The main difficulty consists in the higher degree of skill specialisation resulting from the decentralised system. Any change in technology which makes a certain set of skills redundant will thus meet a relatively stronger degree of resistance than in economies with a lower degree of specialisation. But this means that new technologies take more time to be implemented and hence productivity will grow at a slower pace.

III

As pointed out above, practising economists and other social scientists seem to pursue a variety of different goals. Apart from theoretical explanation, I mentioned description, prediction and control. If my statement of the NMP is correct, why can proponents ignore these alternative aims? There are four possible reasons. A methodologist is justified in ignoring an aim *X* if: (a) *X* is not important; (b) *X* is not attainable; (c) *X* is of no particular methodological interest because how to realise it is already well understood; (d) although he focuses on a different aim *Y*, he recommends a practice that helps to realise both *X* and *Y* simultaneously.

This section considers the first three arguments and the next section the fourth. I will argue that none of the four arguments is successful for the non-explanatory aims of description, prediction and control. Let us consider each argument in turn.

Description, prediction and control are not important. One might argue that a given goal is not important either because no one in fact pursues it or because one ought not pursue it. As I said at the beginning of the chapter, as a matter of fact economists and other social scientists do pursue a number of non-explanatory goals. Thus, from a purely descriptive perspective, it is simply false to deny description, prediction and control any significance. Perhaps practice is the wrong place to look at: one may argue that social scientists uniquely or ultimately *ought* to aim at explaining social phenomena. If practice falls short of this ideal, this only shows that there is something wrong with the social sciences, not with methodology.

Where do normative aims come from? Surprisingly, there is very little indication in the NMP literature about why (perhaps, ultimately) we should take only theoretical explanation seriously. As far as I can see, most proponents simply *presuppose* that the only aim worth pursuing is that of theoretical explanation. Perhaps this is a reaction to a number of anti-realist positions in the philosophy of social science, positions which tended to de-emphasise explanation as a significant goal.

It is clear, however, that methodologists should not prescribe to scientists which goals and values to hold. Apart from prescriptivism and pure descriptivism, there is a third position that is normative, and yet does not impose philosophers' values on scientists. According to this third position, the practice of science should reflect the goals and values of those people affected by it. That is, as Kitcher (2001) argues, it should ultimately be up to the population to decide which research questions are worth pursuing, with what methods and how results are to be implemented. The aims of science, then, ultimately require democratic legitimisation. Kitcher calls a science that reflects the goals and values of people in its lines of research, its methods and dissemination 'well-ordered science'.

It is clear that current science is very remote from the ideal of full democratic legitimisation, and Kitcher himself admits that the specific model he sketches might not be practicable. But a few considerations show that it would be foolish to deny that description, prediction and control are likely to be part of 'well-ordered' social sciences.

Accurately describing aspects of socio-economic systems is often regarded as a preliminary step to the more worthy kinds of scientific activities. While it is certainly true that description sometimes plays a preparatory role, it is also an important end in itself. Especially when social justice is concerned, minimal differences in measurement procedures can lead to great changes in policy results. Consider the two concepts 'inflation rate' and 'rate of unemployment' (for details on inflation measurement, see Chapter 2). The first measures the degree to which the general level of prices – usually but not always thought of as consumer prices – increases over a period of time; the second measures the proportion of unemployed to total members of the workforce. Changes in the measurement procedures associated with both concepts can cause great differences in policy results without concomitant changes in either the policy pursued or our understanding of the causal connections among the relevant variables because the concepts occupy a key place in established policy procedures.

One reason for why policy makers need accurate estimates of the rate of inflation is that a great number of contracts and payments are inflation-indexed. It is sometimes the intention of policy makers to keep the purchasing power of payments such as pension payments constant through time. In other words, the intention is to increase periodical payments by the amount of inflation for that period. The attempt to achieve this objective is frustrated if the price index does not accurately reflect the actual change in the general level of prices. Robert Gordon makes this point forcefully (Gordon 1993: 42f.):

> Price measurement matters. This is particularly true for errors in the rate of inflation over periods of three months to two years. In the American case, the late 1970s and early 1980s provided a textbook case of the follies that occur when policymakers rely on flawed price indexes.

> [. . .] Not only were millions thrown out of work in 1980 and again in 1982, but the distribution of income was permanently distorted as millions of others receiving social security benefits escalated by the CPI enjoyed a windfall gain, since their indexed payments went up by more than the true inflation rate. The unnecessary extra benefit payments caused the government deficit to increase, and higher indexed union wages put more pressure on firms to raise prices and continue the inflation.

Similarly, changes in the definition of the rate of unemployment can have automatic policy consequences in welfare states. If, for instance, the long-term unemployed or people over sixty or under eighteen are excluded from the definition of unemployment after a revision of the counting method (as happened in the United Kingdom during the 1980s), they might either lose benefits altogether or receive a different kind of benefit. In such a case, therefore, a change aimed primarily at improving the accuracy of an index can have real consequences for the people concerned.

Success or failure in our attempts to predict and to control social phenomena, too, are of obvious significance for many people. Any decision (by an individual, a company or a community) about an action whose outcome depends on the future value of some variable would enormously profit from the ability to accurately predict that variable. I'd be rich if I could predict next year's stock market; the entrepreneur could plan his production very efficiently if he could predict future demand and input prices; the community could build sufficient roads, hospitals, kindergartens and power plants if it could only predict future traffic, number of inpatients, fertility rates and energy demand. For policy making we would further like to have the knowledge that allows us to *control* social phenomena. Think of the 'golden triangle' of economic policy – full employment, low or zero inflation and a sustainable rate of growth. Generations of politicians have spent their careers trying to achieve this triple goal, with of course a very mixed success record. Or think of more socio-political goals such as the elimination of poverty, the control of crime, the co-maximisation of liberty and security and so on.

From the point of view of policy making, description, prediction and control are enormously important goals for the social sciences. Moreover, they are scientific goals in themselves, not instrumental for more ultimate scientific goals such as explanatory adequacy. (Of course, most ends are mere means from the point of view of another end: descriptive accuracy may serve social justice, which in turn may serve happiness, and so on. My point here is that there is no immediate other scientific end such as explanation or understanding for which description, prediction and control are instrumental.)

Prediction and control are unattainable. Few people would deny that predictive success and success at controlling social phenomena would be enormously useful for practical and political purposes – if we knew how to attain them. The argument one hears frequently is a rather different one: we should not aim at predicting and controlling social phenomena because doing so with success is impossible. Immanuel Kant argued that 'ought' implies 'can'; if he was right, then 'cannot' implies 'ought not'. (I am not aware of anybody who denies that social phenomena can be accurately described; hence I omit any description in the present discussion. I will consider it again below, in the context of methodology.)

It is fairly obvious, however, that the across-the-board assertion that the prediction of social phenomena can never be successful is plainly mistaken. Pessimists tend to take predictions made in highly regimented physical systems as benchmarks for predictions in 'natural' (i.e. unregimented) social systems. If that is the standard, of course the endeavours of social scientists must fail. The comparison is obviously unfair. It is neither the case that prediction in natural physical systems always works (just think of weather and other complex or chaotic systems) nor that prediction in artificial social systems doesn't (think of some of the results of experimental economics). Further, the fact that predictions in social science fare relatively poorly (relative to what standard?) should not prevent us from trying, as long as we can improve upon mere guesswork.

And that we can improve on guesswork is impressively demonstrated by recent work in financial econometrics. Out of the many examples one could cite, I find this one particularly telling because the belief that financial time series are unpredictable is widespread. Common wisdom holds that, if financial time series were predictable, someone would predict them because he or she could profit from it. His or her action, however, would destroy the basis for the predictability of the series for others. Since this is true for everyone, nobody can systematically predict financial time series. This story underlies the old economists' joke, which is (Lo and MacKinlay 1999: 6)

> about an economist strolling down the street with a companion when they come upon a $100 bill lying on the ground. As the companion reaches down to pick it up, the economist says 'Don't bother – if it were a real $100 bill, someone would have already picked it up.'

For financial markets, this means that price changes must be unpredictable; that is, that financial time series are random walks. Paul Samuelson first applied the Random Walk Hypothesis to financial markets in a theoretical paper (Samuelson 1965). Samuelson's and others' theoretical work (in particular, Fama 1970) has led to the belief that 'a blindfolded monkey throwing darts at a newspaper's financial pages could select a portfolio that would do just as well as one carefully selected by the experts' (Malkiel 1991: 24).

Since the original formulation of the Random Walk Hypothesis, literally thousands of articles with countless theoretical and empirical results have appeared. Importantly, many of these studies are inconsistent with the hypothesis. In particular, it could be rejected as not holding for some markets (see for instance Lo and MacKinlay 1988 on US securities), which suggests that carefully designed active management strategies can outperform mere guesswork in the long term. Of course, this does not mean that making excess profits in these markets is easy. But it does show that investing in forecasting methodology can sometimes pay off.

Whereas prediction is a two-way relationship between a set of information and a set of target variables, control is a three-way relationship between a set of information, a set of actions and a set of target variables. When we say we can control a variable, we mean that our actions are able to bring about a specific value of that variable, a value that it would not have taken in the ordinary course of things. Control is thus prediction in a specific context: we predict the value of the target variable not upon passively observing the information set but rather upon an action designed specifically so as to bring about that value.

Thus, if successful prediction is already impossible, successful control will be impossible *a fortiori*. Consequently, arguments abound to the effect that all efforts to conduct socio-economic policy are futile. Especially following the Lucas critique, many models in the rational expectations literature were used to demonstrate the ineffectiveness of economic policy.

Again, it is crucial here to get the standard right. Control in open, largely unregimented and living systems will be harder than in static systems that can be totally shielded from outside influences and where no ethical considerations matter. However, there are many examples of successful policies – just think of the effective control of inflation worldwide since the 1970s, the success of the crime-control programme in New York City in the Giuliani era or the skill with which Alan Greenspan has been steering the US economy.

Consequently, none of the principled arguments that social technology can never work is convincing. Laissez-faire policies are sometimes justified on the grounds of some of Friedrich von Hayek's work. But all Hayek really said was that across-the-board social planning would have to ignore vast amounts of information that markets generate and thus would likely lead to inferior results. He wasn't an opponent of piecemeal social engineering (though he did not like this Popperian term; see for instance Hayek 1982, vol. III: 204). Similarly, the Lucas critique is sometimes taken to demonstrate that economic policy based on econometric results must be ineffective. However, the Lucas critique is based on the assumption that agents have information about all causally relevant variables at their disposal, including information about unpredictable future events. This is a preposterous requirement. In a more realistic setting, agents will choose the best forecasting model among a number of alternative models, all of which will be mis-specified in one way or another. Now, as we shall see in more detail below, if models are mis-specified and if underlying structures frequently change, simpler, more adaptive models can be more appropriate forecasting tools than causally more adequate models. Sensible agents will use robust forecasting rules. However, a world where agents use simple, adaptive forecasting devices is immune to the Lucas critique (see Hendry 2002).

Description, prediction and control are methodologically trivial. The third argument practically claims the opposite of the second: these aims are not impossible to reach but rather uninteresting because how to reach them is already well understood. In fact, however, all three areas are methodological minefields.

In the context of description, economics, in particular, suffers from a well-recognised but by no means resolved problem: the variables constructed by statistical offices tend to differ quite significantly from the variables that figure in economic theories. This makes the application of theories to data – be it for explanation or prediction or policy – problematic to say the least (see for instance Stigum 2003 for a discussion of the problem).

Suppose a theory predicts that some variable X causes another variable Y and we want to test that theory by running a regression of Y on X. For the moment suppose away all problems about causal confounders. Still, the regression coefficient of X will be biased if X is measured with error. The standard response is to find a so-called instrumental variable Z such that (a) Z is correlated with X but (b) uncorrelated with the measurement error. Including Z in the regression allows the measurement of the coefficient of X without bias. But: it is not guaranteed and, in fact, quite unlikely that a suitable instrument can be found. The error term is by its very nature unobservable. How, then, could we know that some other variable is uncorrelated with it? Consequently, measurement error is widely regarded as a severe problem for empirical modelling. And yet, it has attracted very little interest from methodologists.

Even if the problem is not in the relationship between empirical and theoretical variables, accurate measurement is methodologically intricate. For example, for accurate measurement of the Consumer Price Index (CPI), at least the following issues have to be dealt with (for details, see Chapters 2–4):

- What is the right measurement objective for the CPI?
- How should one deal with product substitutions (i.e. when consumers replace a good whose relative price has increased by one whose relative price has decreased)?
- How should one deal with outlet substitutions (i.e. when consumers replace traditional distribution channels such as grocers with discounters or internet-based traders)?
- How should one deal with quality changes (i.e. when the quality of a good represented in the index changes)?

- How should one deal with new goods (i.e. when goods appear in the market that don't have a direct predecessor such as mobile telephones)?
- How should one deal with taste changes (when for example consumers' preferences change due to changes in income)?
- How should one deal with the fact that different groups differ in salient respects (e.g. employees, old people and poor people)?
- Should expert knowledge play a significant role in price measurement, and if so, which?

Many of the replies to these questions will make a difference to the value of the CPI and hence to the disposable incomes of countless people and to the federal budget. To repeat myself here: price measurement matters.

The work I know best in the area of forecasting and policy analysis methodology is that of David Hendry and his collaborators. Since Hendry *et al.* have published a number of survey articles about these topics, here I will merely summarise what they regard as the most pressing open methodological issues. In a survey of recent work on forecasting, Hendry and Michael Clements list the following ten areas, the increased understanding of which is crucial for our forecasting success (Hendry and Clements 2003: 315):

- pre-testing for the inclusion of intercept corrections;
- modelling shifts;
- inter-forecast smoothing;
- the role of survey information in forecasting;
- pooling of forecasts and forecast encompassing;
- discriminating measurement errors from innovation shifts;
- multi-step estimation for multi-step forecasting;
- the advantages of explicitly checking co-breaking for forecasting;
- attempts to forecast rare events;
- leading indicators in forecasting.

As hinted at above, control is forecasting in a special scenario, namely when a policy variable is deliberately changed. Consequently, some of the methodological issues concerning forecasting are relevant for control, too. Particularly relevant is the role of co-breaking relationships. The time series of two variables are said to be co-breaking if both are subject to deterministic shifts (e.g. to shifts in their unconditional means) but a linear combination removes the shifts. When a policy variable and a target variable co-break, the link can be exploited to control the target variable (see Hendry 2004).

Although tests for co-breaking relationships have been developed, they remain unsatisfactory because they are oversized; that is, the probability of erroneously concluding that no co-breaking is present is higher than the chosen significance level suggests, especially when the degree of autocorrelation is high. Further, all results are asymptotic, which indicates that they have unfavourable small-sample properties (Hendry and Massmann 2007). All that said, one can conclude that methodological problems in measurement (or description), prediction and control abound.

IV

The fourth and perhaps strongest argument for why a methodologist might be justified in ignoring an aim of science is that the practice one recommends simultaneously achieves a plurality of aims. In the present context, one might argue that the focus on explanation is innocuous because investigating causal mechanisms will also further the other objectives of the social sciences. In this section I consider whether investigating causal mechanisms is always a good strategy when the aim is accurate description, successful prediction or control.

Causal-mechanistic models are the best models of data Let us return to the measurement of inflation for a moment. As discussed in detail in Chapter 4, there are three approaches to the problem of index numbers: the axiomatic, the stochastic and the economic approach. Of these three, only the last approach makes use of causal-mechanistic hypotheses by regarding the problem as one of expenditure minimisation given a vector of commodity prices. According to this theory, the right answer to the question 'Which is the best index?' is 'That which measures the change in expenditure for the basket of goods optimising agents would choose were they to maintain a constant level of utility.' The other two approaches are based on very general mathematical and statistical considerations and can therefore be regarded as non-mechanistic.

In this context we could unify our interests in theoretical explanation and accurate description if we could demonstrate that the economic approach is the best answer to the index-number problem. There are, however, two problems with this strategy.

It is true that among economists the economic approach is widely accepted as providing the right answer to the index-number problem. However, and this is the first problem, conceptually it is not clear whether utility is the right quantity to be held constant in a price index (for details, see the discussions in Chapters 2–4). Recall that one of the purposes for which the CPI is used is to insulate benefit recipients from changes in the cost of living. But the 'cost of living' has other connotations than the 'cost for achieving a given level of utility'. Another is the 'cost for achieving a given set of functionings' (in Amartya Sen's sense; see Sen 1999). Yet another requires that the relative position in society is fixed. Yet another asks that a basket of goods that yields an 'acceptable standard of living' is defined. It is easy to see that claiming that only the economic approach provides the correct answer to the index-number problem begs the question against these alternative understandings. And not all of the alternatives will make use of mechanistic information in constructing an index number. A strict price index, for example, which traces the cost for purchasing a fixed basket of goods, is ignorant as to why consumers purchase this rather than another basket.

Second, even if we accept that fixing utility is the right answer to the index-number problem, we can face a trade-off between two different desiderata. For policy purposes, it matters greatly that the index is readily measurable. But a constant-utility index has one major deficiency: it is unobservable. An exact constant-utility index can be measured only if the preference functions of the consumers are known. In practice, of course, they are not. In order to solve this quandary, the effects of various changes that happen in the market are imputed by government statisticians or other experts. If a new good appears, for example, it is estimated whether it is an equivalent replacement of the old good or whether it provides a different amount of utility and how much (the price change is then discounted by the amount of the utility change before it enters the index). But there is something deeply unsatisfactory with this practice. One reason behind the indexation of federal spending programmes was to introduce a mechanical procedure where there had been fortuitous decisions by politicians. Demanding that the CPI be a constant-utility index re-introduces the earlier uncertainty as now statisticians and other experts have to decide how much the cost of living has changed. A constant-utility index may be theoretically more satisfactory but this advantage is bought at the expense of much greater measurement uncertainty. Angus Deaton, for example, argues (Deaton 1998: 38):

> In fact, it is unclear whether a quality-corrected cost-of-living index in a world with many heterogenous agents is an operational concept. I argue that the major problem is not the Consumer Price Index itself, but what it is used for; it is foolish to index benefits thoughtlessly and mechanically to a concept that is hard to define and harder to measure.

If this is true, there are good reasons to believe that causal-mechanistic models aren't always the best models of data. True, they may be more satisfactory from the point of view of theoretical explanation. But the satisfaction of this desire is purchased at the cost of other desiderata, which in some circumstances may be as or more important than theoretical explanation.

Causal-mechanistic models are the best models for prediction This is a version of the old symmetry thesis according to which (causal) explanation and prediction are the two sides of the same coin. Since the symmetry thesis has long gone out of fashion I don't really have to argue that causal-mechanistic models will not always be the best models for prediction. It is useful, however, to consider some recent technical results in the theory of forecasting.

The older theory of forecasting was built on two presumptions: (a) that the econometric model provides an adequate representation of the underlying data-generating structure; (b) that that structure remains stable within the forecasting horizon. In more recent work in this area, it has come to be accepted that: (a) econometric models are almost always mis-specified (i.e. they do not represent the underlying structure correctly); (b) socio-economic systems are subject to frequent structural breaks. Under these conditions, it cannot be proved that causally more adequate models beat models that are not based on causal variables in forecasting competitions. The vital property is that of adaptability: a model that adapts more rapidly to a structural break will beat a model that, after the occurrence of a break, is permanently off track. But since (as of today) causal models tend not to be robust to such shifts, non-causal models often outperform them (Hendry and Mizon 2001: 5):

> A key consequence of these results is that the best available forecasting model need not be based on the 'causal determinants' of the actual economic process, and as the example . . . shows, may be based on 'non-causal' variables, that is, variables which do not enter the DGP [i.e. the data-generating process or *mechanism*].

Causal-mechanistic models are the best models for policy This idea is based on the current version of the symmetry thesis. In this version, the symmetry is between causal explanation and intervention or control. The idea is, roughly, *X* causes *Y* if and only if an intervention (of the right kind) that changes the value of *X* changes the value of *Y* (Woodward 2003). That is, according to this theory, if *Y* is a target variable of interest and *X* is a policy variable we can manipulate, then if and only if *X* causes *Y*, we can use *X* in order to control *Y*. Values of *X* cause values of *Y* and thus, on this account, *X* explains *Y*. At the same time *X* figures as a policy variable through which we can change *Y*.

The problem with this approach in the present context is that an intervention, in order to serve the appropriate role in a theory of causation and explanation, has to have a number of very idealised properties. The theory states that, *if* we were to intervene in just the right way and change the value of the first variable, then the value of the second variable would change if and only if the first caused the second. This formulation is needed because we want to say that, say, past events or event-types we cannot manipulate in the right way are nonetheless causes of other events. However, for policy we need real interventions, not hypothetical ones. Hence, even if it is true that some *X* causes some *Y*, we might not be able to manipulate *X* in just the right way such that a change in *Y* ensues.

Recall James Woodward's definition of an 'intervention' from the previous chapter (Woodward 2003: 98f.):

I1 I causes X.
I2 I acts as a switch for all other variables that cause X [i.e. I breaks all causal laws that have X as an effect].
I3 Any directed path from I to Y goes through X [i.e. if I causes Y, it does so only through X].
I4 I is (statistically) independent of any variable Z that causes Y and that is on a directed path that does not go through X.
I5 I does not alter the relationship between Y and any of its causes Z that are not on any directed path (should such a path exist) from X to Y.

A 'directed path' is a sequence of direct causal relationships (e.g. such that V_1 causes V_2 causes . . . causes V_n). Following this definition, let us call an intervention that satisfies these conditions a 'Woodward-intervention'. This contrasts starkly with ordinary usage, which is stronger and weaker at the same time. According to ordinary usage, it is central that: (R1) I can be set at the will of a human agent (an experimenter, a policy maker or what have you) who aims at changing a policy variable X; and (R2) I sometimes succeeds in changing the value of X. If, say, a central bank intervenes on short-term interest rates (X) by conducting open-market operations (I), it can, on occasion, fail to influence X. However, we would not call a variable an intervention on X if it never affected X. Praying that a dear friend recovers from an illness is not an intervention. Let us call an intervention that satisfies R1 and R2 a 'real intervention'.

With the possible exception of I1 (depending on how we interpret the word 'causes' in I1), any of Woodward's conditions can be violated by a real intervention, and some conditions are very likely to be violated. Few interventions will cancel all causal influence other variables have on the policy variable. An open-market operation is likely to *influence* the short-term interest rate but it won't remove all of its other causes. Some interventions will affect the target via more than one route. Suppose smoking is a policy variable and mortality rates due to lung cancer the target. Banning smoking in bars might affect smoking. But it might, too, change the frequency with which people go to bars, thus triggering alternative activities which may in turn influence mortality rates due to lung cancer. Some interventions will be correlated with other causes of the target variable. The level of the minimum wage in a state is sometimes adjusted in response to favourable economic conditions. If salary is regarded as the policy variable and employment as the target, here the intervention is correlated with another cause of the target, namely 'economic conditions'. Further, many interventions will affect the causal laws of the system themselves. The oil price shocks were interventions that changed many consumers' and producers' attitudes towards petroleum use and are thus likely to have altered the economy's causal laws in important respects.

Therefore, even if X causes Y in Woodward's sense, the relationship will not always be stable under a real intervention on X. What matters for policy is the stable association between the policy variable and the target, not the reason *why* the correlation is stable. Suppose we believe *X* to cause *Y* and *I* to be an intervention, both in Woodward's sense. But let the real structure be such that the correlation is due to a common cause *Z*, and let *I* affect *Z* or, alternatively, *X* and *Y* independently, perhaps such that *X* changes before *Y* changes, so that it looks as if *X* causes *Y*. There is nothing wrong with this alternative structure from a policy point of view. But it would be a mistake to explain the change in *Y* by citing the change of *X*. There is hence a third notion of intervention, that of a policy intervention. A 'policy intervention' adds to the 'real intervention' the requirement that the relationship between policy variable and target remain invariant (cf. the econometric notion of super exogeneity; see for instance Engle *et al.* 1983).

Furthermore, the locution 'there is a causal mechanism between *X* and *Y*' (in the sense relevant for this chapter) is considerably weaker than the locution '*X* causes *Y*' (in Woodward's sense). An intervention (real or Woodward) may, for example, trigger two different mechanisms whose influence on the target variable can be positive, negative or zero. Consider the following example from economist/social theorist Julian LeGrand (LeGrand 1982: 148, quoted from Elster 1999: 50):

> A high marginal tax rate lowers the opportunity cost or 'price' of leisure, and, as with any commodity whose price is reduced, thereby encourages people to consume more of it (and thus do less work). But, on the other hand, it also lowers peoples' incomes, and thereby may induce them to work harder so as to maintain their standard of living. These two effects – the substitution and income effects, in economists parlance – operate in opposite directions, and their net effect is impossible to predict from theory alone.

After the fact, we'll be able to explain the change (if there is any) by citing the two mechanisms. But (in this example) the marginal tax rate does not appear to be a good policy variable if employment is the target.

Another reason why it will not always be enough to have a mechanism that connects *X* and *Y* for using *X* as a policy variable is that causation in Woodward's sense is not always transitive: if *X* causes *Z* and *Z* causes *Y*, it is not guaranteed that *X* causes *Y*. In the social sciences, threshold effects can illustrate possible failures of transitivity. A threshold effect obtains when a cause changes the value of its effect only after reaching a certain critical value. This phenomenon has been reported in the relationship between human capital and income, for instance. Human capital needs to reach a critical level in order to affect income. That is, there is a Woodward-intervention on human capital that changes the value of income, namely one that raises human capital from below to above the threshold level (and thus human capital causes income). Further, let there be a Woodward-intervention on schooling that changes the level of human capital (and thus schooling causes human capital). However, it is well possible that no intervention on schooling affects human capital enough in order to get it above the threshold value (and thus, schooling does not cause income). Hence, we cannot use schooling as a policy variable to control income as the target – despite the causal mechanism running from the policy to the target variable.

In summary, mechanisms and control are distinct, albeit related. Both are causal notions without doubt. But they are causal notions with different characteristics and hence investigating whether one applies will not always be the best strategy for finding out whether the other does also.

V

For reasons discussed above, David Hendry and his collaborators emphasise the distinctness of forecasting and policy (Hendry and Clements 2003: 314): 'Thus, neither forecast success nor failure entails either good or bad policy advice: policy models need policy evaluation.' It seems appropriate to add: data models need data evaluation; forecasting models need forecasting evaluation; and, of course, explanatory models need evaluation in terms of explanation. Economics and other social sciences come with a variety of different ends, and each end brings its own standard of evaluating models.

Maybe I am preaching to the choir here because we've all become pluralists already. Perhaps. But if that is so, it should strike one as odd that measurement, forecasting and policy evaluation are virtually absent from the debates in methodology and the philosophy of economics and other social sciences – and that despite the importance and methodological intricacy of these activities. And there is at least one significant movement in the philosophy of the social sciences that is quite explicit in its neglect or rejection of non-explanatory aims. So maybe some methodologists' declared belief in pluralism is little more than lip service.

Against critical realists and other proponents of the 'new mechanist perspective' I therefore want to urge that methodology and the philosophy of the social sciences can profit from a more explicit endorsement of various non-explanatory aims of the social sciences. Of course, far be it from me to make the same mistake and de-emphasise the explanatory role of social theory. But, to stress it again, explanation is only one important endeavour among many.

9 Social capacities

I

What kind of knowledge do we need for policy applications? What kind of evidence do we need to support policy claims? The aim of this chapter is to address these questions. For various reasons, a number of methodologists have voiced scepticism about the possibility of social policy. Some (in particular, Friedrich August von Hayek) have indeed worried about our ability to ever gather enough evidence that social policies (of certain kinds, to be sure) could be successful. Others (in particular, Tony Lawson and his critical realist acolytes) have worried about the metaphysical presuppositions for social policy. In this chapter I propose to approach the issue with a mild optimism. The reason for the (albeit hesitant) optimism is methodological. I simply don't think that the economy has been studied long enough and with the right methods in order to generate good evidence for policy hypotheses. Perhaps after trying so for a while, we will agree with Hayek that knowledge is too dispersed to allow successful policy applications; or we will agree with the critical realists that economies are open systems that simply do not display enough regularity for policies to be successful. But being unrepentantly cheerful, I would like to see the evidence that policy applications are impossible. Before I see that, I continue to urge: study the economy, not our theories about it; and study it such that the investigation generates evidence relevant for policy hypotheses.

In this chapter I will focus on one problem in learning about policy hypotheses in particular. Policy hypotheses are often causal hypotheses. We would like to know whether money *causes* nominal income because we would like to exploit our control over the money stock for manipulating income; we would like to know whether free trade *causes* growth because we would like to know whether breaking down trade barriers is an efficient strategy for developing countries to fight poverty; we would like to know whether minimum wage increases cause employment because we would like to reduce unemployment. Testing hypotheses to the effect that some variable *X* causes another variable *Y* in some experimental population, even if established successfully, is only part, and probably the easier part, of the work that needs to be done. What we need to know is whether *X continues to cause Y* in the target population – the population our policy hypothesis is concerned with. We don't want to know whether money caused income in the century to 1960 in the United States. We would like to know whether it does so tomorrow and perhaps in other countries. Yet it would not be too informative to point out that there is a good chance that tomorrow will differ from today, and here from there. What we would like to have, thus, is knowledge about causal relationships that are *stable across suitable ranges of circumstances*. Sure, tomorrow differs from today. But perhaps the 1950s United States is in some appropriate sense similar enough to the United States in the twenty-first century such that causal claims established on past data can still be useful for policy. Knowledge that has this property I call knowledge about *social capacities*.

John Maynard Keynes does not think that we can have such knowledge. According to Keynes, the universe consists of bodies 'such that each of them exercised its own separate, independent and invariable effect' (Keynes 1957 [1921]: 249). However (ibid.):

> We do not have an invariable relation between particular bodies, but nevertheless each has on the others its own separate and invariable effect, which does not change with changing circumstances, although, of course, the total effect may be changed to almost any extent if all the other accompanying causes are different.

The contribution a factor makes to a situation is thus dependent on the arrangement of all other factors. In other words, the Keynesian world is 'holistic'. As a consequence, the method of analysis and synthesis cannot be applied. That is, we cannot learn about what happens in a complex situation by analysing the situation into parts that can be more easily handled, studying the parts separately and, in order to make predictions, synthesise what we know about the parts.

In a different context, Nancy Cartwright uses ideas of members of the German Historical School to shed doubt on the reality of capacities in social phenomena. In an encyclopaedia entry on capacities, she writes (Cartwright 1998: 45f., emphasis added):

> Just as the analytic method of Newtonian physics was challenged by Goethe and others in his particular German tradition, the analytic method of classical economics laid out so clearly in Mill was rejected by the Historical School dominant in German political economy at the end of the nineteenth and beginning of the twentieth century. [. . .] Gustav Schmoller, in particular, is famous in methodology for his insistence against Carl Menger that history and political economy could not employ exact universal laws as physics does. For Schmoller, as for Mill, economic phenomena are brought about on each occasion by a myriad of interacting causes. *But for Schmoller, the role each cause plays*

> *depends on the total context in which it is set. So although separate causal factors can be identified and reidentified from one context to another, the separate causes do not have stable capacities.*

Let us then in this chapter study how well founded the scepticism regarding the reality of social capacities really is. Section II examines the capacities concept in detail. Section III shows that popular methods used widely in economics fail to establish knowledge about social capacities. Section IV distinguishes two notions of scepticism about the reality of social capacities and argues that, at best, only the weaker form is warranted. Section V concludes.

II

Saying that some *X* has a capacity to do things means saying three different things (Cartwright, op. cit.). It means, first, that *X* is a *cause*. *X* is a factor that is a genuine producer of change, it is not only a correlate of that change. Further, it tells us something about what *X* does *potentially*: when *X* operates unimpeded, it produces (say) φ. However, even when this process is interfered with, *X* will tend to or try to do φ. In other words, if there are causal factors present that impede on *X*'s action to do φ, *X* will still contribute to the overall result. Third, the ability of *X* to do φ must display some *stability* across some range of circumstances if it is to count as a capacity.

To give a hypothetical example from social science, let us assume that economists have established that the growth of money in an economy has the capacity to raise the general level of prices. According to the conception of capacity just introduced, this means: (a) that the growth of money is not only correlated with the level of prices but it actively produces its increase; (b) that this says nothing about the actual behaviour of the price level, since there can always be factors such as technology shocks or international trade which can interfere with the operation of the money stock – however, even in such a situation, money will *contribute* to the actual behaviour of the price level; and (c) the ability of the growth of money to increase the price level is stable across some range of situations – for example across different capitalist economies, under different monetary regimes etc.; however, it is possible that there are situations (in systems with radically different economic constitutions, say) where money does not have this capacity.

What is the relevance of capacities for social science? The answer is conditional: *if* there are social phenomena that are governed by factors with capacities and they are epistemically accessible, then the social scientist and/or engineer is helped in realising his epistemic and pragmatic aims. Consider three of the aims discussed in the previous chapter: explanation, prediction and control. Knowledge about capacities helps in explaining social phenomena. This is evident from their causal nature and the wide acceptance of causal models of scientific explanation. Capacities can also help in predicting phenomena. It is an analytic truth that capacities allow true conditional predictions to be made about phenomena of the form: 'if nothing interferes, doing *X* will result in φ'. This is an exact prediction but non-vacuously true only if the antecedent is fulfilled. On the other hand, if disturbing factors do occur, the prediction will be inexact and about the contribution of *X* to the overall result.

Knowledge about capacities may also help in planning and control. The matter is, however, slightly more complicated here. When Mill originally introduced the tendencies concept, after which Cartwright modelled her own concept, he did so in order to save the truth or universality of natural laws in the light of apparent disconfirmations due to intervening factors (for a discussion of the difference between Mill's and Cartwright's concepts, see Schmidt-Petri forthcoming). Suppose we have a particle that is subject to two forces, one that pulls in the *x*-direction and another that pulls in a 135° angle to it. When each force operates on its own, the law that describes its behaviour is true. But when both forces operate jointly, the law, understood as a function from forces to actual *results* (in this case, motions), is literally false. This is because part of the motion in the *x*-direction that would have occurred had the first force operated on its own is upset by the second force, and vice versa. The motions do not occur in the way the (individual) laws predict. But if we understand the law as an ascription of a tendency or capacity, its truth is salvaged. This is because, although the motion that actually occurs is not the one predicted by either law, each law is true of the *tendency* to produce its characteristic result and each force contributes to the overall result. Notice that we cannot rescue a law-as-regularity view by claiming that the account presented here simply misdescribes the actual situation because the 'true law' is the *combined* law. The reason is that there are many cases in which the intervening factor cannot be brought under a more comprehensive law. Suppose that the motion in the second direction is brought about by a sudden gust of wind. According to Cartwright, there is no law that describes the operation of this kind of intervening factor in the regularity sense but the capacity (of the first factor) still holds.

Therefore, the kind of stability the concept requires is a stability 'under interferences'. But this does not imply that the *X*–φ relationship must be stable under *all* interferences, and in particular under interferences which destroy the causal structure on account of which the capacity arises. An economic example will illustrate this claim. Let us assume that the Phillips curve has a true causal reading in the capacities sense. That is to say, let us assume that the unemployment gap (the difference between the actual and the 'natural' unemployment rate) has the capacity to decrease inflation. This means: (a) that the unemployment gap causes inflation; (b) that any precise formulation about the exact relationship between the two quantities is true only potentially, that is, in the absence of interferences; and (c) that when other factors capable of affecting the inflation rate are co-present, the unemployment gap still contributes to the overall result. But it does not mean that the capacity must still be there even if there has been any intervention in the economy, for example by changing the wage-setting process. Imagine, for example, an intervention that changes the labour market from a purely centralised and unionised system to a localised and free system. This will surely have effects on the rate with which the unemployment gap changes the inflation rate; that is, on the strength of the capacity, but possible even on its existence (it may change its strength to zero).

The ability to plan and control presupposes knowledge not only of capacities but also of a second kind of stability, which in econometrics is called *autonomy* (see for instance Aldrich 1989). An autonomous relationship is essentially one which remains stable under (some range of) *interventions*. Stability across some range of circumstances is part of the concept of capacity but the difference between the circumstances does not have to involve interventions. All interventions change circumstances though, and hence all autonomous relationships involve a capacity but not necessarily the other way around. However, thus construed, knowledge of capacities again helps in realising (this time, pragmatic) scientific aims; it is just that the economic planner needs to know something more too.

III

If there are stable capacities in a domain of interest, research is aided in a number of ways. Most importantly, claims that have been established with respect to a certain test situation *X* are exportable outside *X*. For example, if we judge on the basis of the Stanford/NASA gyro experiment (see Cartwright 1989, Ch. 2) that coupling has the *capacity* to affect precession in the way the experiment tells us, then we assume that coupling affects precession also outside the experimental situation. True, outside the test situation coupling may *result* in no precession at all. But that means that there is an inhibiting cause which prevents the capacity from being exercised.

Are the methods prominent in economics able to establish knowledge about capacities? In Chapter 5 I have already argued that laboratory experiments in economics are very unlikely to generate knowledge that is particularly stable across different circumstances. Let us now examine the remaining two methods: thought and natural experiments.

Exhibit I: The vanity of rigour In a 1999 paper, Cartwright argues that the thought experiments or 'toy models' we find every so often in theoretical economics do not provide evidence for capacities (Cartwright 1999b). This is due to the fact that these models employ many 'non-Galilean' idealisations, which implies that one cannot attribute the effect to the cause of interest as its 'characteristic effect'.

The concepts of 'Galilean' idealisation and capacity are closely linked. An idealisation is Galilean if it helps in learning about operation of a causal factor free from disturbances. Galileo's own thought experiments on falling bodies are good examples. In one thought experiment, Galileo asks us to imagine two bodies falling from a tower without air resistance, a heavier cannon ball and a lighter musket ball. According to the Aristotelian tradition, the heavier ball falls at a faster rate and hits the ground first. However, if we now suppose that we join the two balls with a string, the Aristotelian theory falls into a contradiction. This is because we can derive that the amalgam falls both faster as well as slower. On the one hand, it falls slower because the lighter ball pulls the heavier one upwards and thus slows down the ensemble. On the other hand, the two balls together are heavier than the heavy ball alone and thus should fall faster. Hence, Galileo argues, in a vacuum all bodies fall at the same rate.

The assumption of no air resistance, then, is a Galilean idealisation as it helps us in learning what the Earth's pull does to falling bodies in the absence of disturbing factors. In other words, it helps us in learning about the capacity of the Earth to attract heavy bodies. Ernan McMullin, in his paper on 'Galilean Idealization' (McMullin 1985), distinguished a number of kinds of idealisation, but in the present context the kind he calls 'causal idealization' is most relevant. McMullin writes (ibid.: 265ff.):

> And it is this sort of idealization that is most distinctively 'Galilean' in origin. His insight was that complex causal situations can only be understood by first taking the causal lines separately and then combining them. [. . .]
>
> The move from the complexity of Nature to the specially contrived order of the experiment is a form of idealization. The diversity of causes found in Nature is reduced and made manageable. The influence of impediments, that is, causal factors which affect the process under study in ways not at present of interest, is eliminated or lessened sufficiently that it may be ignored. Or the effect of the impediment is calculated by a specially designed experiment and then allowed for in order to determine what the 'pure case' would look like. [. . .]
>
> Galileo is convinced that he has discovered the motion that 'nature employs for descending heavy things'. [. . .] It is 'natural' in the sense that it defines what the body *would* do on its own, apart from the effects of causes (like the resistance of air) external to it. These latter are to be treated as 'impediments', as barriers to an understanding of what the 'natural' tendency of body is.

It is a commonplace that the models characteristic of theoretical economics are highly idealised. Cartwright points out that many of the idealisations employed are not of the Galilean kind. Recall Akerlof's lemons model from Chapter 6 (Akerlof 1970). Akerlof's aim was to explain the phenomenon of a large price differential between new cars and cars that have just left the showroom, or, in more general terms, that markets where quality matters often experience lower than expected prices and exchanged quantities. The second-hand car market is an instance of this more general phenomenon.

Akerlof tried to explain the phenomenon by pointing out that in such markets there is an asymmetry in the information distribution: sellers know more than buyers. After they learn about the quality of their cars, owners of lemons (bad-quality cars) will want to sell their cars and exchange them for new ones, while owners of good cars will keep their cars. Since the quality of the car is not observable to buyers, cars are priced at some average rate, which further increases the incentives of owners of bad cars to sell their bad cars and of owners of good cars to keep their good ones. Hence, quality, prices and exchanged quantities drop.

To lend credibility to his story, Akerlof provides a mathematical derivation of the result in addition to a more intuitive thought experiment. As is very common in investigations of this kind, Akerlof makes a large number of assumptions in order to derive the result in the mathematical model. Cartwright points out that making these assumptions is in fact a methodological prerequisite. This is, she claims, because the basic principles of economics (the equivalent to 'laws' in physics) are both few in number and meagre (in the sense that little real-world behaviour is constrained by these principles). As a consequence, the principles do not have much deductive power. But this in turn means that many additional structural assumptions must be made if results are to be deduced mathematically.

Among the assumptions Akerlof makes is that there are two types of traders with distinct utility functions, and both types are von Neumann–Morgenstern maximisers of expected utility, that the cars' quality is distributed uniformly between zero and two, that goods are infinitely divisible and that the price of 'other goods' is one. Few of these are Galilean in nature. That is, few of the assumptions help us learn what asymmetric information does on its own. If one attempts to trace back responsibility for a result, one finds that not only the factor of interest is to blame but all of the assumptions made – otherwise no result would have been obtained. But this in turn means that we have not isolated a tendency.

So what did Akerlof establish? As I have pointed out in Chapter 6, he measured the causal effect of asymmetric information on quality and volume *in the system he envisaged*. To see this, note that his method of proof resembles very closely Mill's 'method of difference'. Recall that the method of difference infers the causal effect of a factor *F* by comparing two situations which are identical except *F* is present in one and absent in the other (and *F*'s effect if there is any). The difference *F* makes to the situation, then, is its causal effect. Akerlof does exactly that. He models a situation with symmetric information and a situation with asymmetric information, and the difference in the market result is then attributed to the difference in the information distribution. But since the result crucially depends on the assumptions made, we can judge it to be present only in systems for which Akerlof's assumptions are true.

The point is this. If we aim at establishing that a factor *X* has the capacity to φ, we had better make our conclusions as independent of the test conditions as possible. This is the lesson one can draw from McMullin's treatment of Galilean idealisations. Due to the particular manner in which results are determined in models such as the lemons model, however, conclusions are highly dependent on test conditions – in this case the model assumptions. Therefore, in themselves, they cannot establish a *capacity* claim.

One might object that the lemons model is a non-starter as a tool for establishing capacities anyway. The model is a piece of theory after all, whereas a capacity claim is a claim about a particular kind of causal relationship in the world. The reason I include theoretical models in my brief survey of methods in social science is that they are frequently taken – in themselves – to provide evidence for capacities. For instance, an argument why third-world labour markets fail might go as follows. In third-world countries labour markets often fail. In these markets quality matters. In markets where quality matters asymmetric information can lead to market failure (we have established that with Akerlof's model). In third-world labour markets, the quality of labour cannot be observed by employers; that is, there is an asymmetry in the information distribution. Hence, in third-world labour markets asymmetric information causes market failure.

This argument is obviously fallacious. One cannot argue from the fact that in a specific situation a causal factor is responsible for a result to the conclusion that it does so too in the envisaged situation. The least we need to do is to rule out all alternative explanations for the result. But worse, the result has been established only for a very unrealistic situation (one where there are only two types of agents, both von Neumann–Morgenstern maximisers of expected utility, distinguished only by their respective utility functions; cars have only one property, namely 'quality', which is uniformly distributed, etc.). Thus one would first need to establish that the conclusion holds in a real experimental situation too before one exports it to other situations. Nonetheless, arguments of this kind can be found, so I wanted to include theoretical models here. Exhibit II examines a case where the conclusion is established experimentally.

Exhibit II: Natural experiments in economics There is a movement in contemporary econometrics which has been labelled the 'natural experiments movement' (see Heckman 2000 and for a discussion Chapter 7 of this book). Its basic strategy can be summarised as follows:

Natural experiments. To measure the causal effect of *C* on *E*, find a set of economic units on which one can measure *E* such that one can partition them naturally, i.e. without intervention, into a treatment group (where *C* is present) and a control group (where *C* is absent) in a way that resembles a controlled experiment. That is, the distribution of factors, which are causally relevant to E, is identical in both the treatment and control groups and the assignment of a unit to a group is independent of any factor that may be causally relevant to E. Then measure the causal effect by taking the difference between the averages of the E-values in the treatment and control groups.

Recall one of the examples from Chapter 7. Economic theory predicts that a rise in the minimum wage leads employers to cut jobs. David Card and Alan Krueger challenged this (universal) prediction with an analysis of a natural experiment that occurred in New Jersey in 1992 (Card and Krueger 1994, 1995). In that year, New Jersey's minimum wage rose from $4.25 to $5.05 per hour. In order to measure the causal effect of the minimum wage rise (C) on the change in employment (E), Card and Krueger surveyed 410 fast-food restaurants in New Jersey and eastern Pennsylvania before and after the rise. The economic units of interest (the fast-food restaurants) fall naturally into two groups (the ones in New Jersey, which form the treatment group, and the ones in eastern Pennsylvania, which form the control group). Several items of background knowledge allow the authors to judge that the natural setup resembles a controlled experiment sufficiently. They argue, for example, that 'New Jersey is a relatively small state with an economy that is closely linked to nearby states' (Card and Krueger 1994: 773) and, therefore, one has no reason to believe that the distribution of factors that could be relevant to employment differs between New Jersey and eastern Pennsylvania. This choice of control group is further tested by means of a second control group, namely restaurants in New Jersey, which initially paid at least $5.00 per hour wage, and thus should not be affected by the rise. In particular, the authors observe that 'seasonal patterns of employment are similar in New Jersey and eastern Pennsylvania, as well as across high- and low-wage stores within New Jersey' (ibid.), such that the 'natural development' of employment, which could confound their result, should be controlled for. There is furthermore no reason to believe that the change in the level of employment is dependent on the assignment to groups, that is, whether the restaurant is in New Jersey or Pennsylvania. Card and Krueger present their results as follows (ibid.: 792, emphasis added):

> . . . we find no evidence that the rise in New Jersey's minimum wage reduced employment at fast-food restaurants in the state. Regardless of whether we compare stores in New Jersey that were affected by the $5.05 minimum to stores in eastern Pennsylvania (where the minimum wage was constant at $4.25 per hour) or to stores in New Jersey that were initially paying $5.00 or more (and were largely unaffected by the new law), we find that the increase in the minimum wage *increased* employment.

I do not want to comment here on whether Card and Krueger are successful in their analysis of the natural experiment (for that, go back to the discussion in Chapter 7). They surely *try* to replicate the structure of a controlled experiment. The point to draw attention to is rather that, *if* their results are valid, they cannot be understood as an ascription of capacity. What I believe they can claim is that, *ceteris paribus*, raising the minimum wage increases employment. But since one way of understanding statements of *ceteris paribus* law is as an ascription of capacity (Cartwright 2002), the difference I want to point out requires elaboration.

To ascribe a capacity to a causal factor means that one believes that certain inductive inferences are licensed. Surely the usual inference to all situations that are relevantly similar to the test situation is made. But, importantly, we know more: even when the conditions of the test situation are not fulfilled, if the causal factor is present, it will still 'try' or 'tend' to produce the result. If it does not succeed, then there must be a very good reason for it, namely a countervailing capacity. For example, saying that the Earth has the capacity to attract heavy bodies means that it will still try to do so even when gravity does not operate on its own. Now, if the Earth does not succeed in attracting a given heavy body, we ascribe this failure to the presence of another capacity, for example a strong magnetic field above the body that pulls it upwards.

Inferences that are licensed by a *ceteris paribus* law in the sense used here are narrower in scope. They allow only the usual induction to cases that more closely resemble the test situation. My point about the Card and Krueger paper is that they can make (at best) only the latter kind of inferences, and not the former, broader kind. They did not find a general truth about minimum wages (nor do they believe they did). Rather, what they found (again, of course, if their results are valid) is a law that under certain conditions raising the minimum wage will increase employment. What these conditions are is difficult to say. Crucially, however, the failure of raising the minimum wage to produce more employment in a very different situation (say, when the minimum wage is already very high, when the rise is very large compared to its level, when economic conditions are radically different and so forth) will not induce us to seek for a countervailing tendency. Rather, we will attribute the failure to a relevant difference between the two situations we have compared. Note that the issue is not one of regularities versus causal powers. I do not want to defend a regularity view of law against a capacities view but rather indicate that the causal powers we find in social phenomena seem to be more fragile than the causal powers we find in many physical phenomena. Social causal powers seem to interact more frequently with other powers when they bring about a result.

One may object that this relevant difference is exactly a countervailing tendency and that the difference is only terminological. However, I think that reading the claim as a capacity claim would be highly unnatural. Let us suppose that there is a second natural experiment involving two different states with characteristics very similar to the Card and Krueger case. One difference is that the minimum wage in these states is initially much higher, say $10.00. Let us also suppose that raising the wage to $12.00 results in a *de*crease of employment. Now it seems to me that it would be absurd to say that there is a capacity of raising the minimum wage (of the first $5.00?) to increase employment, which is offset by a countervailing, stronger capacity (of the second $5.00?) to decrease employment, such that the overall result is negative. Rather, one would say that the situation differs in crucial respects, and that the law we found in the first case is not at work in the second case.

This discussion, I believe, points towards a more general feature about thinking in capacities and thinking in *ceteris paribus* laws. Thinking in capacities presupposes a method of analysis and synthesis. Situations are broken down to tractable parcels, the behaviour of these parcels is analysed severally and, finally, the bits are synthesised to let us know about the initial situation. Among other things, the method of analysis and synthesis presupposes that it makes sense to investigate what the parcels do on their own. Many cases Cartwright examines have this property. It makes perfect sense to talk about bodies, the sole force exerted on them being gravity. Even certain physically impossible scenarios, for instance the behaviour of bodies that have charge but no mass, are relatively easily conceptualised. This verdict is not an artefact of the choice of examples from simple mechanics. Even in more complex systems such as systems described by particle physics the general method employed by physicists remains the same. Often the synthetic step is more involved than adding forces by means of vector addition. But still, the laws of the individual parts contribute in a principled way to the solution of the complex.

In the social sciences the method of analysis and synthesis (in this sense) seems less applicable (cf. the discussion of the results of economic laboratory experiments in Chapter 5 whose analysis is essentially the same). No factor produces anything on its own. It does not even make sense to ask, for instance, what a minimum wage does in the absence of everything else. We need a dense network of causal conditions to produce any result. Furthermore, the result that is actually produced very often depends crucially on the conditions which are present when the factor operates. It seems, then, that in such situations the language of *ceteris paribus* laws is more applicable than the language of stable capacities.

The lesson of this section (and the relevant discussion in Chapter 5) is this. Very widely used and important methods of causal inference in social science fail to yield knowledge about social capacities – for a number of different reasons. We might want to infer from this that John Maynard Keynes', Gustav Schmoller's and Nancy Cartwright's scepticism is warranted. But there is a missing link in the argument. The inference presupposes that these are the best methods indeed to find capacities. In the next section I want to argue that there is something wrong with the way (at least some) social scientists use these methods. If that is true, one may grant that there is no good (positive) reason to believe in the existence of social capacities. But I want to add the caution that there is no good (negative) reason to believe in their non-existence either.

IV

So far, I have tried to give meat to scepticism about the existence of social factors with stable capacities. As with any other form of scepticism, this variety can be read in two basic ways: as a positive disbelief or as a suspension of judgement. In this section I want to argue that we have good reason for the latter but little evidence for the former. In other words, I think agnosticism is a sensible stance regarding the reality of social capacities, while full-blown atheism is ill-founded.

Cartwright herself seems to oscillate between the two forms. A joint statement with Jordi Cat in a paper on the German Historical School sounds pretty dire (Cartwright and Cat 1998: 2):

> The analytic method supposes that the causes of the phenomena of interest can be conceptually separated into distinct factors each of which has its own characteristic law of action. [. . .] Physics has been able to make effective use of this method in the study of motions; but political economy does not seem to lend itself to treatment by the analytic method.

And this is because:

> [The judgement about the above claim] is based on looking at cases of what is judged within the sciences themselves to be good practice . . .

I offer two arguments for the weaker reading according to which it is more sensible to just suspend judgement rather than to claim positively that 'political economy does not seem to lend itself to treatment by the analytic method': a cheap and nasty one and a more involved one.

The cheap and nasty argument is that philosophers of science often make an unfair comparison of social with natural science. I would tend to agree with Cartwright and Cat that '[p]hysics has been able to make effective use of [the analytic–synthetic] method in the study of motions', and in fact in the study of many other phenomena. However, the claim that economics (or even more so social science in general) has failed to make use of this method seems inequitable.

The social and those parts of the natural world where the method of analysis and synthesis has been applied most successfully differ in a number of important and well-known respects. This is not to say, of course, that a great number of cases from the less fundamental 'natural' sciences such as meteorology, geology, engineering and epidemiology don't more closely resemble my characterisation of the 'social' sciences. Let me mention just a few. Social phenomena (of interest) tend to be complex while natural phenomena (of interest) tend to be simple. Social phenomena (of interest) tend to be unstable and evolve over time while natural phenomena (of interest) tend to be stable and immutable. Social kinds tend to be interactive while natural kinds tend to be inert (see Hacking 1999 for this terminology). Social systems tend to prohibit experimentation while natural systems tend to allow it.

In my view, none of these differences motivates a principled distinction between natural and social science but they tend to make causal inference in social science harder. Coupled with the (contingent) fact that social scientists tend to be interested in relatively young phenomena (such as the capitalist economy), it seems unfair to demand from them results comparable with those of their physics colleagues who have had thousands of years to analyse their phenomena.

This argument is cheap and nasty indeed. Let me provide a second, more involved argument. One of Cartwright's methodological principles if one wants to find out about the nature of a subject matter is to investigate the best methods employed in the science that studies the subject matter, and make inferences on that basis. This explains the selection of theoretical modelling in economics and the natural experiments movement that have been discussed above (as well as the laboratory experiments from Chapter 5). I think that this methodological principle, defensible or not for other sciences, fails in the case of economics. The reason is simply that economics' so-called 'best' methods are still characterised by a methodological oddity natural science got rid of in the seventeenth century. The villain is (of course) theory.

The argument, in short, is as follows. Most economists, and increasingly other social scientists as well, presuppose a lot of theory in their empirical work. This, in my view, results in a certain inability to establish the existence of or facts about social phenomena. Knowledge about capacities, however, is parasitic upon knowledge about phenomena. Hence, the theoretical bias also impedes learning about social capacities.

Let us therefore review how social scientists establish phenomena. The best place to look for a sound methodology of social observation and measurement should be the early work of the Cowles Commission. Jakob Marschak, Tjalling Koopmans, Ragnar Frisch and others here established econometrics as a proper branch of economics through a combination of mathematics, statistics and economics. Importantly, at least in the early years, they regarded measurement as central to economics and adopted Kelvin's dictum 'science is measurement' as the motto for the Commission.

However, as much as they were interested in empirical investigation, theory was to play a strong part. In particular, they rejected institutionalist attempts to base economic analysis on empirical and historical investigation without recourse to theory. By contrast, they were aiming at a combination of theory and measurement in which the most fruitful use of both could be made. An apposite statement of this agenda can be found in Koopmans' review of Arthur Burns and Wesley Clair Mitchell's *Measuring Business Cycles* (Burns and Mitchell 1946). He writes (Koopmans 1947: 162):

> . . . this reviewer [Koopmans] believes that in research in economic dynamics the Kepler stage and the Newton stage of inquiry need to be more intimately combined and to be pursued simultaneously. Fuller utilization of the concepts and hypotheses of economic theory . . . as a part of the processes of observation and measurement promises to be a shorter road, perhaps even the only possible road, to the understanding of cyclical fluctuations.

Although I accept that theory sometimes can play a role in observation, measurement and experimentation, I deny that it is necessary and in particular I reject the dogmatism with which economic theory is acknowledged as the *sine qua non* of economic measurement.

In fact, the case studies I have presented in Parts I and II of this book provide excellent reasons for believing that none of the arguments that Koopmans put forward against the 'measurement without theory' perspective can sustain scrutiny. (I am not interested here in the historical question whether or not Mitchell and Burns ever subscribed to such a perspective.)

Koopmans levelled three arguments against the measurement-without-theory approach he ascribes to Burns and Mitchell. His first argument was that, 'for the purpose of systematic and large scale observation [of economic phenomena such as the business cycle], theoretical preconceptions about its nature cannot be dispensed with, and the authors do so only to the detriment of the analysis' (ibid.: 163).

This reasoning can only establish that adequate observation is always purpose-oriented, not that the only purpose of observation is the testing of theory. And in Part I of this book we have seen how economic variables can be measured entirely adequately without presupposing any specific economic theory.

Koopmans elaborates (ibid.: 164):

> But 'good' choices [about which time series can adequately represent salient aspects of business cycles] means relevant choices. What is relevant can only be determined with the help of some notions as to the generation of economic fluctuations, and as to their impact on society. In the light of such notions, wide fluctuations in call money rates may be unimportant if total employment is relatively stable. Fluctuations in the production of durable producers' goods would be less serious if they were approximately offset by opposite fluctuations in the production of consumers' good.

I agree. But there is no need for specific economic theory in determining the causes and effects of the business cycle. Or is there? Koopmans' third argument (the reason for the change in order will be apparent shortly) is that 'the extraction of more information from the data requires that, in addition to the hypotheses subject to test, certain basic economic hypotheses are formulated as distributional assumptions, which often are not themselves subject to statistical testing from the same data' (ibid.: 170). What he alludes to here is the so-called identification problem (for a brief discussion, see Pindyck and Rubinfeld 1991: 292ff.). Suppose we would like to determine the effect of raising tobacco taxes on cigarette prices. According to theory, observed market prices are at an equilibrium point determined by supply and demand. In order to estimate the effect of the new level of tax, we would need to know the price elasticities of supply and demand for cigarettes. At each point in time, however, only the equilibrium point is observable, not the whole schedule. That is, from observing prices and quantities alone, elasticities cannot be identified. But suppose there was a variable, say income, which we knew affected only one side, in this case demand, but not the other side. Including this variable in the regression allows us to identify the demand elasticity (and vice versa for the supply elasticity). It is thus economic theory which tells us what variables to look for in an identification problem.

This is indeed the orthodox way of framing a problem about causal inference in economics. But Koopmans' conclusion is a non sequitur. While most methodologists and philosophers of science now agree that we cannot infer new causal relationships without presupposing causal background knowledge (cf. Nancy Cartwright's slogan 'No Causes In – No Causes Out' in Cartwright 1989), this does not mean that causal background knowledge has to come from economic theory. Again, as we have seen in Chapter 7, we can do sound causal inference without any need for theory.

Koopmans' second argument is, finally, that '[w]ithout resort to theory, in the sense indicated, conclusions relevant to the guidance of economic policies cannot be drawn' (Koopmans 1947: 167). This argument in fact foreshadowed the Lucas Critique (Lucas 1976). It says that the relationships observed (or rather, identified) at the aggregate level are unlikely to remain stable – because of changes in the 'deeper' behavioural parameters, which are responsible for the aggregate relationships – for a variety of reasons, the most relevant of which is policy. In other words, theory-free inference to causal relationships at the aggregate level is unlikely to be a good tool for policy analysis because policy affects the underlying relationships – at the level of individuals, their tastes and environment – themselves. For policy, one has to study relationships at the individual level because only those are invariant to policy changes. And of course, only theory is informative about where to seek such invariant relationships.

Again, Koopmans' analysis is correct but the conclusion a non sequitur. We know that parameters estimated for aggregate variables are often not invariant across different time periods, regions or policy regimes. It is also true (though more contentious) that even relationships that are genuinely causal can break down, especially under policy changes. But from this it doesn't follow that only relationships among individuals and their constraints, that is, those relationships described by economic theory, are invariant to policy changes. Such autonomous relationships can be and have been found at the aggregate level just as much as among individuals. It is also true that not all methods of causal inference produce knowledge about autonomous relationships. But those that do in no way depend on background knowledge informed by economic theory.

Popper is famous for stressing the principle 'theory before observation'. Now, if we accept that in order to make sense observation must be made in relationship to *some* theory, even Popper would regard it as pure dogmatism if it was taken for granted that it must be *a particular* theory and that that theory is beyond questioning. Economic theory (in the sense of a canon of general presuppositions and methods), however, does have such a position. It is no great surprise, then, that the empirical results of the early Cowles Commission have been disappointing.

The Cowles Commission is not the only place to look for this theoretical bias. I used their example because they are the inventors of modern economic measurement and therefore should speak with some authority. To turn to a more contemporary example, reconsider the natural experiments movement. On the face of it, it seems that following this approach one can do solid empirical work without much theory. Of course, I am not saying that one can learn about causal relationships from statistics without *background knowledge*. But that background knowledge can come from a variety of sources, including knowledge about institutions, previous econometric studies, common knowledge and so forth. What I am saying is that background knowledge does not have to include economic theory.

However, a main criticism that has been levelled against it is exactly that the results cannot be interpreted in the light of economic theory and are therefore very limited in their usefulness. Even James Heckman, who himself is a proponent of the natural experiments movement and an ingenious developer of its methods, writes (Heckman 2000: 85):

> Applications of this [natural experiments] approach often run the risk of producing estimates of causal parameters that are difficult to interpret. Like the evidence produced in VAR [vector autoregression] accounting exercises, the evidence produced by this school is difficult to relate to the body of evidence about the basic behavioural elasticities of economics. The lack of a theoretical framework makes it difficult to cumulate findings across studies, or to compare the findings of one study with another. Many applications of this approach produce estimates very similar to biostatistical 'treatment effects' without any clear economic interpretation.

Why do economists get so excited about 'theory' and 'economic interpretation'? One reason is pointed out by Margaret Morrison: sometimes there is a link between theory and our ability to carry experimental results to other contexts. Commenting on Cartwright's analysis of the Stanford/NASA gyro experiment, she writes (Morrison 1995: 168, original emphasis):

> What the *experiment* shows is that in space the dragging effect produces gyro precession but that tells us nothing about frame dragging in other contexts; the *theory* tells us that this is a global effect and since the experiment bears out what the theory predicts will happen in space we consider it confirmed.

Morrison disagrees with Cartwright about whether we need the capacities framework in order to understand such exportability of results. Their disagreement need not concern us in the present context. What is important is Morrison's claim that, *if we have a theory which is universal throughout the specified domain* and *we have good reason to believe our theory to be confirmed by a particular experiment or series of such experiments*, then we also have good reason to believe that our experimental results are exportable to other contexts within that domain.

The complaint recorded by Heckman is, then, because we cannot bring the results achieved by proponents of the natural experiments movement to bear on economic theory – which, after all, is universal in its domain – we do not have an off-the-shelf mechanism which tells us how to export our claims beyond the particular experiment that established it in the first place. Metaphysically, my reaction to this obstacle was to bite the bullet and accept that in economics there may be truths that are entirely local and not at all exportable; that is, to accept that we must understand many of the results of the natural experiments movement as *ceteris paribus* causal laws, where the *ceteris paribus* condition ties the result to the experimental population.

However, this reaction may have been too hasty. There are probably many causal factors in economics that are not as stable as the universal capacities we know from parts of physics but more stable than a *ceteris paribus* causal law. One possible aim of future research in methodology is to find a number of 'off-the-shelf' principles that are informative about how to export claims established by a natural experiment to other contexts. For example, we may ask whether it matters that Card and Krueger's study investigated fast-food restaurants, that the study was conducted on the east coast or that the initial minimum wage was $4.75. Geoffrey Hodgson, I believe, made some advance on this question. In his book *How Economics Forgot History* (Hodgson 2001), Hodgson attempts to answer what he calls the 'problem of historical specificity', namely the problem of knowing how historically (and geographically) specific a claim about socio-economic systems must be, in order to have the potential to be valid. His response consists essentially in relegating concepts and principles to the right level of abstraction, five of which he distinguishes (see his Table 21.2, ibid.: 326–27). Certain concepts and principles pertain to *all* 'open, evolving and complex systems'. At this level, theorising is informed by evolutionary theory, general systems theory and complexity theory. At the second level, concerning all human societies, human instincts and psychology as well as general anthropological principles govern theorising. The usual laws of supply and demand come into play at the third level concerning only 'civilised and complex human societies' while the fourth and fifth levels differentiate between kinds of socio-economic systems.

I understand this schema to be a schema for exporting claims beyond the experimental population. Certain properties are shared by, say, all open, evolving and complex systems. If an experiment establishes a new result about such a property, we should be able to export it to all other open, evolving and complex systems and similarly for the other levels.

In my view, Hodgson's schema fails for a variety of reasons (for a detailed discussion, see Reiss 2002). But what is immensely valuable about it is that it provides a starting-point for research on a topic which I believe to be of fundamental importance for methodology. In their empirical work, economists have usually attempted shortcuts that exploit economic theory in order to, for example, identify causal parameters in an econometric regression or aspects of a measurement procedure. The methodological point of view put forward in this chapter suggests that no such shortcut is possible. We need a methodology that is informative about empirical ways to determine how projectable claims established on the basis of experiments are.

Therefore, I do not believe that the current state of economics is a good place to examine what is possible in economic analysis. The empirical road has not been walked yet and we do not know where it would lead us if we do walk it. Tjalling Koopmans rightly distinguishes a 'Kepler stage' and a 'Newton stage' of scientific inquiry – one of empirical generalisation and one of fundamental law. But he is mistaken in saying that one needs to pursue them simultaneously. Empirical laws do not require fundamental laws to be established. By contrast, fundamental laws are void unless established on the basis of a range of empirical laws. There is no shortcut to fundamental laws that bypasses empirical laws.

The lesson of this section is that, pace Cartwright and Cat, there is no reason to lose hope. Yes, the record of finding social factors with stable capacities is poor. But it is poor because much empirical work done in social science has presupposed a particular theory about human behaviour. In my view, this has incapacitated the ability to establish real social phenomena, which in turn makes learning about social capacities a near impossibility. Giving up reliance on economic theory, and allowing social science to be a more empirical, more Baconian science, may result in learning about real social phenomena governed by real social capacities. Certainly, no one can predict that one day we will find only a single social capacity. However, I believe that there is no reason not to try.

V

The previous section ended with a mild optimism regarding the existence of social capacities. My hope to some day find such things is rooted in the conviction that there is something wrong with the way in which much of social science achieves its results. What I think is wrong is a certain dogmatism in an area one might label 'phenomenal inference'. Phenomenal inference is the establishment of phenomena on the basis of observations and measurements. Phenomena, the object of scientific explanations, do not lie around to be collected by the scientist, neither natural, nor social. To take, I hope, an uncontroversial natural scientific example, consider Newton's method of 'deduction from the phenomena'. What are the things Newton took as a basis for inferences? Surely not the naked observations of dots of light in the night sky (to take an example). Rather, he would construct a phenomenon such as the trajectory of a planet on the basis of observations or measurements made. Bas van Fraassen has recently remarked (van Fraassen 1997, section 3.2):

> Patrick Suppes had long emphasised that theories do not confront the data bare and raw. The experimental report is already a selective and refined representation, a 'data model' as he calls it. This is especially true today, as Fred Suppe has emphasized, now that scientists routinely process gigabytes of data. It was already true in Newton's time when he claimed to deduce laws from the phenomena – for of course he used as basis very smooth functions distilled from thousands of astronomical observations. But it is true even of the idealized, simple observation report discussed by the logical positivists, as they themselves came to agree after some debate.

There is no one way to infer a phenomenon on the basis of 'thousands of observations'. Especially in economics choices decisions about, say, the formula used to construct an index number or the specification of an econometric regression can influence the outcome substantially. As I have described in more detail in the first part of this book, in my view too much use of theoretical considerations is made in these inferences. It is as if Newton used the laws in the process of constructing (or inferring) the phenomena from which he was to deduce his laws. On the other hand, relatively theory-free approaches such as the natural experiments movement are regarded as deficient exactly for the reason that they cannot readily be connected to economic theory. But it is in fact the other way around: presupposing theory in a measurement procedure impedes learning about the validity of the theory.

A more empiricist approach has been sketched in Parts I and II of this book. It starts with an attempt to measure social variables – say, minimum wage (which is trivial) and employment – as accurately as possible using techniques developed in Part I. It then establishes causal relationships among these variables using techniques discussed in Part II; for example the analysis of a natural experiment. Unlike some proponents of natural experiments in econometrics themselves I see nothing wrong with, say, finding out that, under certain conditions, an increase in the minimum wage causes employment to rise – even if that does not tell us much about quantities of theoretical interest such as elasticities. Research would then proceed to investigate the stability of such a law. It would ask under what conditions minimum wages have what effects on employment. Finding a range of different conditions that affect the wage–employment relationship, we may ask whether there are any more abstract factors that would enable the researcher to explain why the minimum wage behaves differently in different situations.

Effectively, this is at least in part what David Card and Alan Krueger do in their 1995 book. After the natural experiment in New Jersey, they analyse a second one in Texas and re-analyse previous state-wide evidence from California and international evidence from Puerto Rico, Canada and Britain. Their aim, however, is only to undermine economists' traditional belief in the universal adverse effect of minimum wages. Hence it is enough for them to present a single case where an increase actually raised employment and to shed doubts on the validity of studies that find evidence for the opposite claim. They stop short of a systematic empirical investigation into the conditions and mechanisms responsible for the wage–employment relationship. Further, they do try to explain their results by means of models of the kind discussed under *Exhibit I* in Section III. Even for Card and Krueger, economic theory is sacrosanct. All they do is amend the simple model that predicts the negative effect slightly such that the resulting model predicts a positive effect.

Natural experiments à la Card and Krueger (as well as other models of causal inference that make little use of theory, such as Kevin Hoover's [Hoover 2001] or the Bayes'-nets approach) do, nonetheless, provide a starting point. On their basis, a range of phenomena can be established, phenomena of the kind 'under conditions *xyz*, increases in the minimum wage lead to higher employment', 'for population *P*, schooling increases earnings' or 'in system *S*, money causes prices'. Phenomena can then be classified according to similarities and dissimilarities, compared and analysed. Again, on the basis of such a classification and analysis, attempts can be made to explain them with reference to underlying mechanisms. If we are lucky, such mechanisms have parts that can be used in the explanation of a range of different phenomena. They may be factors with (relatively) stable capacities.

This Baconian vision of social science is not new. It is essentially what social science would have looked like had the discipline followed Gustav Schmoller's methodological principles (see for example Schmoller 1911). Ironically, then, I suggest that we use Schmoller's ideas to achieve what he himself thought would be impossible. As we have seen near the beginning of this chapter, Schmoller argued against Mill that social factors do not have stable capacities that could be moved from situation to situation, and that, in general, the analytic method is not applicable to social systems. But Schmoller may have been overly hasty in his conclusion. There has never been a prolonged attempt to do social science the way he envisions it. But if we want to find social capacities, I do not currently see any better way.

10 Uncertainty in econometrics

Evaluating policy counterfactuals

(with Nancy Cartwright)

I

There is without question a great deal of uncertainty in planning and policy formation. Our starting point in approaching this uncertainty is that '[c]ounterfactuals are the very guide of life' (paraphrased from the dictum 'probability is the very guide of life'; see Kyburg and Thalos 2003). For rational planning we need counterfactuals because we need to evaluate what would happen were each of the actions under consideration implemented (contributions emphasising the importance of counterfactuals for *policy* include: Fackler and Rogers 1995; Grossman 1984; Lucas and Sargent 1981; Rasche 1995; and Tetlock and Belkin 1996). In terms of the concepts introduced in Chapter 1, we don't only require *valid* evidence – evidence that gives us reason to believe that a claim is true for some population that has already been investigated – we also need *sound* evidence: evidence that licenses actions on future target populations.

For this kind of deliberation there is always a vast amount we do not know – facts, laws, probabilities, people's reactions, etc. This chapter will focus on a more abstract source of ignorance that contributes to uncertainty in planning: We do not know how in principle to evaluate counterfactuals. There is a considerable literature in philosophy on the semantics of counterfactuals and recently contributions in economics itself. The bulk of this literature, we shall argue, puts the problems back to front. It attempts to use counterfactuals to evaluate causal claims; we argue instead that one must use causal claims to assess counterfactuals. That said, there is as yet no general account of how to do so (on the *logic* of counterfactuals, see Edgington 1995; but this kind of work is hard to relate to scientific problems).

The reason the literature has the problems back to front is that parts of both philosophy and economics are still in the grip of the 'Hume problem'. Like David Hume, many philosophers and economists feel that causality is an illegitimate concept. Counterfactuals are called in to secure legitimacy for it. As we shall argue, this skews the study of *genuine* policy counterfactuals – those counterfactuals that can be exploited for policy purposes. The Humean philosophers and economists study a different kind of counterfactuals – counterfactuals that could possibly stand in for causal concepts. But what we need for policy are counterfactuals that describe what would happen were our policies put into place. Unfortunately a semantics geared to the stand-ins for causal concepts fares badly at evaluating policy counterfactuals.

Thus we will argue for two related but independent claims, both concerned with the relationship between causality and counterfactuals. The first is that causal knowledge is required to evaluate policy counterfactuals. The second is that those counterfactuals invoked to stand in for causal concepts are a poor tool for answering the 'What if?' questions policy makers are concerned with.

Section II will argue the case that we need causal models to answer the kinds of 'What if?' questions raised in policy and planning. We shall then point out in Section III a number of ways in which counterfactuals can be ambiguous. A first step in providing counterfactual hypotheses for use in policy and planning, we maintain, is to be clear exactly what counterfactual hypothesis is under consideration, and this requires explicit assumptions about how the counterfactual antecedent is to be implemented. Sections IV and V will describe two attempts to do the job we urge. Section IV will describe Judea Pearl's theory of causal models and counterfactuals, based on his work on Bayes' nets. Section V will look at the work of James Heckman. Section VI concludes.

Both of the accounts we shall look at use counterfactuals to explicate causal notions. Neither, however, is engaged in a full-fledged Hume programme. For both begin, as we urge one must, with a causal model, a model that contains some set of causal principles. The notion of causality involved in the causal principles is left unanalysed. The causal model is used to evaluate counterfactuals and then the causal concept of concern is defined in terms of the counterfactual. Even if this method does not provide a total elimination of causal concepts, if successful it can at least explicate more problematic causal notions in terms of less problematic ones. The cost, however, is in the hope of using the accounts to answer more general kinds of counterfactual questions. The attempt to capture the intended causal notions skews the accounts; whether or not they succeed at explicating the causal notions of concern, neither can double as a semantics for the 'What if?' counterfactuals required for policy formation.

II

Policy analysts are often interested in answers to questions with the structure 'What would have happened to Y (the 'target variable'), had X been x (the 'control variable' and its value, respectively)?' Both control variable and target variable can be binomial or continuous. We might for example ask what would have happened to the profits of British utilities had they not been privatised or whether the 9/11 incidents would have occurred had investments in national security been as high as demanded by some

Democrats. We want to call these questions *genuine* 'What if?' questions (and the corresponding policy counterfactuals, *genuine* policy counterfactuals) because, although formally they refer to hypothetical scenarios, their answers prepare the policy maker for a situation in which what he supposes actually happens.

How does one find answers to a genuine 'What if?' question? We contend that such questions are always answered against a causal model in which the control variable figures as a cause and the target variable as an effect.

Philosophers, and some economists, tend to regard priority the other way around. Many thinkers in the Humean tradition view counterfactuals as more fundamental and causal relationships as derivative. David Lewis, for example, develops a counterfactual theory of causation that takes the following quote from Hume as a starting point (quoted from Lewis 1973: 556):

> We may define a cause to be an object followed by another, and where all the objects, similar to the first, are followed by objects similar to the second. Or, in other words where, if the first object had not been, the second never had existed.

Based on this underlying idea, Lewis develops a theory that defines causal relationships in terms of 'chains of counterfactual dependence'. The details of his theory do not matter here. But in our view, it is peculiar to invoke Hume for this project. Hume was an empiricist of a particular brand. For him, a concept was meaningless unless associated with an idea which itself was a copy of a direct sense impression. Now, it is disputable whether we can have direct sense impressions of causal relationships. Hume certainly believed that we cannot. But it is absurd to suppose that there is a sense impression from which we can copy the idea of the 'object that would never have existed'.

Hume's associationist theory of knowledge has long been out of fashion. In its stead, a contemporary empiricist will demand that our claims are made on the basis of the best evidence at hand. But from the evidential point of view, counterfactuals do not seem to fare any better. No (direct) evidence can be had for a statement that describes a state of affairs which is 'counter to the facts'. The usual strategy, then, is to translate the counterfactual into a different kind of statement; for example, a statement about possible worlds or about laws of nature. Although theories of counterfactuals tend to focus on semantic rather than epistemological issues, eventually the problem of how to justify belief in counterfactuals must be addressed. Robert Stalnaker, for example, notes (Stalnaker 1968: 99):

> For similar reasons, the empiricist may be uncomfortable about a theory which treats counterfactuals as literal statements about non-actual situations. Counterfactuals are often contingent, and contingent

> statements must be supported by evidence. But evidence can be gathered, by us at least, only in this universe . . . It is because counterfactuals are generally about possible worlds which are very much like the actual one, and defined in terms of it, that evidence is so often relevant to their truth. When I wonder, for example, what would have happened if I had asked my boss for a raise yesterday, I am wondering about a possible world that I have already roughly picked out. It has the same history, up to yesterday, as the actual world, the same boss with the same dispositions and habits.

But now it seems that the theorist who regards counterfactuals as more fundamental than causal relationships is in a dilemma. The statement into which the counterfactual is translated either does or does not involve causal concepts. If it does involve causal concepts, the theory is circular and counterfactuals have not been shown to be more fundamental than causal relationships (note for example Stalnaker's own use of the notions 'dispositions' and 'habits' – both are, in our view, causal notions). It is a different question whether the circularity is vicious or virtuous. Below, we will discuss a case where certain causal concepts are defined in terms of counterfactuals, which in turn are evaluated in a causal model. But knowledge about the causal concepts defined in this procedure is not required in the model construction. Thus new causal knowledge is extracted (among other things) from old causal knowledge. This kind of circularity is not vicious but it renders the counterfactual definition superfluous.

If, on the other hand, the statement does not involve causal concepts, the theory is likely to fall prey to one or more of the difficulties that agonise all reductive theories of causation. These difficulties include (see for example Cartwright 1983, 1989):

- the problem of concomitant effects
- the problem of co-extensionality
- Simpson's paradox
- . . .

Of course, one cannot prove that all reductive theories, even future ones, will suffer difficulties like these. However, from the past record of failed attempts it seems a reasonable move to give up trying rather than to go on failing.

Witness that our argument here against counterfactual theories of causation differs from the usual strategy employed when these theories are criticised. The usual strategy consists in choosing a particular formulation of a theory, finding a case where one would intuitively say that x causes y but where the theory yields a negative answer (or the other way around). Bill and Suzy throw rocks at a bottle (for this widely discussed example, see for instance Lewis 2000). Bill's rock hits the bottle a split second before Suzy's does and the bottle shatters. Intuitively, we would say that Bill's throwing the rock caused the bottle to shatter. But had he not thrown the rock, the bottle would have shattered anyway. Thus, according to one naïve formulation of the counterfactual theory, Bill's throwing does not come out as the cause of the shattering. And yet, we would say it is the cause. Thus this version of the theory must be false.

These criticisms, then, are based on intuitions or ordinary language usage. The argument put forward here, by contrast, is based on evidential considerations. It maintains that the evidence in favour of a counterfactual can never be better than the evidence in favour of the associated statement about causal relationships. Therefore, we reject the view that counterfactuals are more fundamental.

Thus far, conditional on the soundness of our argument, we can reject counterfactual theories of causation, but this does not give us a causal theory of counterfactuals. Why, then, believe that counterfactuals can only be analysed in terms of causal models? The reasons for this are mainly pragmatic. There is a great variety of kinds of counterfactuals, and each kind demands its own mode of translation. Just consider a few stock philosophical examples:

- If Bizet and Verdi had been compatriots, Bizet would have been Italian.
- If God had had a daughter, her name would have been Zarines.
- If the pressure in this container had been p, its temperature would have been t.
- If Nixon had pushed the button, there would have been a nuclear holocaust.

To answer whether the first counterfactual is true is a matter of logic and meaning. To be compatriots, Bizet and Verdi would have needed to live in the same country. This could have been Italy, France or any other country for that matter. Thus the truth value is indeterminate. But we do not need *causal* knowledge in order to evaluate it. Living in a country does not cause one to be someone else's compatriot. The second counterfactual is metaphorical. In order to answer it, we may want to ask whether Zarines has a number of characteristics we conventionally ascribe to Jesus, say kind-heartedness and generosity. For the third one, we might invoke a model but (according to many) a purely associational model is sufficient. We do not need to know how the pressure value comes about or how it brings about the temperature. Only the fourth counterfactual seems to require causal knowledge, knowledge about the technological and sociological nexus Nixon lived in.

The point is that different kinds of counterfactuals require different kinds of translations. *A priori*, there is no primacy of translation into causal models. But the topic here is not counterfactuals *simpliciter* but counterfactuals relevant to policy making. It seems thus safe to suppose that counterfactuals which can be addressed on the basis of logical or semantic relationships, or which are metaphorical in nature, do not play an important role.

The matter is not so simple with respect to causal versus associational models. Laws of association (or the models that represent them) *can* be used to evaluate counterfactual claims. Just recall that the gas law – an associational law – was used above with reference to the third example. But in the context of policy making in most cases the formulation of the question is at least partly causal in nature. Usually, we ask whether one can use a certain socio-economic variable as a kind of handle to control another variable – the money stock to control prices, investment in schooling to control education and the latter to influence income and inequality, interest rates to control economic activity. Causal models, then, are the appropriate tools to evaluate these kinds of policy counterfactuals.

There is also another reason. Suppose our counterfactual question was of a kind that could be answered on the basis of an associational law. For instance, we want to know what the unemployment rate would have been had inflation been x – without implying either that we would have *caused* the inflation rate to assume that value or that there is a causal relationship between inflation and unemployment. We may then want to use the Phillips curve to answer that counterfactual. The problem with that suggestion is that the Phillips curve and many other economic 'laws' are at best more or less stable empirical relationships but not ones that deserve the name 'law'. We may calculate measures of association between variables but these do not usually sustain counterfactuals about what would happen under interventions. That such 'laws' fare badly at making policy predictions is a sign of that.

On the other hand, all methods in economics designed to answer counterfactual questions are in fact methods of *causal* (rather than associational) inference. Bayes'-nets methods (Pearl 2000; Spirtes *et al.* 2001), the potential outcome framework (Rubin 1974; for an accessible account, see Holland 1988), Heckman's 'counterfactuals' (Heckman 2000, 2001), natural experiments à la Herbert Simon (Simon 1953, 1954), James Hamilton (Hamilton 1997) and others, Kevin Hoover's invariance account (Hoover 2001), all answer causal questions. Importantly, if they fail to answer these questions (because the method has not been applied correctly or it is inadequate for the situation at hand for instance), they do not answer associational questions either – they answer nothing. We do not want to claim that associational models cannot work. But currently it appears to be the best to evaluate policy counterfactuals in terms of causal models.

What then is a causal model? That, we contend, is the central question. What characterises a causal model depends on what one wants to do with the model. Both Pearl and Heckman provide explicit answers to the question of what constitutes a causal model and both give explicit rules for how to assess the truth values of counterfactuals given a causal model. Both use the counterfactuals they evaluate to define new causal notions. But neither is adequate in general for assessing genuine counterfactuals of direct use in planning and policy formation. That is why we urge that more work needs to be done.

An adequate account of how to evaluate counterfactuals from causal models will require:

- a description of what constitutes a causal model;
- rules for how to evaluate counterfactuals given the model;
- an argument to show that the results are correct: the propositions thus evaluated really are the ones we are trying to assess.

Pearl provides all three ingredients, as a good formal account of counterfactuals and causal models should. Despite this, we shall argue, the counterfactuals he assesses are not in general the ones we need for policy and planning, though they may serve a variety of other purposes, including the definition of new causal notions. Heckman has an explicit proposal for the first two. As to the third, we shall show that, trivially, his characterisation captures the concept of *causal contribution* when applied in linear systems, but it will not double as a semantics for the kinds of counterfactuals that can be put directly to use in planning and policy formation.

III

The question of 'implementing the antecedent' is hugely important for policy purposes. In the philosophy literature the topic is usually discussed under the heading of 'backtracking'. The dominant view is that counterfactuals have to be non-backtracking. That is, for the evaluation of a counterfactual it should not matter how the antecedent is brought about. However, in general the evaluation of the kinds of genuine counterfactuals of direct use for policy will be extremely sensitive to the methods of implementation. Consider a standard example from philosophy. Jack and Jim had a quarrel yesterday and Jack is still furious. The question is: If Jim had asked Jack for a favour today, would Jack have obliged? One plausible answer is 'Yes', since for Jim to ask Jack for a favour there would have had to have been no quarrel before (see for instance Lewis 1979).

Implementation matters all the more for policy. Suppose the counterfactual question of interest is 'Had investment in schooling, I, been i (rather than $i^* \tau < i$, the actual value), what would the income, Z, of the cohort have been?' In the real world, the additional money cannot be manna from heaven – it has to be raised somewhere. And it might matter whether it would have been taken from the defence budget or the social security budget. For in either case, it is very likely that the cohort would have been influenced by the loss (for example because some unemployed would have received less benefit or some recruits would not have been hired) but in an asymmetric way (it is plausible to assume, for instance, that the cohort would have been less influenced had the money come from the defence budget).

So to assess the truth value of any particular counterfactual that we hope to use in policy formation we will need to know what changes are supposed to happen, where often the exact details matter. Sometimes when we consider a policy we have a very definite idea in mind how it will be implemented. We shall call the related counterfactuals 'implementation-specific'. At the other end of the scale, we might have no idea at all; the counterfactuals are 'implementation-neutral'. When we evaluate counterfactuals, we had better be clear what exactly we are presuming.

For counterfactuals that are totally implementation-specific, we know exactly what we are asking when we ask 'What would happen if . . . ?' (or at least, we know it for the factors included in the model). For others there are a variety of different strategies we might adopt. For one, we can employ the usual devices for dealing with epistemic uncertainty. We might, for instance, assess the probabilities of the various possible methods of implementation and weight the probability of the counterfactual consequent accordingly. In the methodology of economics literature we find another alternative: Stephen LeRoy and Daniel Hausman focus on counterfactuals that would be true *regardless* of how they are implemented. We begin with LeRoy.

LeRoy's stated concern is with causal ordering among quantities, not with counterfactuals. But, it seems, he equates '*p* causes *q*' with 'if *p* were to change, *q* would change as well' – so long as we give the 'right' reading to the counterfactual. It is his proposed reading for the counterfactual that matters here. It may help to present his brief discussion of a stock philosophical example before looking to more economic cases – the case of birth control pills and thrombosis.

Birth control pills cause thrombosis; they also prevent pregnancy, which is itself a cause of thrombosis. LeRoy assumes that whether a woman becomes pregnant depends on both her sexual activity and whether she takes pills. Now consider: 'What would happen vis-à-vis thrombosis were a particular woman to become pregnant?' That, LeRoy points out, is ambiguous – it depends on whether the change in pregnancy comes about because of a change in pill-taking or because of a change in sexual activity.

In his formal characterisation LeRoy deals with systems of linear deterministic 'reduced form equations': 'In current usage an economic model is a map from a space of exogenous variables – agents' characteristics and resource endowments, for example – to a space of endogenous variables – prices and allocations' (LeRoy 2004: 1). LeRoy assumes that the equations are functionally correct and that variables designated as 'exogenous' are not caused by any of the remaining (endogenous) variables. Since they are functionally related to the endogenous variables, we may assume that either they are causes of some of the endogenous variables or are correlated with such causes. For LeRoy's purposes it seems we must suppose they are causes.

He also supposes that the possible sources of implementation for a change in an endogenous variable are exactly the members of the minimal set of exogenous variables that will fix the value of the endogenous variable according to the economic model. Together these assumptions constitute a characterisation of the causal model that will be used to evaluate counterfactuals.

For an illustration of his semantics, LeRoy considers a familiar supply and demand model:

$$\begin{aligned} q_s &= \alpha_s + \alpha_{sp}p + \alpha_{sw}w \\ q_d &= \alpha_d + \alpha_{dp}p + \alpha_{di}i \\ q_s &= q_d = q. \end{aligned} \tag{1}$$

Here p is price; q, quantity; w, weather; i, income. LeRoy asks what the effect of a change in price would be on the equilibrium quantity. By the conventions just described, a change in price can come about through changes in weather, income or both, and nothing else. But, LeRoy notes, 'any of an infinite number of pairs of shifts in the exogenous variables "weather" and "income" could have caused the assumed changes in price, and these map onto different values of q' (ibid.: 6). Thus the question has no definite answer – it all depends on how the change in p is brought about.

LeRoy contrasts this model with a different one:

$$\begin{aligned} q_s &= \alpha_s + \alpha_{sw}w + \alpha_{sf}f \\ q_d &= \alpha_d + \alpha_{dp}p + \alpha_{di}i \\ q_s &= q_d = q, \end{aligned} \tag{2}$$

where f is fertiliser. Here fertiliser and weather can change the equilibrium quantity, and no matter how they do so, the change in price will be the same. In this case LeRoy is content that the counterfactual, 'If q were to change from taking the value Q to taking the value $Q + \Delta$, p would change from $P = (Q - \alpha_d - \alpha_{di}I)/\alpha_{dp}$ to $P = (Q + \Delta - \alpha_d - \alpha_{di}I)/\alpha_{dp}$', is unambiguous (and true). The lesson he draws is the following (where we substitute counterfactual language for his causal language): '[Counterfactual] statements involving endogenous variables as [antecedents] are ambiguous except when all the interventions consistent with a given change in the [antecedent] map onto the same change in the [consequent]' (ibid.: 6).

The statement as it stands is too strong. Some counterfactuals are, after all, either implicitly or explicitly implementation-specific. In (1) we could ask, for instance, what the value of q would have been had $p = P$ been brought about by $i = I$. What LeRoy offers instead is a semantics for counterfactuals that is, either implicitly or explicitly, implementation-neutral. In this case the consequent should obtain *no matter what possible change occurs to bring the antecedent about.*

Daniel Hausman seems to have distinguished between implementation-specific and implementation-neutral counterfactuals, too, as we do here, though he does not explicitly say so. He considers an example in which engineers designing a nuclear power plant ask, 'What would happen if the steam pipe were to burst?' (Hausman 1998: 122). The answer, he argues, depends on how it will burst. 'Responsible engineers,' he argues, must look to the origins of the burst 'when the consequences of the pipe's bursting depend on what caused it to burst' (ibid.). That is, in these situations responsible engineers will ask implementation-specific 'What if?' questions.

On the other hand, when Hausman turns to providing some constraints that a general semantics for counterfactuals must satisfy if we are to use counterfactuals to establish causal order, he seems to be concerned with implementation-neutral counterfactuals. It is not worth going into the details here; the results are similar to LeRoy's. Any semantics that satisfies Hausman's constraints should give the same result as LeRoy's prescription when restricted to counterfactuals evaluated via what LeRoy calls an 'economic model'.

So we may have counterfactuals that are implementation-specific; we may have ones that assume some one or another of a range of possible implementations; and we may have implementation-neutral ones where we wish to find out what would happen no matter how the change in the antecedent is brought about. For thinking about policy we had better know which kind of counterfactual we are asserting and ensure that our semantics is appropriate to it.

IV

In our analysis of causal models, we begin with Judea Pearl because his account is the most formal, the most complete and the most powerful of any methods currently available, allowing evaluations of complex counterfactuals and their probabilities. Pearl is famous for his work on artificial intelligence, causal search algorithms and reasoning under uncertainty. In his work on causality, he is an advocate of the so-called Bayes'-nets methods. Although Bayes' nets can be put to a large variety of uses, one prominent application lies in causal inference. Here, they function as a tool for learning causal relationships from conditional probabilities on the basis of assumptions about the system considered.

As tools for causal inference, Bayes'-nets methods are part of what we have called the 'Hume programme': the programme that aims at replacing 'problematic' causal notions with 'unproblematic' ones. We must emphasise that Pearl himself is not a strict Humean. He does not want to eliminate causal talk altogether. But he too uses his system in order to explicate more problematic causal notions, for example those relating to singular causation, in terms of less problematic notions, for example that of a causal model. Pearl's semantics for counterfactuals plays a vital role in his explication of causal notions. Since one might be tempted to think it doubles as a semantics for genuine 'What if?' questions, let us examine his account in more detail here.

Pearl envisages counterfactual statements of the form 'The value that Y would have obtained, had X been x' (Pearl 2000: 204, definition 7.1.5 'Counterfactual'). According to him, counterfactual statements are always evaluated within a causal model. A *probabilistic causal model* is defined as a quadruple $<U, V, F, P(u)>$, where (this is actually a merger of two of Pearl's definitions; for the precise formulations, see Pearl 2000: 204f., definitions 7.1.1, 'Causal Model', and 7.1.6, 'Probabilistic Causal Model'):

(i) U is a set of variables that are determined by factors outside the model;
(ii) V is a set of variables that are determined by variables in the model;
(iii) F is a set of functions $[f_1, f_2, \ldots, f_n]$ such that each f_i is a mapping from $U \cap (V \backslash V_i)$ to V_i and such that the entire set F forms a mapping from U to V;
(iv) $P(u)$ is a probability function over the domain of U.

Condition (iii) says that each f_i gives the value of V_i given the values of all other variables in $U \cap V$, which is unique in case the system is recursive or 'acyclic' ('acyclic' is a term from graph theory which basically means that there are no loops in the system). Each f_i is supposed to be functionally correct in the situation modelled and the quantities on the right-hand side are supposed to be a complete set of 'direct causes' of the quantity on the left (a *direct* cause is a cause that makes a contribution to the effect that is not mediated via other variables represented in the model).

An important notion in Pearl's system is that of a *submodel*. A submodel M_x of a model M is relative to realisations x of a set of variables X. It is formed by deleting all functions in M that have members of X as an effect and replacing them with the constant function $X = x$. The effect of action 'set X to x', in short $do(X = x)$, on M is given by the submodel M_x. Finally, a counterfactual of the form 'The value Y that would have obtained, had X been x' on M is defined as the solution of M for Y under the action $do(X = x)$, that is, of M_x. The counterfactual value Pearl also calls 'potential response' and abbreviates it with $Y_x(u)$.

Pearl introduces a theorem according to which a counterfactual can be evaluated using three steps (see Pearl 2000: 206, Theorem 7.1.7). The theorem shows how to assess the conditional probability $P(B_A \mid e)$ of a counterfactual statement of the form 'If it were A then B', given evidence e:

1 Abduction – Update $P(u)$ by the evidence e to obtain $P(u \mid e)$.
2 Action – Modify M by the action $do(A)$, where A is the antecedent of the counterfactual to obtain the submodel M_A.
3 Prediction – Use the modified model . . . to compute the probability of B, the consequence of the counterfactual.

Let us then examine one of Pearl's policy analysis examples so that we can understand the definitions. The example consists of two equations (ibid.: 215ff.; the symbol 'c =' replaces Pearl's '=' and reads 'functionally equivalent and the variables on the right hand side cause the variables on the left hand side'):

$$q \text{ c} = b_1 p + d_1 i + u_1, \tag{3}$$

$$p \text{ c} = b_2 q + d_2 w + u_2, \tag{4}$$

where q is the quantity demanded for some good, p is its price, i is income, w is the wage rate and u_1 and u_2 are error terms. Given the modularity assumption – each equation represents an autonomous mechanism – (3) and (4) constitute a causal model with Q and P as endogenous and U_1, U_2, I and W as the exogenous variables ($M = < [U_1, U_2, I, W], [Q, P], [(3), (4)], P(u) >$).

Pearl considers the policy question 'Given that the observed price is $P = p_0$, what would be the expected value of the demand Q had we controlled the price to be $P = p_1$?' The required probability, $P(Q_{P=p1} \mid P = p_0)$, can be evaluated as follows, using the three steps.

1 Abduction – Update $P(u_1)$ by the evidence $P = p_0$ as well as $I = i$, $W = w$ to obtain $P(u_1 \mid P = p_0, I = i, W = w)$.
2 Action – Modify M by the action $do(P = p_1)$. That is, formulate the submodel $M_{P=p1}$:

$$q \text{ c} = b_1 p + d_1 i + u_1 \tag{3}$$

$$p = p_1. \tag{4'}$$

3 Prediction – Use the modified model to compute the probability of Q. This yields for the expected value of Q:

$$E(Q_{P=p1} \mid p_0, i, w) = b_1 p_1 + d_1 i + E(U_1 \mid p_0, i, w). \tag{5}$$

One of the advantages of Pearl's semantics is that it ties in very nicely with purely philosophical accounts. In particular, it can be shown that under certain conditions Pearl's and Lewis's semantics yield *the same* results for recursive systems (Pearl 2000: 238ff.). In order to achieve this equivalence, the counterfactual $Y_x(u) = y$ in Pearl's notation is equated with Lewis's A → B (and A with the proposition that $X = x$ holds and B with the proposition that $Y = y$ holds).

In Lewis's account, the counterfactual antecedent is brought about 'by miracle'. That is, the laws that are responsible for A to obtain are broken and A is brought about *ex nihilo*. Equivalently, Pearl explicitly breaks all causal laws that have X as an effect and replaces these laws with the constant $X = x$.

What seems to be an advantage from a philosophical point of view is detrimental from the point of view of the policy maker. For Pearl's semantics to work, it is required that the law for each variable in the system (P and Q in the example) be separately manipulable, and he reads the counterfactuals as supposing that the implementations can be represented by changes only in the laws governing the antecedent and no others. To evaluate a counterfactual, we model the implementation in one special way: by destroying one set of causal laws – (4) in the example, replacing it with another set – (4′) in the example, and leaving the rest of the system intact – (3) in the example. It is of course always possible to evaluate a counterfactual according to Pearl's method *assuming* the truth of a model with the right properties (as we have done in the example). Thus, whether or not real socio-economic systems have these properties does not matter. Pearl is explicit, however, that he understands causality and related notions to apply to the world, rather than a model (or our language, say). Models represent real features of the world. For policy considerations, then, we want the model to be true of the world and therefore the system in the world, not just the model, must have the right properties.

Do all socio-economic systems of interest for policy making behave like this? We believe not. We shall illustrate this by pointing to one large class of systems relevant for policy making that is familiar in economics. These are systems where agents' expectations play a role in determining the relationships between the control variable and the target variable (the well-known 'rational expectations' models represent a special case of these). Consider a simple model of the money market:

money demand:

$$m_t = p_t + y_t - \lambda i_t \tag{6}$$

money supply:

$$m_t = m^* + \gamma(y^* - y_{t-1}) + v_t, \tag{7}$$

where m = money, p = price level, y = real output, i = nominal interest rate, m^* = exogenous money supply, y^* = potential output and v = white noise. We present this model for expositional purposes only; we omit the goods side of the economy, which contains the expectations parameters.

Let us consider the counterfactual question 'What would the value of the price level p have been, had the money supply been m_c?' How would we model that counterfactual à la Pearl? He asks us first to replace the feedback mechanism (7) with a constant law:

$$m_t = m_c, \tag{8}$$

where the m_c defines some constant value of m. What would the agents in the economy make out of it? As far as we know, there is no uniform answer in the literature but here are a number of possible replies.

First and foremost, the reply will depend on what the agents know. It seems that the most natural reply to Pearl's question would be that, despite the central bank's regime change, the agents would believe that (7) is still intact. Since m_c is a possible realisation of (7), namely in the case:

$$v_t = m_c - m^* - \gamma(y^* - y_{t-1}),$$

the agents might still use (6)–(7) in their decision making. The point is that Pearl wants us to model the shift from the actual to the counterfactual situation minimally. Thus he replaces one law in the system with another one. If that means that agents' expectations remain the same, the central bank can change as much as it wants, and agents' expectations would be formulated on the basis of (6)–(7) rather than (8). In this case, we would have to formulate Pearl's question more precisely as 'What would the value of the price level p have been, had money supply been m_c due to a realisation of the error term of $v_t = m_c - m^* - \gamma(y^* - y_{t-1})$?' In order to evaluate this counterfactual, we would just update the agent's beliefs using (7)–(8) and the realisation of v_t. Pearl's semantics would not apply.

Alternatively, we could mean the counterfactual to say that central bank policy has now changed (temporarily? permanently?) to a fixed-policy regime. Fixed-policy regimes, however, are usually not modelled as (8) but as a mix of a deterministic term plus a random component. Economic agents are usually not assumed to believe that the central bank can perfectly control the money supply. Thus we have, for instance,

$$m_t = m_c + \varepsilon_t. \tag{9}$$

This comes closest to Pearl's suggestion. It would answer the question 'What would the value of the price level p have been, had money supply been m_c due to (a) a credible switch of monetary policy to a fixed regime and (b) the realisation of $\varepsilon_t = 0$?'

Another alternative is to have the agents believe that the central bank has changed its policy to a so-called regime-switching system. This could be represented by

$$m_t = \begin{cases} m^* + \gamma(y^* - y_{t-1}) + v_t \text{ with probability } q \\ m_c + \varepsilon_t \text{ with probability } (1-q). \end{cases} \tag{10}$$

The counterfactual question we answer with this model would be very similar to the preceding one but we would have 'regime-switching system' instead of 'fixed-policy regime'. None of the preceding models models the expectations formation process of the agents very thoroughly. In particular, one can assume that the agents realise that the central bank's decision to set the value for the money supply is itself an outcome of a rational procedure.

For example, they might believe that the central bank aims at minimising the following loss function:

$$L = E_{t-1}(p_t - z_{t-1})^2, \tag{11}$$

where z is an exogenous target value. The central bank would then set the money supply m_c such that $E_{t-1}(p_t) = z_{t-1}$. A change in m_c, then, would imply that the target variable z has changed.

The moral of this story is that, if expectations matter, Pearl's semantics might not be applicable. Pearl assumes that we can change each law on its own. However, if some laws in a system contain expectations, the *actual* changes may be of little relevance. What matters more is what agents can be made to believe. And in order to make them believe the right thing, many more things might have to change than the one law Pearl envisages.

This is not, however, a problem confined to cases of rational expectations but a general one for Pearl's account. Pearl evaluates one particular kind of implementation-specific counterfactual, where the counterfactual antecedent is brought about by a precise incision that changes only the laws governing the counterfactual antecedent and nothing else *at all* (except what follows causally from just that difference). When we consider implementing a policy, we want to know what would happen were the policy really set in place – and this may well involve a variety of changes beyond those Pearl admits.

The problem is not with implementations that involve complex changes, each of which can be represented in the overall scheme as a change in the value of one of the variables. Although we have not described it here, Pearl offers a detailed account of how to deal both with cases where our actions are complex – they involve changes in a number of different variables at once – and also where our complex actions may be conditional in specified ways on the values that other variables take. The problem is rather with implementations that result in changes in some of the causal laws that describe the system.

We might most easily locate this problem in Pearl's characterisation of a causal model. Recall, a causal model for Pearl contains a set of equations, one for each effect. The effect is to be written on the left-hand side; on the right is a full set of direct causes of that effect, where the values of these causal variables fix the value of the effect. Note first that this means that Pearl's scheme cannot be used to evaluate counterfactuals in systems where causes may act purely probabilistically. Nor can it deal with systems where the causal laws themselves may be affected by our policies; for instance, where the causal laws are tied together so that, if one changes, so too will others, or so too probably will others.

This is a familiar phenomenon and we are not always out of our depths in dealing with it. Occasionally we understand what will happen to the laws of the system as we implement different kinds of change and as a result can provide a scientific account of the system. This is one of the central aims of rational expectations theory, which is why we have used a rational expectations case as an example. Rational expectations methods cannot be encompassed by Pearl's scheme. But this is only an example. The general problem with Pearl's scheme is that it provides no place for encoding information that we might well have about how the changes we envisage will affect the causal laws by which the system operates. His characterisation of what constitutes a causal model is too narrow.

We should note that there is one suggested quick solution to this problem that will not do: simply add more causal laws to express the information needed. In its first preliminary form the answer will not do because we need information about how changes in causal laws are correlated with each other and it does not make sense to write down causal laws that take causal laws themselves as both antecedents and consequents.

A different version of the answer supposes that where these problems arise it must always be because we are focusing on the wrong set of causal laws, a set of causal laws at the 'wrong level'. This view takes as a paradigm the situation in which there is some set of fundamental laws that have no connections with each other: each can change separately. From these, given certain specified boundary conditions, some further less fundamental laws can be derived. Under this picture, if there is a change in some targeted derivative law (keeping the boundary conditions fixed), there must necessarily be a change in the fundamental laws; this in turn might well lead to changes in other derivative laws beyond the one targeted. In this kind of situation, so the answer goes, counterfactuals should be evaluated relative to a causal model that describes the fundamental laws, not one that employs the derivative.

There are a number of problems with this way of defending the universal applicability of Pearl's scheme. The first concerns what the character of economic laws really is. We agree that the story of two tiers of causal laws, one more fundamental than the other, does show how correlations among laws can come about. But we have no reason to think that it is the only way. Moreover, whether there is one tier or many, it does not seem likely – no matter how far 'down' we go – that the principles for economic systems need ever have the kind of independence from each other that Pearl's scheme demands (see for example Estrella and Fuhrer 1999).

The second set of problems concern the more realistic issues of how best to deploy what we know. Even if the two-tier story is the right account for why changes in certain economic principles occur in tandem, it is very often much harder to learn about the 'more fundamental' tier given even our best methods for empirical inference in economics. Nor do we need to know the principles at this level to evaluate our counterfactuals. What we need to know and to encode in our causal models is how the principles we propose using to make counterfactual judgements are likely to change given our envisaged implementations, and that is something we often come to learn, or to have good bets about, without having to calculate it from a 'more fundamental' theory.

Last, we should notice that rational expectations theory itself does not fit Pearl's scheme. Notoriously the theory does offer a two-tier account of why certain 'observational' regularities may well not be stable as we try to use them to implement policy. The observational regularities are supposed to be a consequence of the behaviour of rational agents and those agents will – because they are rational – change their mode of behaviour if they foresee that a new policy will be implemented. Thus the observational regularities that arise under the older modes of behaviour may well no longer obtain were the policy to be implemented (or were agents to expect it to be implemented).

Nevertheless the methods suggested by rational expectations theory for calculating what would happen were a new policy undertaken are more complex than those proposed by Pearl. We do not just replace the law for the policy variable with a new one setting the value at the proposed level, then deduce from the 'fundamental' laws in their original unchanged form with parameters fixed what the values of the target variables will be. For there is an interaction envisaged between the two tiers – a 'self-consistency' requirement is invoked. The variables that appear in the 'fundamental' laws include expectations (in the sense of beliefs and predictions) that the agents have about macro variables; the values of these are supposed to match the expectations (in the statistical average sense) of those macro variables in the less fundamental laws. This provides a method – albeit not formalised – for calculating simple (non-complex, non-conditional) counterfactuals. But so far as we can see, it cannot be fitted into Pearl's scheme.

Why does Pearl focus on this one kind of implementation, where variables change as the counterfactual antecedent is implemented, but no laws, excepting those governing the counterfactual antecedent? One reason is to resolve the problems of ambiguity. As we discussed in Section III ordinary language counterfactuals are open. They have different truth values depending on how they are supposed to be implemented. We have advocated disambiguating the counterfactual before trying to evaluate it; so too does Pearl. His detailed work on how to assess counterfactuals with complex and conditional antecedents is testimony to that.

Pearl is also worried about the problems of ambiguity that arise if laws can change. His solution here is to treat all counterfactuals the same. He insists that the laws of a causal model can be changed one at a time and that the right reading of the counterfactual is the one that supposes that that is just what happens: the laws governing the antecedent change and only those laws. This will work sometimes, but, as we have argued, it does not allow us to answer all the 'What if?' questions we want to ask. On the other hand, Pearl's is the most complete and well-developed formal apparatus available for assessing counterfactuals in science. This is why we are keen to bring this issue to the fore.

One of the tasks that Pearl's particular semantics undertakes is that recommended by the Hume programme, that is, the elimination of 'problematic' causal notions in favour of non-causal ones. For example, Pearl defines *the causal effect* of one variable on another in terms of counterfactuals and then shows how to calculate the causal effect from the probabilities of propositions that employ neither causal nor counterfactual notions. As we noted, this is just the kind of programme that philosophers have been heavily engaged in; in particular Pearl's account is very similar to that of David Lewis (see Lewis 1973, 1979, 1986). Pearl's account like Lewis's is skewed towards the job of evaluating counterfactuals that can deliver the right verdicts on the targeted causal concepts. Correlatively it fails to provide the right answers to large numbers of genuine 'What if?' questions we want to ask.

What then of our claim above that Pearl provides a proof that his semantics is indeed a semantics for counterfactuals? The proof is in the form of a representation theorem. He first provides some independent characteristics that counterfactuals are supposed to satisfy, then shows that these characteristics hold for the propositions his semantics evaluates and, conversely, that, for any set of propositions for which these characteristics hold, there is a causal model that renders them true under his semantics.

The trouble is with Pearl's characteristics for counterfactuals. One is called *composition*. Pearl describes it this way: 'Composition states that, if we force a variable (W) to a value w that it would have had without our intervention, then the intervention will have no effect on other variables in the system' (Pearl 2000: 229). Composition is fine when antecedents are implemented by miracles of the kind employed by Pearl and Lewis. But it is not a characteristic of counterfactuals in general. Most ways of implementing a counterfactual antecedent will produce knock-on effects different from what would have obtained had the antecedent occurred without the implementation. That is particularly true of the kinds of real-life implementations available to us in complex policy situations.

Pearl's scheme can serve as a model for what is needed. It has the three requisite ingredients for a semantics for counterfactuals and it is both rich in detail and formally set up to allow for the proof of a variety of important and interesting results. But it itself does not do the job of providing a semantics for genuine 'What if?' counterfactuals.

V

Counterfactuals are an important topic in economic methodology today, especially since they have been championed by Nobel Prize winner James Heckman (Heckman 2000, 2001). Superficially the way the counterfactuals are shown to work by Heckman is much as we have urged. A causal model is postulated and rules are supplied for how to calculate answers to specific 'What if?' questions from the model. But when it comes to setting counterfactuals to use there is a big difference. For the counterfactual analysis provided by Heckman cannot in general answer 'What if?' questions of the kind we pose in planning, policy and evaluation. Nor does Heckman claim that it can. The analysis is offered, rather, as in the philosophy literature, as a causal surrogate. We wish to underline the fact that the two jobs are different. We cannot assume that what serves for the one job will serve for the other.

This does not mean, however, that the causal-surrogate counterfactuals are irrelevant for policy and planning. We shall point out that they can serve as *inputs* for constructing the causal models employed in generating the genuine policy counterfactuals needed for planning as outputs. This will require, however, a weaker interpretation than that put on the causal-surrogate counterfactuals.

As in the philosophy literature, Heckman's counterfactuals are offered as a way of defining causal concepts in terms of presumably less problematic non-causal concepts. We propose to view them instead as a way for finding out about independently understood causal relationships in special situations. Entirely separate sets of considerations may then tell us whether we can export knowledge about these causal relationships to new situations, for which we need to construct causal models and generate counterfactual outputs.

What kinds of considerations are required? The distinction between internal and external validity is of use here. A causal claim is internally valid if it is correct for the experimental system in which it was established. By contrast, the claim is externally valid if in addition it is correct for (possibly non-experimental) situations outside the original system (see Chapter 5). There is no systematic answer available to the question of how to establish external validity. We make only one small contribution here. The counterfactuals that are on offer as causal surrogates have little external validity when they are conceived as counterfactuals. Indeed they very often do not even make sense in the new situation. They only become relevant if they can be taken as measures of causal relationships that hold in the situations in which the causal-surrogate counterfactuals are evaluated and that might (or might not) hold in the target situation.

We have talked about the importance of counterfactuals to questions of policy. Similarly when we want to evaluate the effectiveness of a trial programme we need answers to counterfactual questions: What if the programme had not existed? Or had existed in some other form? Or were set up more widely without the trial controls? These are just the kinds of questions Heckman considers in his applied work on the evaluation of labour-market programmes, where he is at pains to point out that the question itself must be carefully formulated.

We have stressed the ambiguity in ordinary counterfactuals about how the antecedent will be implemented. Heckman points out other sources of ambiguity. We may for instance want to know what the wages of workers in the population at large would have been had the programme not existed; more commonly we end up asking what the wages of workers *in the programme* would have been. Or we may want to know what the GDP would have been without the programme. We also need to take care about the contrast class: Do we want to know the difference between the results of the programme and those that would have occurred had no alternatives been present or the difference compared to other programmes, real or envisaged?

Heckman begins his treatment with *causal functions*. As with LeRoy's starting point, causal functions are a special kind of sparse causal model. The models describe special kinds of systems, systems that mimic experiments: 'Causal functions are ... derived from conceptual experiments where exogenously specified generating variables are varied . . . The specification of these hypothetical variations is a crucial part of model specification and lies at the heart of any rigorous definition of causality' (Heckman 2001: 14).

Heckman tells us three things about causal functions: (i) They 'describe how each possible vector of generating variables is mapped into a resulting outcome', where the generating variables 'completely determine' the outcome (ibid.: 12). (ii) They 'derive from' – or better, we think, 'describe' – conceptual experiments. (iii) Touching on questions of realism and of model choice, models involving causal functions are always underdetermined by evidence; hence, as Heckman sees it, causality is just 'in the head' since the models relative to which it is defined are just in the head. From this we take it that causal functions represent (a probably proper subset of) the causal principles under which these special experiment-like systems operate, where the right-hand-side variables – the ones Heckman calls the 'generating variables' – form a minimal complete set of causes of the quantity represented on the left (or, keeping in mind Heckman's view that causality is only relative to a model, the right-hand-side variables record what the model designates as causes) and where each cause can each vary independently of the others; that is, they are variation-free: a set of variables (x_1, $x_2, \ldots, x_n$) is variation-free if $(x_1, x_2, \ldots, x_n) \in X_1 \times X_2 \times \ldots \times X_n$. This is why we say that Heckman's starting point is a causal model.

Imagine that the causal function for an outcome y is given by

$$y \text{ c} = g(x_1, \ldots, x_n). \tag{12}$$

The *causal* or *counterfactual effect* (Heckman seems to use the terms 'causal effect' and 'counterfactual effect' interchangeably) of x_j on y fixing the remaining factors in the causal function is defined thus:

Causal effect of x_j on y:

$$[\Delta y/\Delta x_j = x'_j - x''_j] \equiv g(x_1, \ldots, x'_j, \ldots x_n) - g(x_1, \ldots, x''_j, \ldots x_n). \tag{13}$$

Read in terms of counterfactuals we have here the evaluation, relative to a specific assignment of values to all x_j, $j \neq i$, of the difference between the value y would have were $x_i = x_i'$ and the value y would have were $x_i = x_i''$.

As Heckman insists, in order for this definition 'to be meaningful requires that the x_j can be independently varied when the other variables are fixed so that there are no functional restrictions connecting the arguments ... it is thus required that these variables be variation-free' (Heckman 2001: 18). We shall call the counterfactual effect as thus defined a *Galilean effect* since it is just the kind of effect we look for in a Galilean experiment, where a single cause is varied controlling for all other relevant features in order to observe the effect of that cause 'acting alone' (cf. the discussion of Galilean idealisation in the previous chapter).

Heckman considers simultaneous supply and demand equations as an example. For simplicity we can look at the specific equations that we have already considered in discussing LeRoy, where we have added the additional equilibrium constraint on price:

$$\begin{aligned} q_s &= \alpha_s + \alpha_{sp} p_s + \alpha_{sw} w \\ q_d &= \alpha_d + \alpha_{dp} p_d + \alpha_{di} i \\ q_s &= q_d = q \\ p_s &= p_d = p. \end{aligned} \tag{14}$$

Heckman points out that these equations do not fit Pearl's scheme since they are not recursive and hence Pearl's method for assessing counterfactuals will not apply. This fits with familiar remarks about these kinds of systems: p and q are determined jointly by exogenous factors. It seems then that it makes no sense to ask about how much a change in p will affect a change in q. To the contrary, according to Heckman. We can still assess causal efficacy using his definition – so long as certain 'exclusion' conditions are met.

Say we want to assess the causal/counterfactual effect of demand price on quantity demanded. We first look to the reduced form equations:

$$\begin{aligned} q &= (z_d, z_s) \\ p &= (z_d, z_s), \end{aligned} \tag{15}$$

where z_d is the vector of exogenous variables in the demand equations and z_s, those in the supply equations. In LeRoy's equations (14), $z_d = i$ and $z_s = w$. Heckman takes these to be causal functions, otherwise the causal model has not properly specified the 'exogenous' variables. That means that the exogenous variables are 'generating variables' for p and q and that they are variation free. Now the task is easy: 'Assuming that some components of [z_d] do not appear in [z_s], that some components of [z_s] do not appear in [z_d], and that those components have a non-zero impact on price, one can use the variation in the excluded variables to vary [p_d or p_s in the reduced form equations] while holding the other arguments of those equations fixed' (Heckman 2001: 36). The result (using the equality of p_d and p_s and of q_d and q_s) is

$$\partial q_d/\partial p_d - (\partial q/\partial z_s(e))/(\partial p/\partial z_s(e)), \tag{16}$$

where $z_s(e)$ is a variable in z_s that is excluded from z_d and that, as he puts it, 'has an impact on' p_d. In (14) this job can be done by w; the causal effect thus calculated of p_d on q_d is α_{dp}.

Notice how much causality is involved here. By definition we are supposed to be evaluating the change in q_d holding fixed all the factors in a causal function for q_d except p_d. What we actually do is hold fixed z_d while z_s varies. Presumably this is okay because z_s is a cause of p_d that can produce variations in p_d while z_d is fixed; and z_d being fixed matters because z_d constitutes, along with p_d, a minimal full set of causes of q_d. So when the exclusion condition is satisfied, the demand equation is a causal function and the counterfactual definition of causal effect is meaningful.

Now consider a slightly altered set of equations:

$$\begin{aligned} q_s &= \alpha_s + \alpha_{sp}p_s + \alpha_{sw}w + \alpha_{si}i \\ q_d &= \alpha_d + \alpha_{dp}p_d + \alpha_{di}i + \alpha_{dw}w \\ q_s &= q_d = q \\ p_s &= p_d = p. \end{aligned} \tag{14'}$$

In this model the demand equation cannot be treated as a causal function and the question of the causal effect of demand price on quantity demanded is meaningless. This is true despite the fact that α_{dp} still appears in the equation and it still represents something – something much the same one would suppose – about the bearing of p_d on q_d. The intermediate case seems even stranger. Imagine that $\alpha_{sw} = 0$. Now α_{sp} measures a Galilean effect but α_{dp} does not.

We propose an alternative interpretation of what is going on. We begin with causal principles. One can be a realist about the principles of a causal model. They are correct if and only if they approximate well enough to the causal laws that govern the operation of the system in question. Heckman, it seems, is not a realist. But that does not matter here since he himself has introduced the notion of a causal function. A causal principle is just like a causal function but without the restriction that the causes (or 'generating variables') are variation-free. We shall continue to restrict attention to linear causal models of the kind both LeRoy and Heckman use for illustration. Then define for any linear causal model, *the contribution a cause* x_c *makes to an effect* x_e ≡ the coefficient of x_c in any causal principle for x_e in the model. This supposes that all principles in the model with x_c on the right-hand side and x_e on the left will have the same coefficient. This will be the case given a proper statement of 'transitivity' and the definitions for the form of causal principles outlined in Cartwright (2003). On a minor point, for any linear causal model where Heckman's measure for the causal/counterfactual effect of x_c on x_e applies, it has the same value as the contribution x_c makes to x_e.

Given this characterisation the contribution of p_d to q_d is the same in (14) and (14′). What is different is that in (14) we have a particular way to find out about it that is not available in (14′). Equation (14) is what we call *an epistemically convenient system* (for a definition see Cartwright 2003): having an epistemically convenient system implies among other things that it is possible to find out what a cause, x_c, contributes to an effect, x_e, in one particular simple way – hold fixed all the other contributions that add up to make the effect the size it is, then vary the cause and see how much x_e varies. Any difference has to be exactly the contribution that x_c adds. This does not mean, however, that, for systems where this independent variation is not possible, all is lost. There are hosts of other legitimate ways of defending claims about the size of causal contributions that apply both in systems with independent variation and in those without.

There are two advantages to the account that takes Heckman's causal surrogate counterfactuals as measures of causal contributions rather than as mere counterfactuals. First, few systems we confront are governed by principles in which the causes are variation-free. The vast majority are not. In these systems Heckman's counterfactuals are irrelevant.

Second, even if we are studying a system where the causes are variation-free, there is a puzzle about why we should wish to ask just these implementation-specific questions. If we are thinking of setting policy or evaluating the success of some programme in the system, then these, with their special method of implementation, might be relevant sometimes. But there is no necessity to implement policies in the single way highlighted by Heckman; generally we would want to consider a variety of different methods of implementation and frequently to assess implementation-neutral counterfactuals as well. Even where causes are variation-free, the counterfactual changes that Heckman studies generally have no privileged role.

There are two familiar enterprises where they do have a special role. The first is in trying to determine if, and to what degree, one factor contributes causally to another. In an epistemically convenient system we can ask Galilean-type counterfactual questions; and the answers we obtain will double as answers to our causal questions. They are a tool for finding out answers to our causal questions. But note that they are only a tool for finding out about causes in special epistemically convenient systems. For other systems we cannot even ask these counterfactual questions, let alone let the answers to them supply our causal answers as well.

The other is in Heckman's own field, evaluation. In setting up new programmes, we might try to set them up in such a way that the causal contribution they make to the result can be readily disentangled from the contribution of other factors. Of particular concern are other factors that might both contribute to the effect independently of the programme and also make it more likely that an individual entered (or failed to enter) the programme. If we can arrange the setup of our programme so that it is epistemically convenient, then again we can ask Galilean counterfactual questions – 'What difference would there be in outcome with the programme present versus the programme absent, holding fixed all other contributions to the outcome?' And again these counterfactual questions will tell us the contribution the programme makes, since in these circumstances the difference in outcome between when the programme is present and when it is absent must be exactly the contribution the programme makes. So we can use information about Galilean effects to learn about the causal contributions of the programme we set up. Still, all we learn is about that programme in those special epistemically convenient circumstances.

In either case, whether it be experimental systems or programme setups that we engineer to make the measurement of causal contributions easy, we need to ask, 'Why should we be interested in causal contributions in these special – and rare – kinds of systems?' The answer is clear. Generally we want this information because we hope it will tell us something about causal contributions in other systems. But we confront here the familiar problem of internal and external validity. In an epistemically convenient (linear) system, using counterfactual differences as a measure of causal contributions is provably valid: internal to the situation this method is bound to give us correct results about the question of interest. But nothing said in this discussion bears on external validity: When will the results that we can be sure are correct in an epistemically convenient system hold elsewhere?

So how do these odd Galilean counterfactuals bear on more useful 'What if?' counterfactuals? In a very indirect way, it seems. We can use Galilean counterfactuals to tell us about causal contributions in Galilean experiments. Then, to the extent that we can expect the facts about causal contributions to remain stable across situations of interest, we can use the information about causal contributions in Galilean experiments to help build causal models for new non-Galilean situations. And we can use the causal models so constructed for these new situations to answer real 'What if?' questions that we want to ask about these new situations. Galilean counterfactuals are one of many inputs in a multi-step process that yields as outputs counterfactuals of immediate use in policy and planning. Figure 10.1 lays out this picture.

It is important to stress, however, that assumptions about when information about causal contributions learned in one setting will obtain in others are not justified by anything we have discussed so far, and in particular not by any information about counterfactuals of the kinds we have explored. Showing that results on causal contributions have external validity – and how far and of what kind – requires a different methodology altogether (cf. the results of Chapter 9). This is one of the reasons we have been at pains to distinguish input counterfactuals from output counterfactuals.

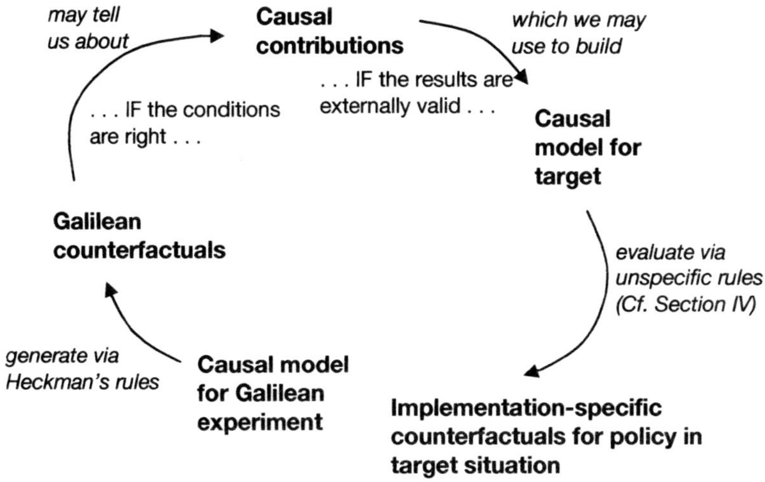

Figure 10.1 How counterfactuals relate to causal models.

Recent work in economics like that of LeRoy and Heckman provides some clear formal characterisations of how to evaluate special counterfactuals with very particular assumptions about their methods of implementation. But they leave us a long way from any characterisation of counterfactuals whose implementations are the ones we are generally interested in. For we have no good rules for how to judge external validity; that is, for when we can export what we learn from a Galilean effect to build a causal model for a non-Galilean situation. And then, as we saw in discussing Pearl, we have only a meagre start on how to use a causal model to answer the 'What if?' questions we ask for planning and policy.

VI

The lesson we want to draw from the preceding discussion can be captured by the slogan 'Disambiguate before you evaluate'. All three accounts we have been looking at – LeRoy, Pearl and Heckman – provide an unambiguous semantics for counterfactuals. But they do so at the cost of seriously constraining the range of admissible counterfactual questions. More importantly, they often provide a semantics for counterfactuals that has no relevance for policy analysis whatsoever. What we urge instead is to disambiguate the question first and subsequently use a semantics that is tied closely to precisely that kind of question.

First and foremost, we will need to know whether the counterfactual at stake is a Heckman-style Galilean counterfactual of the kind we have discussed in Section V or a genuine policy counterfactual as discussed in Sections II–IV. A Galilean counterfactual helps us to evaluate the contribution of a causal factor to a quantity of interest in very specific – that is, epistemically convenient – systems. Without further tests, the results of this evaluation tell us nothing beyond the experimental system at hand. But we may be lucky and find that test results are exportable or 'externally valid'. In this case, we can use the knowledge gained in one particular system as a building block for the evaluation of a genuine policy counterfactual.

Let us assume that we have knowledge of all causal laws governing a particular socio-economic system. If we now want to evaluate a genuine policy counterfactual, we have to decide whether it is meant in an implementation-specific or implementation-neutral sense. Implementation-neutral counterfactuals are true no matter how the antecedent is brought about. These come in particularly handy in case we don't know how to implement the antecedent. But this kind of epistemic uncertainty is neither necessary nor sufficient for evaluating counterfactuals in an implementation-neutral way. On the one hand, we might just want to know what the answer to our counterfactual question was in case it didn't matter how we implemented the antecedent. On the other hand, there are other strategies available for situations of epistemic uncertainty. And these are important if the causal structure of the socio-economic system that we contemplate does not lend itself to implementation-neutral evaluation (recall for instance that there was no answer to LeRoy's question for system (1), where the price variable appeared in both equations).

Turning to implementation-specific counterfactuals, finally, once more both metaphysics and epistemology matter. For systems which are characterised by the axioms of Pearl's formalism, we can use his semantics and implement the antecedent without disturbing any other relationship in the system. But for many socio-economic systems that will not do, so we may have to use the more involved (and less formal) modelling strategies of, say, rational expectations economics. In both cases we assume that we have a clear idea of how the antecedent is to be brought about.

If we do not have a clear idea, we must fall back on alternative strategies to deal with epistemic uncertainty. Though we may not know for sure where the money for the new schooling programme comes from, we may know that it is far more likely to be raised by a tax increase than by cutting defence. Thus we can use our best guess as to the probability of each possible implementation and weigh the results accordingly.

The main message of our musings about the use of counterfactuals in policy advice is, then, to make the underlying assumptions as transparent as possible. Answering a counterfactual question can amount to a myriad of things. We believe we had better be clear about precisely what issues are involved and give answers that are tailored to the specific case at hand, rather than provide a semantics that yields results across the board but in so doing fails to resolve the question we are in fact interested in.

Glossary

Allais Paradox An empirical violation of the von Neumann–Morgenstern theory of choice under uncertainty. In a large number of experimental studies subjects have been found to violate the Independence of Irrelevant Alternatives axiom, which says that, if X is preferred to Y out of the set of alternatives $\{X, Y\}$, then introducing a third alternative Z should not reverse the preference between X and Y in the larger set of alternatives $\{X, Y, Z\}$. More formally, letting '$X > Y$' denote 'X is (strictly) preferred to Y', the axiom says 'If $X > Y$, then $pX + (1 - p)Z > pY + (1 - p)Z$ for all Z and $p \in (0, 1)$'. Here is a numerical example. Respondents can choose between two lotteries X and Y, where X yields \$1,000 for sure and Y yields \$1,500 with a 80% chance and zero otherwise. A great majority of respondents chooses X over Y. Let Z now be \$0 and $p = 25\%$. The compound lottery $pY + (1 - p)Z$, where people win \$1,500 with a 20% chance and zero otherwise, is then preferred by a great majority to the compound lottery $pX + (1 - p)Z$, where people win \$1,000 with a 25% chance and zero otherwise. Intuitively, this kind of behaviour makes some sense: people prefer receiving a certain payoff for sure to gambling, even if the expected value of the gamble is higher; however, if they are gambling anyway, they prefer the lottery with the higher expected payoff. This phenomenon led to various reformulations and generalisations of expected utility theory aimed at rationalising the observed choice behaviour.

Analysis and Synthesis, Method of A scientific method that goes back to at least Aristotle. The principal idea is that complex phenomena are to be studied by breaking them down into simple and manageable parts, investing the behaviour of the parts severally, and then deriving results for the complex by adding up the operation of the parts using a law of composition. In economics, John Stuart Mill championed the use of this method. He thought that economic phenomena could be studied analogously to certain mechanical phenomena. Empirical work however suggests that what an economic factor does depends on the whole setting in which it is embedded, so that the method of analysis and synthesis is less useful in this context.

Auctions An auction is an institution in which goods are sold to the highest bidder following specific rules. Some important types are as follows. In an *English auction* bids are made in a succession of rounds (starting with the reservation price in the first round), and in each round the bid is increased by a minimum increment. It is finished when no one is willing to go above the last bid made. In a *Dutch auction* the price is gradually lowered until there is a bid. In a *first-price auction*, the highest bidder pays the price of his or her bid. In a *second-price auction*, the highest bidder receives the auctioned good but pays only the price of the second-highest bid. In an *open auction* bids are announced publicly while in a *sealed-bid auction* bids are known only to the bidder and the auctioneer.

Capabilities In Amartya Sen's theory of justice alternative combinations of functionings.

Checkerboard Model Thomas Schelling's model of geographic segregation (Schelling 1971, 1978). Schelling asks us to distribute pennies and dimes (representing two social groups such as men and women, blacks and whites, students and tutors or members of two opposing football teams) randomly on a checkerboard and then to use some dynamic rule of individual decision. For instance, any penny will move unless at least a third of its neighbours are also pennies and vice versa for dimes. Using different initial distributions and different dynamic rules we will see that patterns of segregation will often emerge. That is, the initial randomly distributed coins will end up in relatively homogenous penny areas and dime areas.

Context of Discovery versus Context of Justification A distinction between the process by which a scientific theory is generated and the process by which reasons for believing it are provided. According to the logical positivists and Karl Popper only the latter but not the former can be rationalised. That is, these philosophers hold that there are certain fixed rules that describe and prescribe how to justify a scientific theory but no such rules pertain to the invention of theories. The latter is thus a matter of mere psychology, not philosophy.

Deduction A type of inference which consists in a sequence of sentences within a formal system of proof. Typically it begins with an axiom and each subsequent element is either an axiom or a sentence that follows from the preceding statements by a rule of transformation of the system.

Deductive–Nomological Model of Scientific Explanation A theory of scientific explanation according to which an explanation is a type of argument. The premisses of the argument form the so-called explanans (or 'that which explains') and the conclusion forms the explanandum (or 'that which is to be explained'). The model is 'deductive' because the explanandum is thought to follow deductively from the explanans; it is 'nomological' because at least one of the premisses must be a law of nature (from Greek *nómos* = habit, law).

Deductivism A perspective on science according to which scientists proceed by conjecturing theories, deriving predictions from them and testing these predictions against observations. If the prediction is borne out by the data, the theory is regarded as 'corroborated' and can temporarily be retained; if it conflicts with the data, the theory is regarded as 'falsified' and must be discarded. Strict deductivism means that we never have any positive reason to believe in a theory; a corroborated theory is one that has not been falsified yet. This view is mostly associated with Karl Popper.

Dictator Game There are two players in a dictator game. The game consists of only one move: player 1 divides the total of $\$M$ between himself and player 2. Since player 2 has no say in the game, the profit-maximising strategy for player 1 is to keep the total $\$M$. In experiments, subjects typically give some share to player 2, albeit smaller shares than in the ultimatum game.

Endowment Effect The empirical phenomenon that people tend to value a good higher once their property rights to it have been established; in other words that people tend to ask for more money to give up a good they own than they would be willing to pay to acquire it. A significant implication of the divergence between 'willingness to pay' and 'compensation to accept' is that the Coase Theorem does not hold. The Coase Theorem, which is of great importance for economic analyses of government regulation, says that in the absence of transaction costs the allocation of resources between bargaining parties is independent of the initial distribution of property rights. Results of field experiments suggest that the endowment effect shrinks with increasing market experience of the participants.

Equation of Exchange Irving Fisher's version of the quantity theory. In this formulation, $MV = PT$, where: M – money stock; V – velocity of money (the number of times a monetary unit is exchanged during a given period); P – price level; and T – trade (that is, GDP).

Expensive Tastes, Problem of The egalitarian, a person who believes that a just distribution of resources is one that leaves everyone equal, faces the issue 'Equality of what?' for we could require to distribute income, wealth, primary goods (such as health etc.), capabilities or what have you equally, and each answer would yield a different result. The welfare egalitarian answers that 'welfare' or 'utility' is the unit that requires an equal distribution. Suppose that some society has managed to distribute welfare equally. But now consider a person who develops 'expensive tastes', who, say, takes a wine-tasting course, learns to appreciate the differences between different types of oysters and so on. That person's welfare will drop if he or she is endowed with only ordinary wine and food. It will thus take more of the society's resources to maintain that person's welfare. That is, everyone else's welfare will have to be reduced in order to satisfy him or her. Most people would judge that this is not what justice requires and that hence welfare egalitarianism must be wrong.

Falsificationism The thesis, originally due to Karl Popper, that the demarcation criterion between scientific and 'non-scientific' statements is falsifiability. Only statements that in principle could empirically be shown to be false count as scientific. This is sometimes accompanied by the view that science proceeds by conjecturing bold hypotheses and attempts to refute them. In economic methodology, falsificationism has been very popular until recently. Contributions include Blaug (1992), Boland (2003) and de Marchi (1988).

Framing Strategic choices in games appear to depend on how the alternatives are presented to the participants, how they are 'framed'. Playing a dictator game with identical payoffs, for example, the dictator will make different offers depending on whether the game was described as the 'Let's split a pie' game or the 'Dutch tipping' game (offers tend to be higher in the first game). To give another couple of examples, it matters whether people face a '70 per cent survival rate' or a '30 per cent chance of dying' and whether they are presented with probabilities or natural frequencies.

Functionings In Amartya Sen's theory of justice the various things a person may value doing or being, such as being adequately nourished, being healthy, being mobile, being able to take part in social life and having self-respect.

General Equilibrium Theory A branch of theoretical economics that studies the interaction between consumption, production, saving and investment. Unlike partial equilibrium theory, general equilibrium theory seeks to solve the coordination problem for all markets simultaneously.

Generalised Axiom of Revealed Preference The axiom says 'If an allocation X is revealed preferred to Y, then Y cannot be strictly directly revealed preferred to X' (with slight alterations from Varian 1992: 132). Essentially, this is a restriction that enables observed choice behaviour to be rationalised by an underlying utility maximisation process.

Hume's Fork According to David Hume, all statements fall into one of two categories: relations of ideas and matters of fact. Relations of ideas can be verified by logic alone; matters of fact require experience and observation. One major consequence of this view is the idea that very general principles about the world such as 'all events have a cause' are themselves empirical, they follow the same rules of verification and therefore can always turn out to be false.

Induction The inference from statements about past observations to either universally qualified statements or statements about the future. An instance of an inductive inference is, for example, 'All hitherto observed swans have been white; therefore, all swans (including as of yet unborn ones) are white'. David Hume pointed out that such inferences are not certain or 'truth preserving' because it is always conceivable that some future instance turns out not to fall into the observed pattern. Ever since Hume philosophers have been wondering how significant his insight really is.

Induction, New Riddle of Suppose that all emeralds examined before a certain time *t* are green. This evidence, says Nelson Goodman, equally supports two alternative hypotheses, namely 'All emeralds are green' and 'All emeralds are grue', where 'grue' means 'Examined before *t* and green or unexamined and blue' (Goodman 1954, Ch. III). That is, depending on how one describes one's evidence, the evidence can lend support to conflicting hypotheses. Philosophers debate whether Goodman's problem is just a different way of stating Hume's problem of induction or whether it is a problem in its own right.

Inductivism (in economics) Besides (hypothetico-)deductivism, inductivism is a second major perspective on science. It holds that scientists proceed by collecting evidence and generalising from the individual instances to laws and causal relations. To my knowledge, in economics inductivism was explicitly endorsed as a scientific method only by the German Historical School.

Innate Ideas In Early Modern Philosophy (roughly, the period in Western philosophy that began with Bacon or Descartes and culminated in Kant) the term 'idea' denotes an aspect of the contents of our minds, i.e. a perception, feeling or thought. One major issue between the empiricists (most notably, Locke, Berkeley and Hume) and the rationalists (most notably, Descartes, Spinoza and Leibniz) was regarding the existence of innate ideas, that is, principles every human is endowed with by virtue of being human. John Locke famously held that there are no such things as innate ideas; when a human is born, his or her mind is a 'blank slate'.

Kind, Interactive A term due to Ian Hacking (Hacking 1999, Ch. 4). Interactive kinds are objects or people the classification of which or whom interacts with our theories and ideas about them. Whether or not an electron is 'charged' is independent of our theories and ideas about electrons in a way that whether or not a child is 'hyperactive' is not.

Kind, Natural A classification of objects or people that is 'natural' rather than 'artificial'. Usually, the classified objects or people are thought to share essential properties – properties without which they would not be the object or person they are classified as.

Lemons Model George Akerlof's model of markets in which quality matters and in which information can be distributed asymmetrically. In his seminal paper, Akerlof showed that markets can break down when sellers know more about the quality of some good than buyers (Akerlof 1970). Akerlof himself applied the model to second-hand car markets (hence the name 'lemons' model; a poor-quality car is called a 'lemon' in the United States), and insurance, labour and credit markets. The paper is generally regarded as pivotal for the development of the economics of information.

Mill's Methods John Stuart Mill developed some of Francis Bacon's methods of causal inference and systematised these as the 'Method of Agreement', the 'Method of Difference', the 'Method of Residues' and the 'Method of Concomitant Variations'. The Method of Agreement seeks two situations in which the phenomenon under investigation occurs and that differ in all but one factor. That factor is then inferred to be the cause or effect of the phenomenon. The Method of Difference seeks two situations in which the phenomenon occurs that are identical with respect to all factors but one. That factor is then inferred to be the cause or the effect of the phenomenon. This is essentially the method of controlled experimentation. The Method of Residues deducts from a phenomenon a part that is known to be caused by certain factors. The residue is then inferred to be caused by the remaining factors. The Method of Concomitant Variations seeks phenomena that systematically co-vary and infers that one is the cause of the other or that they are connected through some other fact of causation.

Operationalism (also Operationism) A theory of concept formation according to which the meaning of the concepts of a scientific theory consist in the measurement procedure or operation that connects the concepts with observations. Behaviourism and revealed preference theory are related doctrines. Behaviourism in psychology is the view that (observable) behaviour defines corresponding mental states. The revealed preference theory in economics defines utility in terms of observable choices.

'Post hoc ergo propter hoc' Fallacy From Latin 'After this, therefore because of this'. We cannot infer from the fact that an event *A* is (regularly) followed by another event *B* that *A* is the cause of *B*. For example, a common cause that precedes both *A* and *B* may be responsible for the succession of the two events.

Prisoner's Dilemma The story behind the Prisoner's Dilemma, one of the most widely discussed scenarios in game theory, is the following. Two prisoners are being interrogated separately. The judge makes each of them an offer: if one confesses and the other denies, the confessing villain is released and the other receives a very long sentence; if both confess, both get a long sentence; and if both deny, both get a short term in prison. Given this structure, both prisoners have an incentive to confess: given the choice of the other, choosing to confess yields the better result (given prisoner 2 chooses to deny, confessing results in a release while denying yields a short term for prisoner 1; given prisoner 2 chooses to confess, confessing results in a long term while denying yields an even longer term).

More abstractly, any game with the following strategic form is a Prisoner's Dilemma:

		Player 2	
		Cooperate	Defect
Player 1	Cooperate	c, c	a, d
	Defect	d, a	b, b

Figure G.1 The Prisoner's Dilemma.

where for the payoffs or utilities $d > c > b > a$. Thus, no matter whether player 2 chooses to cooperate (deny) or to defect (confess), defecting yields a higher utility for player 1 and vice versa. This choice problem is a 'dilemma' because there seems to be a social optimum when both parties cooperate but there are individual incentives to defect from that optimum and thus reach a situation that yields a lower utility for both parties.

Protocol Sentence A statement that describes the immediate experience or perception of an observer and was held to provide the foundation of all knowledge by members of the logical positivism movement.

Public Good A pure public good is a good with two characteristics: non-rivalry and non-excludability. A good is non-rival when one person's consumption of it does not reduce the ability to consume it for another. Many goods that are copyright protected are non-rival in this sense – for instance, music, films and literature. While the physical copy (a CD, DVD, book) of such a good may be rival (if I listen to a particular CD, my friend in Tokyo can't), the good itself isn't (my listening of a certain kind of music doesn't reduce anybody else's potential enjoyment of it). Goods are non-excludable when consumers cannot be prohibited from benefiting from the good. That is, once the good is provided, everybody will enjoy it (think of water dams, national security or clean air).

Quantity Theory of Money It is not easy to state what 'the' quantity theory really says as there are numerous versions, and each version is importantly different from other versions. What all versions share is a relation between money on the one side and prices, income and other nominal variables on the other. According to John Locke, money and prices vary *proportionally* – but he did not specify any causal order among the quantities. Commonly it is thought to be part of the quantity theory that money *causes* the other quantities. But this is ambiguous: Is money the only cause or a mere contributing cause? And does this mean that money is exogenous, that is, that money is not caused by the other quantities? Milton Friedman, for instance, did not exclude the latter and equivocated on the former. A further ambiguity is the time frame: Does money cause nominal quantities instantaneously or after the passage of time? Friedman asserted that *in the long run* money and prices are proportional. But when exactly does the long run start? Apart from Locke and Friedman, Jean Bodin (who is sometimes credited as the originator of the theory), William Petty, Richard Cantillon, David Hume, Irving Fisher and John Maynard Keynes made significant contributions to the development of the quantity theory.

Screening-Off Suppose variables X and Y are probabilistically dependent: $P(Y \mid X) > P(Y)$. A third variable Z is then said to 'screen off' the probabilistic dependence between X and Y just in case: $P(Y \mid X, Z) = P(Y \mid Z)$. That is, X and Y are unconditionally dependent but independent conditional on Z.

Statement, Analytic The distinction between analytic and synthetic statements or propositions is Immanuel Kant's version of Hume's Fork. An analytic statement is one whose truth can be determined by analysis of its meaning alone. Another way to put it is that the negation of an analytic statement is self-contradictory. A popular example is 'All bachelors are unmarried'. Since bachelor means 'unmarried man', the statement amounts to 'All unmarried men are unmarried', which is a tautology.

Statement, Synthetic A synthetic statement or proposition is true in virtue of how the world is, in virtue of the 'facts'. It therefore transcends logic. An important aspect of the disagreement between empiricists and rationalists is whether or not there are 'synthetic *a priori*' statements – statements about the world – which can be verified by reason alone, prior to experience. Empiricists reject the thesis that there are synthetic *a priori* statements; they hold that only analytic statements can be verified *a priori* while all synthetic statements must be tested against experience.

(Non-)Stationary Time Series Consider a time series $X = X_t, X_{t+j1}, \ldots, X_{t+jn}$. The process for X_t is said to be *covariance* or *weakly* stationary if neither the mean $\mu_X = E(X_t)$ nor the autocovariance $\gamma_j = E(X_t - \mu_X)(X_{t+j} - \mu_X)$ depend on date t (for all t and j). The process is strictly stationary if for any values of j_i the joint distribution of $(X_t, X_{t+j1}, \ldots, X_{t+jn})$ depends only on the intervals separating the dates, not on the date t itself. Non-stationarity is usually the negation of strict stationarity. In less technical terms, non-stationary time series have a 'memory', which implies that the exact time when samples are taken matters. Most processes described by economic time series are non-stationary.

Strategy, Dominant A strategy is a rule in a game that tells the player which action to choose at each instant of the game. A strategy is dominant if it never yields a lower payoff than all alternative strategies, and sometimes a higher payoff, no matter what the other players choose.

Subgame-Perfect Equilibrium Consider the following coordination game called 'Follow the Leader' (cf. Rasmusen 1994: 93ff.). There are two players who choose disk sizes between large and small. Both their payoffs are greater if they choose the same size and greatest if they both choose large. Unlike in the Prisoner's Dilemma game, where players choose simultaneously, the players here choose sequentially. Player 1 (S) chooses first, so his strategy set is (small, large). Player 2 (J) has to specify a strategy for each of player 1's choices, for instance (small, large), which says that player 2 chooses small if player 1 chose small and large if player 1 chose large or (large, large), which says that player 2 chooses large independently of what player 1 chose. There are three equilibria in this game, [large, (large, large)], where player 2 chooses large no matter what player 1 chooses and player 1 chooses large, [large, (large, small)] and [small, (small, small)]. But only the second of these is subgame perfect. The extensive form of this game is:

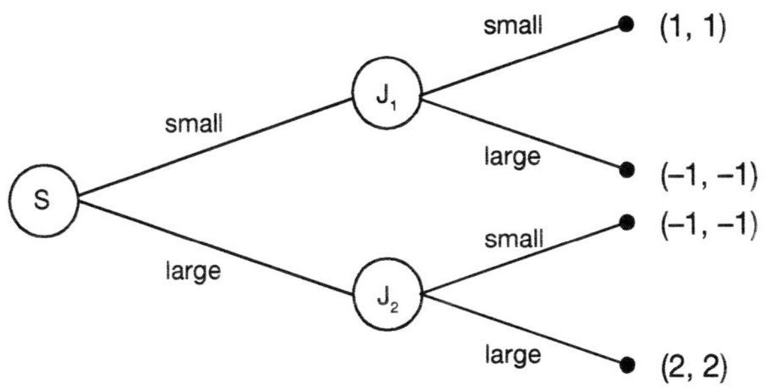

Figure G.2 'Follow the leader' game.

There are three subgames in this game: the two that start with player 2's choices and the whole game. Thus we can see that only [large, (large, small)] is subgame perfect: only that strategy profile is an equilibrium in all three subgames. For example, [large, (large, large)] is not an equilibrium in the subgame that starts at J_1 because, given player 2 chooses large, it is not optimal for player 1 to choose small.

Ultimatum Game There are two players in an ultimatum game. Player 1 (the 'proposer') makes an offer of $\$X$ from a total of $\$M$ to player 2 (the 'respondent') or, alternatively, a *share* of X/M. If player 2 accepts the offer, then player 1 is paid $\$(M–X)$ and player 2 receives $\$X$; if player 2 rejects the offer, each gets zero. The subgame-perfect equilibrium and therefore predicted outcome in this game are ($X = \varepsilon$, accept), that is, player 1 offers the smallest amount possible and player 2 accepts it. However, in economic experiments outcomes with much higher offers ($X/M \approx 45\%$) are typically observed and, when offers are low (but positive), they typically get rejected.

Unification Model of Scientific Explanation One of the competitors for an adequate account of scientific explanation. The intuition behind it is that satisfactory explanations unify a range of diverse phenomena under a common scheme. It shares with the deductive–nomological model the idea that explanations are kinds of arguments. In Philip Kitcher's version an explanation is a deduction of a description of a phenomenon from an argument pattern that can be used again and again in describing different kinds of phenomena (Kitcher 1981). This model has certainly some appeal in economics because economists often regard the power to unify an important desideratum of an explanation (witness, for example, how Akerlof's lemons model can be used to explain phenomena in goods, credit, labour and insurance markets).

Winner's Curse The problem for successful bidders in auctions of winning a Pyrrhic victory because the offered price exceeds the intrinsic value of the auctioned good. The problem obtains particularly in sealed-bid and first-price auctions in which the good has a value that is common to all participants but not known to the bidders. As the value is not known to the bidders, some will underestimate, others overestimate it. But since the highest bidder receives the good, that bidder who makes the largest positive error will receive it. To ameliorate the winner's curse the auction can be held openly (because then bidders can learn about other bidders' estimations) or, if a sealed-bid auction, it can be specified that the winner pays the price of the second highest bid.

Bibliography

Abraham, Katherine 1997, 'The CPI Commission: Discussion', *American Economic Review* 87 (2): 94–95

——2003, 'Toward a Cost-of-Living Index: Progress and Prospects', *Journal of Economic Perspectives* 17 (1): 45–58

Achinstein, Peter 2001, *The Book of Evidence*, Oxford: Oxford University Press

Aiyagari, Rao 1995, 'The Econometrics of Indeterminacy: An Applied Study, a Comment', *Staff Report* 196, Minneapolis, MN: Federal Reserve Bank of Minneapolis

Akerlof, George 1970, 'The Market for "Lemons": Quality Uncertainty and the Market Mechanism', *Quarterly Journal of Economics* 84 (3): 488–500

Aldrich, John 1989, 'Autonomy', *Oxford Economic Papers* 41: 15–34

——1992, 'Probability and Depreciation: A History of the Stochastic Approach to Index Numbers', *History of Political Economy* 24 (3): 657–87

Alexandrova, Anna 2006, 'Connecting Economic Models to the Real World: Game Theory and the FCC Spectrum Auctions', *Philosophy of the Social Sciences* 36 (2): 173–92

Andreoni, James 1995, 'Cooperation in Public Goods Experiments: Kindness or Confusion?', *American Economic Review* 85 (4): 891–904

Angner, Erik 2006, 'Economists as Experts: Overconfidence in Theory and Practice', *Journal of Economic Methodology* 13 (1): 1–24

Angrist, Joshua 1990, 'Lifetime Earnings and the Vietnam Era Draft Lottery: Evidence from Social Security Adminstrative Records', *American Economic Review* 80 (3): 313–36

Bahry, Donna and Rick Wilson 2006, 'Confusion or Fairness in the Field? Rejections in the Ultimatum Game under the Strategy Method', *Journal of Economic Behavior and Organization* 60: 37–54

Baily, Martin and Robert Gordon 1988, 'The Productivity Slowdown, Measurement Issues, and the Explosion of Computer Power', *Brookings Papers on Economic Activity* 19 (2): 337–420

Baker, Dean (ed.) 1997, *Getting Prices Right: The Battle over the Consumer Price Index*, Armonk, NY: M.E. Sharpe

Banks, Jeffrey, John Ledyard and David Porter 1989, 'Allocating Uncertain and Unresponsive Resources: An Experimental Approach', *Rand Journal of Economics* 20: 1–22

Banzhaf, Spencer 2001, 'Quantifying the Quantitative: Quality-Adjusted Price Indexes in the United States 1915–61', in Judy Klein and Mary Morgan (eds), *The Age of Economic Measurement*, Durham, NC: Duke University Press, 345–70

Bardsley, Nicholas 2005a, 'Altruism or Artefact? A Note on Dictator Game Giving', *CeDEx Discussion Paper* 2005–10, University of Nottingham

——2005b, 'Experimental Economics and the Artificiality of Alteration', *Journal of Economic Methodology* 12 (2): 239–51

Bartels, Larry 1991, 'Instrumental and "Quasi-Instrumental" Variables', *American Journal of Political Science* 35 (3): 777–800

Benhabib, Jess and Roger Farmer 2000, 'The Monetary Transmission Mechanism', *Review of Economic Dynamics* 3 (3): 523–50

Bernt, Ernst, Iain Cockburn and Zvi Griliches 1996, 'Pharmaceutical Innovations and Market Dynamics: Tracking Effects on Price Indexes for Anti-Depressant Drugs', *Brookings Papers on Economic Activity: Microeconomics* (1): 133–88

Blanchard, Olivier 2005, *Macroeconomics*, 4th edn, Upper Saddle River, NJ: Pearson/Prentice Hall

Blaug, Mark 1992, *The Methodology of Economics or How Economists Explain*, 2nd edn, Cambridge: Cambridge University Press

Bogen, James and James Woodward 1988, 'Saving the Phenomena', *Philosophical Review* 97: 302–52

Boland, Lawrence 2003, *The Foundations of Economic Method: A Popperian Perspective*, 2nd edn, London: Routledge

Boskin, Michael, Ellen Dulberger, Robert Gordon, Zvi Griliches and Dale Jorgensen 1996, *Final Report of the Advisory Commission to Study the Consumer Price Index*, Washington, DC: US Government Printing Office

Boumans, Marcel 2001, 'Fisher's Instrumental Approach to Index Numbers', *History of Political Economy* 33 (Supplement): 313–44

Brante, Thomas 2001, 'Consequences of Realism for Sociological Theory-Building', *Journal for the Theory of Social Behaviour* 31 (2): 167–94

Bridgman, Percy 1927, *The Logic of Modern Physics*, New York: Macmillan

Bureau of Labor Statistics 1997, 'Measurement Issues in the CPI', Washington, DC: US Department of Labor

Burns, Arthur and Wesley Clair Mitchell 1946, *Measuring Business Cycles*, Studies in Business Cycles, Vol. 2, New York: National Bureau of Economic Research

Caldwell, Bruce 2001, 'There Really Was a German Historical School: A Comment on Heath Pearson', *History of Political Economy* 33 (3): 649–54

Callon, Michel and Fabian Muniesa 2007, 'Economic Experiments and the Construction of Markets', in Donald MacKenzie, Fabian Muniesa and Lucia Siu (eds), *Do Economists Make Markets? On the Performativity of Economics*, Princeton, NJ: Princeton University Press, 163–89

Card, David and Alan Krueger 1994, 'Minimum Wages and Employment: A Case Study of the Fast Food Industry in New Jersey and Pennsylvania', *American Economic Review* 84 (4): 772–93

——1995, *Myth and Measurement: The New Economics of the Minimum Wage*, Princeton, NJ: Princeton University Press

Carpenter, Jeffrey, Stephen Burks and Eric Verhoogen 2005, 'Comparing Students to Workers: The Effect of Social Framing in Distribution Games', in Jeffrey Carpenter, Glenn Harrison and John List (eds), *Field Experiments in Economics*, Amsterdam: Elsevier, 261–90

Cartwright, Nancy 1983, *How the Laws of Physics Lie*, Oxford: Oxford University Press

——1989, *Nature's Capacities and Their Measurement*, Oxford: Clarendon

——1998, 'Capacities', in John Davis, D. Wade Hands and Uskali Mäki (eds), *The Handbook of Economic Methodology*, Cheltenham: Edward Elgar, 45–48

——1999a, *The Dappled World*, Cambridge: Cambridge University Press

——1999b, 'The Vanity of Rigor in Economics: Theoretical Models and Galileian Experiments', *CPNSS Discussion Papers* DP {43/99}, London: Centre for Philosophy of Natural and Social Sciences

——2001, 'Modularity: It Can – and Generally Does – Fail', in Domenico Constantini, Maria Carla Galavotti and Patrick Suppes (eds), *Stochastic Causality*, Palo Alto, CA: CSLI Publications, 65–84

——2002, 'In Favor of Laws That Are Not *Ceteris Paribus* after All', *Erkenntnis* 57: 425–39

——2003, 'Two Theorems on Invariance and Causality', *Philosophy of Science* 70 (1): 203–24

——forthcoming, *Hunting Causes – and Using Them*, Cambridge: Cambridge University Press

Cartwright, Nancy and Jordi Cat 1998, 'Abstract and Concrete Knowledge: Why the Historical School Should Matter to How We Do Economic Theory Today', unpublished manuscript, London School of Economics

Cason, Timothy and Vai-Lam Mui 1998, 'Social Influence in the Sequential Dictator Game', *Journal of Mathematical Psychology* 42: 248–65

Chang, Hasok 2004, *Inventing Temperature*, Oxford: Oxford University Press

Clements, Kenneth and H.Y. Izan 1987, 'The Measurement of Inflation: A Stochastic Approach', *Journal of Business and Economic Statistics* 5 (3): 339–50

Coase, Ronald 1959, 'The Federal Communications Commission', *Journal of Law and Economics* 2: 1–40

Cox, James, Samuel Dinkin and Vernon Smith 1999, 'The Winner's Curse and Public Information in Common Value Auctions: A Comment', *American Economic Review* 89 (1): 319–24

Cramton, Peter 1998, 'The Efficiency of the FCC Auctions', *Journal of Law and Economics* 41: 727–36

Croson, Rachel 1996, 'Information in Ultimatum Games: An Experimental Study', *Journal of Economic Behavior and Organization* 30: 197–212

——2002, 'Why and How to Experiment: Methodologies from Experimental Economics', *University of Illinois Law Review* 2002: 921–45

Croson, Rachel and Melanie Marks 1998, 'Identifiability of Individual Contributions in a Threshold Public Goods Experiment', *Journal of Mathematical Psychology* 42: 167–90

Cutler, David, Mark McClellan, Joseph Newhouse and Dahlia Remler 1996, 'Are Medical Prices Declining?', *Working Paper* 5750, New York: National Bureau of Economic Research

de Marchi, Neil (ed.) 1988, *The Popperian Legacy in Economics*, Cambridge: Cambridge University Press

Deaton, Angus 1998, 'Getting Prices Right: What Should Be Done?', *Journal of Economic Perspectives* 12 (1): 37–46

Diewert, W. Erwin 1976, 'Exact and Superlative Index Numbers', *Journal of Econometrics* 4 (2): 115–45

——1987, 'Index Numbers', in John Eatwell, Murray Milgate and Peter Newman (eds), *The New Palgrave: A Dictionary of Economics*, Vol. 2, London: Macmillan

——1993, 'The Early History of Price Index Research', in W. Erwin Diewert and A.O. Nakamura (eds), *Essays in Index Number Theory*, Vol. 1, Amsterdam: Elsevier, 33–66

——1997, 'The CPI Commission: Discussion', *American Economic Review* 87 (2): 95–96

——2001, 'The Consumer Price Index and Index Number Purpose', *Journal of Economic and Social Measurement* 27: 167–248

——2004, 'The Economic Approach to Index Number Theory: The Single Household Case', in International Labour Organization (ed.), *Consumer Price Index Manual: Theory and Practice*, Geneva: ILO Statistical Office

Edgington, Dorothy 1995, 'On Conditionals', *Mind* 104: 235–329

Elgin, Catherine 1996, *Considered Judgment*, Princeton, NJ: Princeton University Press

——1997, *Between the Absolute and the Arbitrary*, Ithaca, NY: Cornell University Press

Elster, Jon 1983, *Explaining Technical Change: A Case Study in the Philosophy of Science*, Cambridge: Cambridge University Press

——1985, *Making Sense of Marx*, Cambridge: Cambridge University Press

——1989, *Nuts and Bolts for the Social Sciences*, Cambridge: Cambridge University Press

——1998, 'Introduction', in *Deliberative Democracy*, Cambridge: Cambridge University Press, 1–18

——1999, 'A Plea for Mechanisms', in Peter Hedström and Richard Swedberg (eds), *Social Mechanisms: An Analytical Approach to Social Theory*, Cambridge: Cambridge University Press, 45–73

Engle, Robert, David Hendry and Jean-François Richard 1983, 'Exogeneity', *Econometrica* 51 (2): 277–304

Ericsson, K.A. and A.C. Lehmann 1996, 'Expert and Exceptional Performance: Evidence of Maximal Adaptation to Task Constraints', *Annual Review of Psychology* 47: 273–305

Estrella, Arturo and Jeffrey Fuhrer 1999, 'Are "Deep" Parameters Stable? The Lucas Critique as an Empirical Hypothesis', *Working Paper* 99–4, Boston, MA: Federal Reserve Bank of Boston

Fackler, James and John Rogers 1995, 'Output, Inflation and Stabilization: A Counterfactual Analysis', *Journal of International Money and Finance* 14 (5): 619–40

Fama, Eugene 1970, 'Efficient Capital Markets: A Review of Theory and Empirical Work', *Journal of Finance* 25: 383–417

Farmer, Roger and Jang-Ting Guo 1995, 'The Econometrics of Indeterminacy: An Applied Study', *Carnegie Rochester Conference Series on Public Policy* 43

Feenstra, Robert 1992, 'New Goods and Index Numbers: US Import Prices', unpublished manuscript, University of California, Davis

Fisher, Franklin M. and Karl Shell 1968, 'Taste and Quality Change in the Pure Theory of the True Cost-of-Living Index', in John Wolfe (ed.), *Value, Capital, and Growth: Papers in Honour of Sir John Hicks*, Edinburgh: University of Edinburgh Press, 97–139

——1972, *The Economic Theory of Price Indices: Two Essays on the Effects of Taste, Quality, and Technological Change*, New York: Academic Press

Fisher, Irving 1911, *The Purchasing Power of Money: Its Determination and Relation to Credit and Crisis*, New York: Macmillan

——1921, 'The Best Form of Index Number', *Journal of the American Statistical Association* 17: 533–37
——1922, *The Making of Index Numbers: A Study of Their Variety, Tests and Reliability*, Boston, MA: Houghton Mifflin
Forsythe, Robert, Joel Horowitz, N.E. Savin and Martin Sefton 1994, 'Fairness in Simple Bargaining Experiments', *Games and Economic Behavior* 6: 347–69
Friedman, Milton 1953, 'The Methodology of Positive Economics', in *Essays in Positive Economics*, Chicago, IL: University of Chicago Press
——1956, *Studies in the Quantity Theory of Money*, Chicago, IL: University of Chicago Press
Friedman, Milton and Anna Schwartz 1963, 'Money and Business Cycles', *Review of Economics and Statistics* 45 (1, Part 2, Supplement): 32–64
Frisch, Ragnar 1930, 'Necessary and Sufficient Conditions Regarding the Form of an Index Number Which Shall Meet Certain of Fisher's Tests', *Journal of the American Statistical Association* 25 (172): 397–406
——1936, 'Annual Survey of General Economic Theory: The Problem of Index Numbers', *Econometrica* 4 (1): 1–38
Gigerenzer, Gerd 2002, *Reckoning with Risk*, London: Penguin
Gillie, Oliver 2004, *Sunlight Robbery: Health Benefits Are Denied by Current Public Health Policy in the UK*, London: Health Research Forum
Glennan, Stuart 2002, 'Rethinking Mechanistic Explanation', *Philosophy of Science* 69 (PSA 2000): S342–53
Glymour, Clark and Gregory Cooper 1999, *Computation, Causation, and Discovery*, Menlo Park, CA: American Association for Artificial Intelligence
Godfrey-Smith, Peter 2003, *Theory and Reality: An Introduction to the Philosophy of Science*, Chicago, IL: University of Chicago Press
Goodman, Nelson 1954, *Fact, Fiction and Forecast*, Atlantic Highlands, NJ: Athlone Press
Gordon, Robert 1990, *The Measurement of Durable Goods Prices*, Chicago, IL: University of Chicago Press (for National Bureau of Economic Research)
——1993, 'Measuring the Aggregate Price Level: Implications for Economic Performance and Policy', *Working Paper* 3969, New York: National Bureau of Economic Research
——1996, 'The Sears Catalog Revisited: Apparel and Durable Goods', unpublished manuscript, Northwestern University, Evanston, IL
——2000, 'The Boskin Commission Report and Its Aftermath', *Working Paper* 7759, Cambridge, MA: National Bureau of Economic Research
Greene, William 2000, *Econometric Analysis*, 4th edn, Upper Saddle River, NJ: Prentice-Hall
Grether, David and Charles Plott 1979, 'Economic Theory of Choice and the Preference Reversal Phenomenon', *American Economic Review* 69: 623–38
Griliches, Zvi 1971, *Price Indexes and Quality Change*, Cambridge, MA: Harvard University Press
——1997, 'Commentary', *Federal Reserve Bank of St. Louis Review* 79 (3): 169–73
Griliches, Zvi and Iain Cockburn 1994, 'Generics and New Goods in Pharmaceutical Price Indexes', *American Economic Review* 84 (5): 1213–32
Gross, Bill 2004, 'Con Job Redux', *PIMCO Bonds Investment Outlook* (October)
Grossman, Herschel 1984, 'Counterfactuals, Forecasts, and Choice-Theoretic

Modelling of Policy', *Working Paper* 1381, Cambridge, MA: National Bureau of Economic Research

Guala, Francesco 2001, 'Building Economic Machines: The FCC Auctions', *Studies in the History and Philosophy of Science* 32: 453–77

——2005, *The Methodology of Experimental Economics*, Cambridge: Cambridge University Press

Hacking, Ian 1983, *Representing and Intervening*, Cambridge: Cambridge University Press

——1992, 'The Self-Vindication of the Laboratory Sciences', in Andrew Pickering (ed.), *Science as Practice and Culture*, Chicago, IL: University of Chicago Press, 29–64

——1999, *The Social Construction of What?*, Cambridge, MA: Harvard University Press

Hamilton, James 1996, 'Measuring the Liquidity Effect', *UCSD Discussion Paper* 96–19, University of California, San Diego

——1997, 'Measuring the Liquidity Effect', *American Economic Review* 87 (1): 80–97

Hammond, Daniel 1996, *Theory and Measurement: Causality Issues in Friedman's Economics*, Cambridge: Cambridge University Press

Hands, D. Wade 2001, *Reflection without Rules: Economic Methodology and Contemporary Science Theory*, Cambridge: Cambridge University Press

Häuser, Karl 1989, 'Gründe des Niedergangs: Überlebendes und Überlebenswertes', in Michael Bock (ed.), *Gustav Schmoller heute*, Berlin: Duncker und Humblot

Hausman, Daniel 1992, *The Inexact and Separate Science of Economics*, Cambridge: Cambridge University Press

——1998, *Causal Asymmetries*, Cambridge: Cambridge University Press

Hausman, Daniel and James Woodward 2004, 'Modularity and the Causal Markov Condition: A Restatement', *British Journal for the Philosophy of Science* 55: 147–61

Hausman, Jerry 1996, 'The Valuation of New Goods under Perfect and Imperfect Competition', in Timothy Breshnahan and Robert Gordon (eds), *The Economics of New Goods: Studies in Income and Wealth*, Chicago, IL: University of Chicago Press

Hayek, Friedrich von 1982, *Law, Legislation and Liberty*, London: Routledge

Hazlett, Thomas 1998, 'Assigning Property Rights to Radio Spectrum Users: Why Did FCC License Auctions Take 67 Years?', *Journal of Law and Economics* 41 (2): 529–75

Heckman, James 1996, 'Comment', *Journal of the American Statistical Association* 91 (434): 459–62

——2000, 'Causal Parameters and Policy Analysis in Economics: A Twentieth Century Perspective', *Quarterly Journal of Economics* 115 (1): 45–97

——2001, 'Econometrics Counterfactuals and Causal Models', unpublished Keynote Address, International Statistical Institute, Seoul

Hedström, Peter and Richard Swedberg (eds) 1999a, *Social Mechanisms: An Analytical Approach to Social Theory*, Cambridge: Cambridge University Press

——1999b, 'Social Mechanisms: An Introductory Essay', in *Social Mechanisms: An Analytical Approach to Social Theory*, Cambridge: Cambridge University Press, 1–31

Hendry, David 2002, 'Forecast Failure, Expectations Formation, and the Lucas Critique', *Economics Papers* 2002-W8, Oxford: Nuffield College, University of Oxford
——2004, 'Causality and Exogeneity in Non-Stationary Economic Time Series', *Causality: Metaphysics and Methods Technical Reports* CTR {18/04}, London: Centre for Philosophy of Natural and Social Sciences
Hendry, David and Michael Clements 2003, 'Economic Forecasting: Some Lessons from Recent Research', *Economic Modelling* 20: 301–29
Hendry, David and Michael Massmann 2007, 'Co-Breaking: Recent Advances and a Synopsis of the Literature', *Journal of Business and Economic Statistics* 25: 33–51
Hendry, David and Grayham Mizon 2001, 'Forecasting in the Presence of Structural Breaks and Policy Regime Shifts', *Economics Papers* 2002-W12, Oxford: Nuffield College, University of Oxford
Henrich, Joseph, Robert Boyd, Samuel Bowles, Colin Camerer, Ernst Fehr, Herbert Gintis and Richard McElreath 2001, 'In Search of Homo Economicus: Behavioral Experiments in 15 Small-Scale Societies', *American Economic Review* 91 (2): 73–78
Hodgson, Geoffrey 2001, *How Economics Forgot History*, London: Routledge
Hoffmann, Elisabeth, Kevin McCabe and Vernon Smith 1996, 'On Expectations and the Monetary Stakes in Ultimatum Games', *International Journal of Game Theory* 25: 289–301
Hogarth, Robin 2005, 'The Challenge of Representative Design in Economics and Psychology', *Journal of Economic Methodology* 12 (2): 253–63
Holland, Paul 1988, 'Statistics and Causal Inference', *Journal of the American Statistical Association* 81 (396): 945–60
Homann, Harald 1989, *Gesetz und Wirklichkeit in den Sozialwissenschaften*, Tübingen: Brenner
Hon, Giora 2003, 'The Idols of Experiment: Transcending the "Etc. List"', in Hans Radder (ed.), *The Philosophy of Scientific Experimentation*, Pittsburgh, PA: Pittsburgh University Press: 174–97
Hoover, Kevin 2001, *Causality in Macroeconomics*, Cambridge: Cambridge University Press
Horsey, Richard 2002, 'The Art of Chicken Sexing', *UCL Working Papers in Linguistics*, London: University College London
Hulten, Charles 1997, 'Quality Change in the CPI', *Federal Reserve Bank of St. Louis Review* 79 (3): 87–100
Jevons, William Stanley 1884 [1863], 'A Fall in the Value of Gold Ascertained, and Its Social Effects Set Forth', in William Stanley Jevons (ed.), *Investigations in Currency and Finance*, London: Macmillan, 13–118
——1884 [1869], 'The Depreciation of Gold', in William Stanley Jevons (ed.), *Investigations in Currency and Finance*, London: Macmillan, 151–59
Kagel, John and Dan Levin 1986, 'The Winner's Curse and Public Information in Common Value Auctions', *American Economic Review* 76 (5): 894–920
Kagel, John and Alvin Roth 2000, 'The Dynamics of Reorganization in Matching Markets: A Laboratory Experiment Motivated by a Natural Experiment', *Quarterly Journal of Economics* 115 (1): 201–35
Kelly, Thomas 2006, 'Evidence', in Edward Zalta (ed.), *The Stanford Encyclopedia of Philosophy*, Palo Alto, CA: CSLI

Keynes, John Maynard 1909, 'Index Numbers', in Donald Moggridge (ed.), *The Collected Writings of John Maynard Keynes*, Vol. 11: Economic Articles and Correspondence Academic, London: Macmillan, 49–173

——1930, *A Treatise on Money*, Vol. 1: The Pure Theory of Money, London: Macmillan

——1957 [1921], *A Treatise on Probability*, London: Macmillan

Kincaid, Harold 1996, *Philosophical Foundations of the Social Sciences*, New York: Cambridge University Press

——2004, 'Contextualism, Explanation and the Social Sciences', *Philosophical Explorations* 7 (3): 201–18

Kincaid, Harold, John Dupré and Alison Wylie 2007, *Science and Values: Ideal or Illusion?*, Oxford: Oxford University Press

Kitcher, Philip 1981, 'Explanatory Unification', *Philosophy of Science* 48: 507–31

——2001, *Science, Truth and Democracy*, Oxford: Oxford University Press

Klemperer, Paul 2004, *Auctions: Theory and Practice*, Princeton, NJ: Princeton University Press

Koopmans, Tjalling 1947, 'Measurement without Theory', *Review of Economic Statistics* 29 (3): 161–71

Kosso, Peter 1993, *Reading the Book of Nature: An Introduction to the Philosophy of Science*, Cambridge: Cambridge University Press

Krantz, David 1971, 'Measurement Structures and Psychological Laws', *Science* 175 (4029): 1427–35

Krantz, David, R. Duncan Luce, Patrick Suppes and Amos Tversky 1971, *Foundations of Measurement*, Vol. 1: Additive and Polynomial Representations, New York: Academic Press

Kyburg, Henry and Miriam Thalos 2003, *Probability Is the Very Guide to Life*, Chicago, IL: Open Court

Laidler, David 1991, *The Golden Age of the Quantity Theory: The Development of Neoclassical Monetary Economics*, Hemel Hempstead: Philip Allan

Lambert, Karel and Gordon Brittan 1987, *An Introduction to the Philosophy of Science*, 4th edn, Atascadero, CA: Ridgeview

Lawson, Tony 1997, *Economics and Reality*, London: Routledge

——2003, *Reorienting Economics*, London: Routledge

Laymon, Ronald 1985, 'Idealizations and the Testing of Theories by Experimentation', in Peter Achinstein and Owen Hannaway (eds), *Experiment and Observation in Modern Science*, Boston, MA: MIT Press, pp. 147–73

Leamer, Edward 1978, *Specification Searches: Ad Hoc Inferences with Non-experimental Data*, New York: Wiley

Lebow, David and Jeremy Rudd 2003, 'Measurement Error in the Price Index: Where Do We Stand?', *Journal of Economic Literature* 41 (March): 159–201

LeGrand, Julian 1982, *The Strategy of Equality*, London: Allen and Unwin

LeRoy, Stephen 2004, 'Causality in Economics', *Causality: Metaphysics and Methods Technical Reports* 20/04, London: Centre for Philosophy of Natural and Social Sciences

Levy, Ed 2001, 'Quantification, Mandated Science and Judgment', *Studies in the History and Philosophy of Science* 32 (4): 723–37

Lewis, David 1973, 'Causation', *Journal of Philosophy* 70 (8): 556–67

——1979, 'Counterfactual Dependence and Time's Arrow', *Noûs* 13 (4): 455–76

——1986, 'Postscripts to "Causation"', in *Philosophical Papers*, Vol. 2, Oxford: Oxford University Press, pp. 172–213

——2000, 'Causation as Influence', *Journal of Philosophy* 97 (4): 182–97

Lipton, Peter 2004, *Inference to the Best Explanation*, 2nd edn, London: Routledge

List, John 2002, 'Testing Neoclassical Competitive Market Theory in the Field', *Proceedings of the National Academy of Sciences* 99 (24): 15827–30

——2003, 'Does Market Experience Eliminate Market Anomalies?', *Quarterly Journal of Economics* 118 (1): 41–71

——2005, 'Dictator Game Giving Is an Experimental Artifact', *Working Paper*, University of Chicago

List, John and Daniel Millimet 2005, 'Bounding the Impact of Market Experience on Rationality: Evidence from a Field Experiment with Imperfect Compliance', *Departmental Working Papers* 0505, Southern Methodist University, Dallas, TX

Little, Daniel 1991, *Varieties of Social Explanation*, Boulder, CO: Westview

——1998, *Microfoundations, Method, and Causation: On the Philosophy of the Social Sciences*, New Brunswick, NJ: Transaction Publishers

Lo, Andrew and Craig MacKinlay 1988, 'Stock Market Prices Do Not Follow Random Walks: Evidence from a Simple Specification Test', *Review of Financial Studies* 1: 41–66

——1999, *A Non-Random Walk Down Wall Street*, Princeton, NJ: Princeton University Press

Lucas, Robert 1976, 'Econometric Policy Evaluation: A Critique', *Carnegie-Rochester Series on Public Policy* 1: 19–46

——1982, *Studies in Business Cycle Theory*, Cambridge, MA: MIT Press

Lucas, Robert and Thomas Sargent 1981, 'Introduction', in Robert Lucas and Thomas Sargent (eds), *Rational Expectations and Econometric Practice*, London: George Allen & Unwin, xi–xxi

McAfee, Preston and John McMillan 1996, 'Analyzing the Airwaves Auction', *Journal of Economic Perspectives* 10 (1): 159–75

McCloskey, Deirdre 2003, *How to Be Human (Though an Economist)*, Ann Arbor, MI: University of Michigan Press

McCloskey, Donald 1994, *Knowledge and Persuasion in Economics*, Cambridge: Cambridge University Press

McDermott, Michael 1995, 'Redundant Causation', *British Journal for the Philosophy of Science* 46: 523–44

Machamer, Peter, Lindley Darden and Carl Craver 2000, 'Thinking about Mechanisms', *Philosophy of Science* 67: 1–25

McMillan, John 1994, 'Selling Spectrum Rights', *Journal of Economic Perspectives* 8 (3): 145–62

——1995, 'Why Auction the Spectrum?', *Telecommunications Policy* 19 (3): 191–99

McMullin, Ernan 1985, 'Galileian Idealization', *Studies in the History and Philosophy of Science* 16: 247–73

Mäki, Uskali (ed.) 2002, *Fact and Fiction in Economics: Models, Realism and Social Construction*, Cambridge: Cambridge University Press

Malkiel, Burton 1991, *A Random Walk Down Wall Street*, 5th edn, New York: Norton

Mankiw, Gregory 2002, *Macroeconomics*, 5th edn, New York: Werth

Mankiw, Gregory, Julio Rotemberg and Lawrence Summers 1985, 'Intertemporal

Substitution in Macroeconomics', *Quarterly Journal of Economics* 100 (1): 225–51
Mas-Colell, Andrew, Michael Whinston and Jerry Green 1995, *Microeconomic Theory*, Oxford: Oxford University Press
Menger, Carl 1963, *Problems of Economics and Sociology*, translated by F.J. Nock, Urbana, IL: University of Illinois Press
Merton, Robert 1968 [1948], 'The Self-fulfilling Prophecy', in Robert Merton (ed.), *Social Theory and Social Structure*, New York: Free Press, 475–90
Milgrom, Paul 2004, *Putting Auction Theory to Work*, Cambridge: Cambridge University Press
Milgrom, Paul and Robert Wilson 1993, 'Affidavit of Paul R. Milgrom and Robert B. Wilson', *PP Docket* No. 93–253, Comments of PacBell
Mill, John Stuart 1844, 'On the Definition of Political Economy; and On The Method of Investigation Proper to It', in *Essays On Some Unsettled Questions of Political Economy*, London: Parker
——1872, *A System of Logic*, 8th edn, London: Longmans, Green, Reader and Dyer
Mirowski, Phil and Edward Nik-Khah 2007, 'Markets Made Flesh: Performativity, and a Problem in Science Studies, Augmented with Consideration of the FCC Auctions', in Donald MacKenzie, Fabian Muniesa and Lucia Siu (eds), *Performing Economics: How Markets are Constructed*, Princeton, NJ: Princeton University Press, 190–224
Mitchell, Wesley Clair 1915, 'The Making and Using of Index Numbers', *Bulletin of the US Bureau of Labor Statistics* 173 (July): 5–114
——1927, *Business Cycles: The Problem and Its Setting*, New York: National Bureau of Economic Research
Morgan, Mary 2005, 'Experiments versus Models: New Phenomena, Inference and Surprise', *Journal of Economic Methodology* 12 (2): 317–29
Morrison, Margaret 1995, 'Capacities, Tendencies and the Problem of Singular Causes', *Philosophy and Phenomenological Research* 55 (1): 163–68
Moulton, Brent and Karin Moses 1997, 'Addressing the Quality Change Issue in the Consumer Price Index', *Brookings Papers on Economic Activity* (1): 305–49
Moyer, Albert 1991a, 'P.W. Bridgman's Operational Perspective on Physics. Part I: Origins and Development', *Studies in the History and Philosophy of Science* 22: 237–58
——1991b, 'P.W. Bridgman's Operational Perspective on Physics. Part II: Refinements, Publications, and Receptions', *Studies in the History and Philosophy of Science* 22: 373–97
Murphy, J.J., A. Dinar, R.F. Howitt, S.J. Rassenti and Vernon Smith 2000, 'The Design of "Smart" Water Market Institutions Using Laboratory Experiments', *Environmental and Resource Economics* 17 (4): 375–94
Neumark, David and William Wascher 2000, 'Minimum Wages and Employment: A Case Study of the Fast-Food Industry in New Jersey and Pennsylvania: Comment', *American Economic Review* 90 (5): 1362–96
Nik-Khah, Edward 2005, 'Designs on the Mechanism', unpublished PhD dissertation, University of Notre Dame, Notre Dame, IN
——2006, 'What the FCC Auctions Can't Tell Us about the Performativity Thesis', *Economic Sociology* 7: 15–21
Nixon, Richard 1969, Special Message to the Congress on Social Security, 25 September 1969, available at www.ssa.gov/history/nixstmts.html

Palfrey, Thomas 1983, 'Bundling Decisions by a Multiproduct Monopolist with Incomplete Information', *Econometrica* 51: 363–88

Pearl, Judea 1993, 'Mediating Instrumental Variables', *Statistical Science* 8 (3): 266–73

——1997, 'The New Challenge: From a Century of Statistics to an Age of Causation', unpublished manuscript, University of California, Los Angeles

——2000, *Causation: Models, Reasoning and Inference*, Cambridge: Cambridge University Press

Pearson, Karl 1911, *The Grammar of Science*, London: Walter Scott

Pettit, Philip 2001, 'Deliberative Democracy and the Discursive Dilemma', *Noûs* 35 (Supplement 1): 268–99

Pindyck, Robert and Daniel Rubinfeld 1991, *Econometric Models and Economic Forecasts*, New York: McGraw-Hill

Plott, Charles 1991, 'Will Economics Become an Experimental Science?', *Southern Journal of Economics* 57 (4): 901–19

——1997, 'Laboratory Experimental Testbeds: Application to the PCS Auction', *Journal of Economics and Management Strategy* 6 (3): 605–38

Pollak, Robert 1980, 'Group Cost-of-Living Indexes', *American Economic Review* 70 (2): 273–77

——1989, 'The Treatment of the Environment in the Cost-of-Living Index', in *The Theory of the Cost-of-Living Index*, Oxford: Oxford University Press, 181–85

Porter, Theodore 1995, *Trust in Numbers: The Pursuit of Objectivity in Science and Public Life*, Princeton, NJ: Princeton University Press

——2001, 'On the Virtues and Disadvantages of Quantification for Democratic Life', *Studies in the History and Philosophy of Science* 32 (4): 739–47

Putnam, Hilary 2002, *The Collapse of the Fact/Value Dichotomy and Other Essays*, Cambridge, MA: Harvard University Press

Quine, Willard van Orman 1953, 'Two Dogmas of Empiricism', in Willard van Orman Quine (ed.), *From a Logical Point of View*, Cambridge, MA: Harvard University Press, 20–46

Rasche, Robert 1995, 'Pitfalls in Counterfactual Analyses of Policy Rules', *Open Economies Review* 6: 199–202

Rasmusen, Eric 1994, *Games and Information*, 2nd edn, Cambridge, MA: Blackwell

Read, Daniel 2005, 'Monetary Incentives, What Are They Good for?', *Journal of Economic Methodology* 12 (2): 265–76

Reichenbach, Hans 1956, *The Direction of Time*, Berkeley, CA: University of California Press

Reinsdorf, Marshall and Jack Triplett 2004, 'A Review of Reviews: Ninety Years of Professional Thinking about the Consumer Price Index and How to Measure It', unpublished manuscript, Washington, DC: US Bureau of Commerce

Reiss, Julian 2001, 'Natural Economic Quantities and Their Measurement', *Journal of Economic Methodology* 8 (2): 287–311

——2002, 'Review of *How Economics Forgot History* by Geoffrey Hodgson', EH.Net, downloadable at: www.eh.net/bookreviews/library/0567.shtml

——2004, 'Evidence-Based Economics: Some Questions and Preliminary Answers', *Analyse & Kritik* 26: 346–63

——2005, 'Causal Instrumental Variables and Interventions', *Philosophy of Science* 72 (PSA 2004): 964–76

Rosenberg, Alex 1992, *Economics: Mathematical Politics or Science of Diminishing Returns?*, Chicago, IL: University of Chicago Press

Roth, Alvin 1995, 'Introduction to Experimental Economics', in John Kagel and Alvin Roth (eds), *Handbook of Experimental Economics*, Princeton, NJ: Princeton University Press, 3–110

Roth, Alvin and Elliott Peranson 1999, 'The Redesign of the Matching Market for American Physicians: Some Engineering Aspects of Economic Design', *American Economic Review* 89 (4): 748–80

Rubin, Donald 1974, 'Estimating the Causal Effects of Treatments in Randomized and Nonrandomized Studies', *Journal of Educational Psychology* 66: 688–701

Russell, Bertrand 1913, 'On the Notion of Cause', *Proceedings of the Aristotelian Society* 13: 1–26

Sackett, David, William Rosenberg, Muir Gray, Brian Haynes and Scott Richardson 1996, 'Evidence-Based Medicine: What It Is and What It Isn't', *British Medical Journal* 312: 71–2

Salmon, Merrilee, John Earman, Clark Glymour, James Lennox, Peter Machamer, James McGuire, John Norton, Wesley Salmon and Kenneth Schaffner 1992, *Introduction to the Philosophy of Science*, Englewood Cliffs, NJ: Prentice-Hall

Samuelson, Paul 1965, 'Proof That Properly Anticipated Prices Fluctuate Randomly', *Industrial Management Review* 6: 41–49

Samuelson, Paul and William Nordhaus 2001, *Economics*, 17th edn, Boston, MA: McGraw-Hill

Samuelson, Robert 2005, 'Time to Toss the Textbooks', *Washington Post*, June 22: A21

Sayer, Andrew 2000, *Realism and Social Science*, London: Sage

Schelling, Thomas 1971, 'Dynamic Models of Segregation', *Journal of Mathematical Sociology* 1: 143–86

——1978, *Micromotives and Macrobehavior*, New York: Norton

——1999, 'Social Mechanisms and Social Dynamics', in Peter Hedström and Richard Swedberg (eds), *Social Mechanisms: An Analytical Approach to Social Theory*, Cambridge: Cambridge University Press, 32–44

Schmidt-Petri, Christoph forthcoming, 'Cartwright and Mill on Capacities and Tendencies', in Luc Bovens and Stephan Hartmann (eds), *Nancy Cartwright's Philosophy of Science*, London: Routledge

Schmoller, Gustav 1911, 'Volkswirtschaft, Volkswirtschaftslehre und-methode', in Heino Heinrich Nau (ed.), *Gustav Schmoller: Historisch-ethische Nationalökonomie als Kulturwissenschaft*, Marburg: Metropolis, 215–368

Schram, Arthur 2005, 'Artificiality: The Tension between Internal and External Validity in Economic Experiments', *Journal of Economic Methodology* 12 (2): 225–37

Schultze, Charles and Christopher Mackie (eds) 2002, *At What Price? Conceptualizing and Measuring Cost-of-Living and Price Indexes*, Washington, DC: National Academy Press

Schumpeter, Joseph 1954, *History of Economic Analysis*, New York: Oxford University Press

Sell, Jane and Rick Wilson 1991, 'Levels of Information and Contributions to Public Goods', *Social Forces* 70 (1): 107–24

Selvanathan, E.A. and D.S. Prasada Rao 1994, *Index Numbers: A Stochastic Approach*, Basingstoke: Macmillan

Sen, Amartya 1999, *Development as Freedom*, Oxford: Oxford University Press

Shanteau, James and Thomas Stewart 1992, 'Why Study Expert Decision Making? Some Historical Perspectives and Comments', *Organizational Behavior and Human Decision Processes* 53: 95–106

Shapiro, Matthew and David Wilcox 1996, 'Mismeasurement in the Consumer Price Index: An Evaluation', *Working Paper* 5590, Cambridge, MA: National Bureau of Economic Research

Sills, David (ed.) 1968, *International Encyclopedia of the Social Sciences*, Vol. 10, New York: Macmillan and the Free Press

Simon, Herbert 1953, 'Causal Ordering and Identifiability', in William Hood and Tjalling Koopmans (eds), *Studies in Econometric Method*, New York: John Wiley, 49–74

——1954, 'Spurious Correlation: A Causal Interpretation', *Journal of the American Statistical Association* 49 (267): 467–79

Smith, Vernon 1987, 'Experimental Methods in Economics', in John Eatwell, Murray Milgate and Peter Newman (eds), *The New Palgrave: A Dictionary of Economics*, London: Macmillan

——1994, 'Economics in the Laboratory', *Journal of Economic Perspectives* 8 (1): 113–31

——2003, 'Autobiography', in Tore Frängsmyr (ed.), *Les Prix Nobel – The Nobel Prizes 2002*, Stockholm: Nobel Foundation

Smith, Vernon and James Walker 1993, 'Monetary Rewards and Decision Costs in Experimental Economics', *Economic Inquiry* 31 (2): 245–61

Spirtes, Peter, Clark Glymour and Richard Scheines 2001, *Causation, Prediction, and Search*, 2nd edn, Cambridge, MA: MIT Press

Stalnaker, Robert 1968, 'A Theory of Conditionals', in Nicholas Rescher (ed.), *Studies in Logical Theory*, Oxford: Basil Blackwell, 98–112

Steel, Daniel 2004, 'Social Mechanisms and Causal Inference', *Philosophy of the Social Sciences* 34 (1): 55–78

Stigler, George, Dorothy Brady, Edward Denison, Irving Kravis, Philip McCarthy, Albert Rees, Richard Ruggles and Boris Swerling 1961, *The Price Statistics of the Federal Government*, New York: National Bureau of Economic Research

Stiglitz, Joseph and Carl Walsh 2006, *Principles of Macroeconomics*, New York: Norton

Stigum, Bernt 2003, *Econometrics and the Philosophy of Economics: Theory-Data Confrontations in Economics*, Princeton, NJ: Princeton University Press

Stinchcombe, Arthur L. 1993 [1991], 'The Conditions of Fruitfulness of Theorizing about Mechanisms', in A. Sørensen and S. Spilerman (eds), *Social Theory and Social Policy: Essays in Honor of James S. Coleman*, Westport, CT: Praeger, 23–41

Sugden, Robert 2000, 'Credible Worlds: The Status of Theoretical Models in Economics', *Journal of Economic Methodology* 7 (1): 1–31

——2005a, 'Experiment, Theory, World: A Symposium on the Role of Experiments in Economics', *Journal of Economic Methodology* 12 (2): 177–84

——2005b, 'Experiments as Exhibits and Experiments as Tests', *Journal of Economic Methodology* 12 (2): 291–302

Sunstein, Cass 1993, *The Partial Constitution*, Cambridge, MA: Harvard University Press

Suppes, Patrick 1970, *A Probabilistic Theory of Causality*, Amsterdam: North-Holland

Tetlock, Philip 2006, *Expert Political Judgment: How Good Is It? How Can We Know?*, Princeton, NJ: Princeton University Press

Tetlock, Philip and Aaron Belkin (eds) 1996, *Counterfactual Thought Experiments in World Politics: Logical, Methodological and Psychological Perspectives*, Princeton, NJ: Princeton University Press

Tobin, James 1970, 'Money and Income: Post Hoc Ergo Propter Hoc?', *Quarterly Journal of Economics* 84 (2): 301–17

Trajtenberg, Manuel 1990, 'Product Innovation, Price Indices and the (Mis) Measurement of Economic Performance', *Working Paper* 3261, New York: National Bureau of Economic Research

Triplett, Jack 1997, 'Measuring Consumption: The Post-1973 and the Research Issues', *Federal Reserve Bank of St. Louis Review* 79 (3): 9–42

US Congress 1993, 'Omnibus Budget Reconciliation Act', 'Communications Licensing and Spectrum Allocation Improvement', *Report* 103–213, August 4

van Fraassen, Bas 1997, in Maria Luisa Dalla Chiara *et al.* (eds), *Logic and Scientific Methods: Vol. 1 Tenth International Congress of Logic, Methodology and Philosophy of Science*, Dordrecht: Kluwer, 511–30.

Varian, Hal 1992, *Microeconomic Analysis*, 3rd edn, New York: Norton

Vogt, Arthur and Barta Janos 1997, *The Making of Test for Index Numbers*, Heidelberg: Physica Verlag

Walsh, Vivian 1987, 'Philosophy and Economics', in John Eatwell, Murray Milgate and Peter Newman (eds), *The New Palgrave: A Dictionary of Economics*, Vol. 3, London: Macmillan, pp. 861–69

Walter, Maila 1990, *Science and Cultural Crisis: An Intellectual Biography of Percy Williams Bridgman (1882–1961)*, Stanford, CA: Stanford University Press

Walton, Douglas 1989, 'Reasoned Use of Expertise in Argumentation', *Argumentation* 3: 59–73

Wilcox, Nathaniel 1993, 'Lottery Choice: Incentives, Complexity and Decision Time', *Economic Journal* 103 (421): 1397–417

Woodward, James 1989, 'Data and Phenomena', *Synthese* 79: 393–472

——1997, 'Explanation, Invariance and Intervention', *Philosophy of Science* 64 (PSA 1996): S26–41

——2002, 'What Is a Mechanism?', *Philosophy of Science* 69 (PSA 2000): S366–77

——2003, *Making Things Happen*, Oxford: Oxford University Press

Author index

Subject index